The Ingham Lectures.

A

COURSE OF LECTURES

ON

THE EVIDENCES

OF

NATURAL AND REVEALED RELIGION.

DELIVERED BEFORE THE

OHIO WESLEYAN UNIVERSITY,

DELAWARE, OHIO.

CLEVELAND:
INGHAM, CLARKE AND COMPANY.
CINCINNATI: HITCHCOCK & WALDEN.
NEW YORK: NELSON & PHILLIPS.
1873.

PREFACE.

THE Ohio Wesleyan University and the public are indebted for this volume to the liberality of WILLIAM A. INGHAM, ESQ., of Cleveland, Ohio. Besides other benefactions and provisions for the future growth of the University, of which he is one of the trustees, Mr. Ingham placed, four years ago, at the disposal of the Faculty of the University, a very generous sum, to be expended in securing the delivery, before the University, of a course of lectures on the Evidences of Natural and Revealed Religion. The selection, both of the lecturers and of the several themes, he referred wholly to the Faculty.

This foundation for a course of lectures met one of the wants of the University, and received the hearty approval of the Faculty and other friends of the institution.

The Faculty, holding their positions by the appointment of the Church, as educators of the young men of the Church, have always felt that the most important part of their work was to secure the religious culture and establish the religious faith of the hundreds of minds annually committed to their care. To this end, there has been, from the beginning of the University, among the stated religious exercises, a regular appointment, on the Sabbath afternoon, of a *lecture*, for the discussion of topics connected with the faith,—the evidences, doctrines, and morals of Christianity. This lecture, usually delivered by the President of the University, or one of the professors, has embraced, besides other religious instruction, not only occasional single discourses on the Evidences of Religion, natural or revealed, but, from time to time, several series of discourses on the different branches of the great argument. These efforts of their own, for the religious instruction of the students, and especially their establishment in the faith, the Faculty were very glad to supplement with a course of lectures in this direction by distinguished men from abroad. They accordingly very gratefully accepted the duty imposed on them by Mr. Ingham, and prepared a programme for the course, and selected the lecturers.

The limits which the Faculty had to prescribe to themselves, as well as the special aim of the course, determined the themes to be selected. The subject-matter of the Evidences of Religion is, no doubt, practically inexhaustible; yet each age has its own particular phase of the one great conflict between faith and unbelief. The great battle of the present age is fought on these three questions: 1. The existence of a personal God; and, that being conceded, 2. Whether he can make, and has made, a special revelation of himself; and, a revelation being granted, 3. The person and position of Christ. These are the live questions discussed in this volume. It is needless to state here the bearing and the shape which each argument assumes, as this is so much better, and more fully, done in the pages following. The lecturers are competent to speak for themselves; and, unless we have much mistaken the ability and conclusiveness of the discussions, they have well and satisfactorily uttered what will be accepted as the thought of the common Church, in defense of the faith, on these great vital questions.

Each lecture, except the first three by Bishop Foster, is independent of the others, and complete in itself. If there be found some repetition in the course of thought in the volume, as is almost inevitable in the case of many writers discussing cognate themes without previous consultation, there is certainly no collision of views; and the parallelism will, at least, not detract from the force of the several arguments, or from the value of the book.

The lectures were not delivered in the order in which they are here given. As there was no necessary interdependence in the lectures, the convenience of the authors was consulted as to the time and order of their delivery. Yet they have been restored, in the published volume, to the order which the logical sequence of the subjects seems to indicate.

By the arrangement of the publisher, the profits of this volume are to be devoted to the purposes of the original foundation, and will lead to additional lectures, from time to time, before the University, on the great themes found in the department of Apologetic Theology.

W. G. WILLIAMS.

OHIO WESLEYAN UNIVERSITY,
Delaware, O., June 1, 1872.

CONTENTS.

LECTURE I.

PERSONAL CAUSE.

BY THE

REV. RANDOLPH S. FOSTER, D. D., LL. D.,

President of the Drew Theological Seminary,

MADISON, NEW JERSEY.

LECTURE I.

PERSONAL CAUSE.

THE Bible is either the most adventurous and astounding fraud that has ever gained currency among men, or the most sublime and momentous system of verities that has at any time appeared upon earth. If the former, it ought not to be impossible to expose the imposture; if the latter, it ought to be possible to command for it the respect of unprejudiced reason and the acceptance of rational faith. That after so many ages it is still in debate, might, to a superficial observer, seem to be to the discredit of its claim. A more astute and careful judge would find the explanation to consist, in part, of the unique nature and intrinsic difficulty of the claim itself, and, in part, of the peculiar relations of the jury to the question in dispute.

The claim laid by the Bible is, that, entire, it is either a direct revelation from God, delivered by inspiration to different persons in widely separated ages, or a statement of facts under authority of Divine sanction, and that it is of complete and permanent authority over the faith and conduct of men on all the subjects of which it enunciates.

The compositions are in some parts historic, in some poetic, in other some didactic. They meddle with all subjects. Adventuring beyond the highest sweep of imagination, they lay bare the secrets of the infinite. Beginning with the primal creative act, they boldly announce a cosmogony; detail the order and method of the origination of worlds; give the history of cosmical development and changes anterior to life; state the chronological order of the advent of the different kinds of animate existence. Especially, they minutely describe the origin of man, his place in the scale of being, the mysterious junction of spirit and matter in his composition, and his inauguration to the lordship and sovereignty of the world. Then follows the history of the first forty centuries, tracing all existing nations to root-stock, specifying the rise of the earliest arts and inventions; the probable origin of written and spoken language; the institution of sacrifice; the inauguration of the moral law; deific appearances to men at many times and in divers manners; inspirations, and miracles attending; the incarnation of the Godhead; his utterances and supernatural works while in the flesh; his death, with preternatural signs accompanying; his resurrection and translation; the publication of the Gospel; and signs authenticating the apostolic ministry, with an endless minutia of public and private events spread over four millenniads. They discourse of all occult questions; of the nature and perfections of God; of the source and origin of evil; of fundamental ethics, divine and human; of the origin and significance of pain and death; of the immortality of man; of the unique doctrine of the resurrection; of a final universal judgment; of angels and demoniac spirits; of the employments and limitations of each order; of heaven and hell; in a word, of almost all subjects that have ever interested human thought, as matters either of speculative or practical concernment.

It can not be occasion of surprise that an utterance so manifold, passing upon so many difficult and vexed subjects, claiming such exactness and perfection of truth, and withal, boasting an origin so unique and pre-eminent, should have been met, not with simple challenge alone, but confronted with spontaneous objurgation, and resisted with long-continued and unrelenting opposition, especially by a race to whom not alone were its ethical requirements grievous, but its historical statements criminatory, and the future it held forth, threatening and alarming in the extreme.

The broad, almost infinite, area of its discussions, both as to time and space, opened so many sides to attack; introduced so many points irritant of opposition; placed it in so many short antagonisms with ancient prejudices and fondly cherished superstitions, faiths, and practices; brought humanity into such angry and uncomfortable moods with itself in so many ways, that it can create no astonishment if the unextinguished resentment of centuries burns still fiercely to-day; if the defenders of the faith find themselves still beleaguered by armies of defiant and derisive enemies. The hate and persistent oppugnance the revelation has encountered is what, *a priori*, was to be expected.

Nor ought it to excite wonder or discouragement

if the chosen defenders of the faith have not always been most wise and skillful in their methods. If the revelation was God-given, we ought not to forget that the trust was committed to men. It may even be a question, whether friends or foes have most weakened the holy keep; whether the defenders or assailants of the sacred trust have most postponed the day of its coronation; the former by their follies, or the latter by their hate. In fact, the fables man-invented, not the faith God-given, have protracted the struggle. The human filaments inwrought into the holy vestments have been their weakness. The debris piled about the walls are the fragments of the human stucco, daubed over the hewn stone. It is time to have done with this expensive folly.

As might have been anticipated, the phases of attack have been constantly changing. One form of opposition has been obviated only to make way for another. Olympus has been stormed, and its mob of mythic gods put to the rout, only to discover the strongholds of more insidious adversaries. To-day the battle rages along the whole line of Christian defenses as really and as fiercely as when Paul went up and down from Syria to Rome, preaching, against pagan idols, the new doctrine of Jesus and the resurrection.

Past successes forbid us to doubt the issue; but it is not to be disguised that, finally to silence, and, more still, to convince, disputants fecund of every scholarly art, and animated equally by pride, ambition, and hate, will continue to lay under tribute the best brain, the broadest learning, and most noble and tireless zeal Christendom can elaborate. As has been well said by the late learned and excellent Doctor Barnes: "The battle, under a new form, may be to be re-fought in each successive generation. The triumph of Christianity at any one time is by no means a permanent triumph, or even in itself a proof of permanent triumph at all; and the apparent triumph at any time of infidelity is by no means a demonstration of permanent and ultimate victory. Celsus, Porphyry, and Julian act their part and disappear; Hobbes, Chubb, and Morgan follow, and then vanish from the stage; Volney, Gibbon, Hume, attack the system and retire from the conflict; Strauss and Rénan, Hegel and Comte, follow after. A host of scientific warriors rushes on the arena for an attack on the religion that is fixed and unchangeable, deriving their means of attack from a system that is fixed and unchangeable as Christianity itself; and the warfare assumes new forms, and is to be fought with new weapons. Whether these two systems, equally fixed and unchangeable, are *really* in conflict, or will be found ultimately to coincide and harmonize, is the question which is now before this age, and which is perhaps to be before the world in the development of future ages."*

The favorite form of attack in our time is that which patronizes religion, but throws contempt on revelation. Its boast is, that science has obsoleted the Bible. There are two ways in which it is supposed that science reaches this result, and so closes the ages' long debate. The first disports itself with compliments; it acknowledges that the Bible was once a very respectable book, much superior to the age in

* "Evidences of Christianity, pp. 362, 363.

which it was written; that it contained many useful lessons, and did good service; but insists that it belongs to the childhood of the world, and has only shared the inevitable fate of every good thing in its supersedence by something better; its nursery-clothes have simply become too small for the grown-up man, and must be laid aside. Moses and Isaiah were great, and Jesus and Paul, in their respective periods; but it was their misfortune to have lived too early, and so they must retire—be snuffed, put out, or lost amid the blaze of modern luminaries. This was a darling idea of Theodore Parker, and often appears rehashed in the orations and essays of the Boston *littérateurs*, who still wax lustrous in the sheen of his profane babblings. There is so much semblance of truth in this arrogant and dangerous flattery, that it goes further than many arguments. The world is wiser than it used to be; the child has become the stalwart man; the nursery-rattle will no longer suffice; the fables and the thumb-screws have been cast away; a new and glorious day has come. Since the world began, there has been no parallel to the progress of the time in which we live. But it does not follow that the new age has no further need of the old master who inaugurated its splendors, and set the coronet of its glories upon its brow. Who knows what other inexhaustible riches are still to be dug from the same mines which have already enriched the ages? The second method would retire the venerable Book, not alone because the world has found something better adapted to its ripeness, but because science has found its staple facts to be fables—that it is even false as it is useless.

This is the precise point I am here to discuss. It is incisively presented in the question: Do the discoveries of science collide with the statements of the Bible, and so vacate its claim as a revelation from God? By the discoveries of science, we mean those facts and theories which have become established by the inductive or Baconian method; the knowledges, as distinguished from conjectures. There is a dispute among scientists themselves as to precisely where the boundary is between philosophy, which aims at ultimate cause, and science, which aims at the knowledge of definite facts and laws. We include under the term all knowledge founded on experiment and observation, and such generalizations as are arrived at by a fair use of the inductive method.

Before we proceed to examine the point in dispute, it will be proper to mention a few things as incidental, and yet important to the right conduct of the discussion. First, it ought to be noted, that if it should be found that there is no such conflict as is alleged by the enemies of the Word, this discovery will not leave the Christian cause in the same condition in which it was before—*simply uninvalidated;* but, on the contrary, must greatly redound to its advantage; must, indeed, become a most conclusive and unanswerable proof in support of its claim to inspiration. If the contradiction of science would vacate its claim, as we admit it would, its coincidence with science establishes its claim. This would not be a sequitur in every case, but certainly is in this. It is so important a point that we must beg especial attention to it. The position we assume is this: the Bible, if uninspired, would inevitably have violently collided with the modern findings of science; if, therefore, it be found not so to collide, it must be because it was inspired—indited by a higher than human intelligence.

The ground upon which we rest this position is briefly this: The Biblical writings were indited at a time when there was no knowledge extant on the subjects of which modern science treats; at a time when it was *impossible* that the writers, if dependent merely upon human resources, should have been able to reach even proximate truth; at a time when, it is now known, all conjectures were shallow, empty, and false; in the very infancy of knowledge on all subjects. Now, if it shall so turn out that these writers, under the circumstances, alone of all men, announced in substance what after-ages of great scientific research prove to be true, there is no way of accounting for this fact except on the hypothesis of inspiration; what they did not know themselves, and could not, for want of access to the means of knowledge, they must have received from a supernatural intelligence. Thus the coincidence of the story read from the rocks to-day, and from the very particles of matter, with what was written on the sacred pages ages before, supports the authority and inspiration of the record.

The next point to be noted is this: It is most important that the disputants in the case do justice to each other and to the common cause of truth, which ought to be equally dear to both. They have no right to assume the attitude of factionists. Truth is one and harmonious wherever found, whether in the Bible or in the rocks, and can not conflict.* Some scientists ill conceal a discreditable animus against the Bible—an animus just enough as against priestly ignorance and intolerance, but the grossest injustice as against revelation. Some theologians, so called, on the other hand, exhibit venom against science, and cease not to denounce it as atheistic. Let us have done with this. In debating the point whether the findings of science collide with the statements of revelation, the disputants insult their readers and stultify themselves when they interlard the discussion with caricatures of each other.

The scientist finds his facts and laws. He does so with perfect independence and freedom. He asks no permission from any class of men, or from any book. His only business is to find out truth and make it known to his fellows, and his only limitation is to be faithful and honest in his chosen work. All good men must rejoice in his success. The theologian has a book which he believes to be inspired, and therefore infallible. His business is to ascertain its contents, expound and defend them; but he has no other interest in it than is found in its truth; his obligation to defend it has no other ground than its truth. If it be true, it can not disagree with other truth; therefore his pledge to it can not make it necessary that he should make war upon other truth. But it is said that science takes away his book and destroys his occupation! Let his book go, then, and the sooner the better, and let him seek some other and more worthy occupation. But before he surrenders his book and his occupation, he surely has the right to see whether any such necessity

* "Reign of Law," chap. ii.

exists. If he may not denounce or renounce the science, he certainly may look searchingly into the question whether it requires him to renounce himself or not. Now, in conducting that examination, there is both a true and a false method.

The false method is not uncommon with the theologian, and betrays conscious weakness. It shows fear that the book can not stand the test of trial by the rigorous requirements of criticism. It would therefore deny the venue. It will have nothing to do with science—it will ignore it. As well might the criminal ignore the executioner. The book can not survive such a method as this. It can not preserve its life by skulking in the dark. It must reign in the blaze of day with the homage of enlightened faith, or must relinquish its throne, willingly or reluctantly, to another and more deserving king. Of the same kind is the defense which has been attempted on the ground that the Bible is not a scientific book, and, therefore, can not be required to agree with science; as if it might be false to science and yet true to truth. To take such a position is the most damaging thing that could happen to the book, for it shows two fatal weaknesses: first, that the defender himself believes that facts are against him; and second, that he is stupid enough to hold on to his faith against the facts. The Bible will accept of no such defense as this!

While it would be unreasonable to object to any assumed revelation on the ground that it did not contain an exhaustive treatment of the encyclopedia of science, when it professes only to announce certain spiritual laws, it would be perfectly legitimate to discard it as false and wholly unworthy of trust, if it could be shown that it had uttered as fact any statement which after-knowledge proved to be not fact, even though the fact had no bearing on the special subject of which it claimed to make revelation. But its announcements must be interpreted, even in such cases, by just rules of criticism. "*Ab uno disce omnes*," is in this case a just rule. "*Falsus in uno, falsus in omnibus.*" There may be no reason why the revelation should make an announcement; but if it announce at all, it must be in accord with truth. No error can have the sanction of a "Thus saith the Lord."

It is not with a pretended revelation as it is with a confessedly merely human essay. The latter may be known to err, and yet retain a measure of respect and authority. It has more truth if it has some error. A revelation acquires all its authority from the fact of its divine source. When you convict it of error in a single instance, you destroy the sanction of divinity, and its entire authority is taken out of it. It may have good and truth in it; but it is not what it pretended to be, a revelation.

We must be content with the most rigorous criticism; hold ourselves amenable to the same tests we apply to others. We do not hesitate to say that the defenders of the Bible, if they were so disposed, can not afford to "whistle science down the wind." *No clearly established truth of science can be set aside by any evidence now known as supporting the truth of Biblical utterances.* In an absolute conflict, it is not a question which must ultimately go to the wall. The evidence for the Divine authority of the Bible is assumed to be clear and conclusive; but once demonstrate that its statements collide with fact, and its evidences crumble in a moment as "the baseless fabric of a vision."

The utmost the defenders of revelation can demand is, that in any supposed or seeming conflict between its received statement and a newly discovered knowledge, they have time for re-examination and a new departure, aided by the light the new knowledge furnishes. If they can make it appear that the conflict is only one bearing against their interpretation, but not against another construction which the text will allow, they are entitled to ask that the text be not held responsible for their ignorance. Candid criticism will not dare to push the objection, when it perceives that it is the interpretation and not the word that is at fault. But in such a case the discoverers of the new knowledge have a right to ask that the old error of interpretation be abandoned, and that they receive the credit to which their discovery entitles them. Had this been the uniform custom, I doubt not a better understanding would prevail between Biblical and scientific critics.

It is proper we should say yet further: the discussion is not a causeless one. There is, confessedly in several cases, the appearance of conflict between the two records. There is positive conflict between the popular rendering of the one and the unequivocal conclusions of the other. So much ought to be admitted before any discussion is commenced; and consequent on the admission ought to be the unreserved renunciation of the traditional interpretational faith, and candid and grateful recognition of the service rendered in exposing its error. But it ought also to be remembered, that if believers have made mistakes of construction, and have not always been apt scholars in discovering their blunders, and prompt in correcting them, scientists themselves have not always proved to be safe masters. All literature is full of vagaries, once proclaimed scientific verities. So-called science often turns out to be nescience. So, while we must hold ourselves ready and eager to close with any and every new truth, we have a right to ask that we be allowed time to scrutinize carefully each pretender, before we join the mob of its following. Especially, as we think we have very high proof of the authority of our book, if an unknown guide should ask us to renounce it, it can not be unreasonable that we demand a little time to get familiar with his voice. It ought to suffice that we accept conclusions when they are reached; or, at most, no more ought to be required of us than that we aid in reaching them.

Once more: it is important at the outstart that we be guarded against a mistake into which some have fallen, and into which the very terms of the question in debate are liable to plunge us—the mistake of supposing that scientists, as a class, and by virtue of their science, are unbelievers in the inspiration of the Bible; or, what is the same, that they believe there is irreconcilable disagreement between their findings and Biblical statements. There could be no greater mistake than this. It is not only certain, as we expect to show, that there is no such conflict, but it is also true that the best and most learned devotees of science are, and have been, the purest and noblest Christians, the simplicity of their faith keeping step with the breadth and depth of their researches. The scientists who have attained to eminence in their respective departments, who reject the sacred record, may be counted on the fingers of the two hands, whilst those who bow to its authority are both numerous and pre-eminent. Here, then, we make our departure, having full confidence in the inspiration and, hence, infallible truth of the Bible; and having full and cordial sympathy with the spirit, and unalloyed and hearty confidence in the success, of science; in the truth of its already grand discoveries, and awaiting with eager desire its yet greater triumphs,—here, I say, we take our departure, to show that between these two revelations, the one by inspiration, the other by discovery, there is, and can be, no conflict; because both are true. The *true scientist* shall lead nowhere where we will not follow.

That there has been a wonderful enlargement of knowledges within a century or two, on all subjects, can not be disputed. Especially has material nature been cultivated with marvelous results. Not only have scientific methods conducted to solid and certain knowledge of the facts of nature as extended in space; the elements and composition of bodies; the forces—mechanical, chemical, and vital; the structural arrangements and functions of organisms; the laws of propagation, variation, and destruction in the realm of life, and whatever besides is existing within and around us in the processes of both mind and matter; but the same methods have conducted to a knowledge of events as extended in time of almost incalculable duration. "Thus it is that we have those great sciences which extend themselves beyond the limits of our experience, and from slight signs educe the knowledge of what has been, but never met the eye of man; and of what will be, but will never meet the eye of him who predicts it; which does not even in imagination come before the eye of the thinker as he predicts it, but is understood through symbols only. Astronomy, geology, botany, zoölogy, are among these. The distance in space or time; the long sequences of causes through the ages; the metamorphoses which the forms of nature, animate or inanimate, have gone through in the progress to their present state, are rendered comprehensible by such sciences as these."* They have carried us back along the march of ages too great for our arithmetic, and disclosed to our view the monumental remains of races and creations, extinct myriads of millenniums before our race became denizens of the earth. We can not too much admire the vast progress that has been made, and is constantly making, in all the departments of knowledge.

Upon any theory but the inspiration of the Bible, inevitable conflict, as we have seen, must have arisen between its statements, made in the time of ignorance, and these wonderful discoveries. No other book has survived intact a single century. Nor could it have been more fortunate if merely a human book. What, then, are the points upon which it is assumed there is conflict? It is strange they are so few. They may be reduced to four; and these are so related as without

* *North British Review*, Oct. '70.

great strain to be brought to unity. The sixty books and the thousand pages, hailing from patriarchal climes and patriarchal times, pass the ordeal of scientific criticism with but four signs of dissent. And our hope is to show that with regard to these the collision is imaginary; a strife, in fact, between groundless interpretations of the text and science, and not the text itself.

The points upon which there is supposed conflict may be reduced to the following:

First. The question of a personal God, distinct from, and the creator of, all other being.

Second. The question of the time and manner of creation, or the origin and method of the cosmos.

Third. The question of the origin of man, and the unity, development, and antiquity of the race.

Fourth. Some incidental allusions to astronomical facts, and the question of miracles in general.

There have been other points mooted; but they have either been retired by a fair reconcilement, or are too trivial to require special attention. The above are the grand points which are at present occupying the thought of the learned world. Let us consider them in their order. Our limits will necessitate brevity, and we must assume for our audience a considerable amount of learning on the subjects under discussion; but we will endeavor fairly to present, and, on the part of the Bible, relieve the supposed difficulty.

First. We are to consider the question of a personal God, distinct from, and the creator of, all other being.

It is just to say that the question here is rather a

question as between philosophy and the Bible, than between science and the Bible; but science, as positivism, has become so far a party in the interest of philosophy, that it fairly joins the issue as against the Bible, and must be known in the answer.

The postulate of the Bible, repeated in so many forms that it is impossible to mistake it, is: "*A personal God, self-existent and eternal, the absolute creator of all other being and beings, visible and invisible.*" Positivism, by the school of Auguste Comte, and developmentism, by its most conspicuous expounders, Darwin and Huxley, attempt to show that science reaches a solution of the problem of the origin and permanent order of the cosmos without any such being. They are careful not to deny his existence, and even to profess faith in it; but the whole drift and boom of their reasonings serve to create the impression that he is a needless factor; that, in reality, for the purposes assigned in the Bible, he is not required, absolutely not found, *non est.* This they boldly and constantly assert upon the authority of science. They scientifically construct the universe without God. The conflict between science and the Bible, made thus by them, is found in this, that the Bible positively assigns one cause for the cosmos; science, it is alleged, demonstrates a totally different one.

Here we join issue. The exact point of the issue we make is this: We *deny* that scientists of any school are able to account for the cosmos without including the exact quantity set forth in the Bible as a personal God, an absolute creator. We insist, rather, that science leads us directly to him, and does him reverent homage and worship. Let us examine the case. The importance of the issue must be apparent on the slightest reflection. It involves the key-stone of the arch. Demonstrate that the Bible is false in its postulate, and of course the debate is closed.

We have already said, and now wish to repeat it with greater emphasis and fullness, that the Bible postulates the existence of a *personal* God, the absolute creator of all other existence. It declares him to be a spirit; non-material in his essence, eternal in duration, infinite in power and knowledge. It differentiates between the substances of the uncreated and the created, as fundamentally distinct and different; the one wholly unlike the other in the sources of being, and in the perfections and modes of being; the one unoriginated, the other caused. This Biblical thesis of a personal God, it is declared, has been set aside by the discovery, scientifically made, of the essential unity and eternity of all substance, which substance either consists of, or inherently possesses, certain eternal, impersonal, and necessary forces, and is known as matter, by the action of which all cosmical changes have been and will be produced. We deny that any such discovery has been made, and will proceed to show that the thing supposed is absolutely impossible in fact, and that the conjecture is destroyed by the very science which is made to assert it.

It is conceded that there is such a substance as matter, and that it is invariably characterized by certain necessarily-acting impersonal forces, known as chemical and mechanical; and that it is found occasionally to have associated with it another force, or cluster of forces, known as vital. But it is denied that it is the only substance, or that it is eternal, or that the inhering forces are original to it, or that it accounts for all cosmical changes. The ground of our denial is not simply that the case is not made out, but that it is self-destructive and impossible. How this appears we will proceed to show. In two ways science demonstrates, with absolute certainty, that the material cosmos exists under the conditions of time, both as to its substance and fashion.

By means of geological records we are conducted back over the track of cosmical history, through a succession of well-defined changes, until, having penetrated below the earliest memorial of life, we find ourselves standing upon the glowing crystals of a newly formed world. The demonstration is complete, that all life, and all conditions of possible life, had beginning. In fact, we find the dates legibly traced when each event occurred. Science is no more certain of any thing than it is of this. Chemical science takes up and continues the history. It conducts us to a still more primitive condition. Seizing the solid substances of the glowing mass, it decomposes them, and reduces them to their original molecular elements. This, it tells us, was the primal condition of the universe, the original state of all known compounds. The demonstration thus carries us not simply to the dawn of life, but to a period antedating the organization of matter itself. All that remains to us are the ultimate atoms, the primordial elements, the absolute protoplasts. But these immediately discover to us that each and every infinitesimal part is the home of a definite force, which will unerringly, and without shadow of variation, determine its alliances and necessitate its combinations forever. It is a truth, therefore, that when we form the acquaintance of matter in its most rudimental and primitive state, it is the home of a force, or, rather, forces, which necessarily evolve.

But now observe the insurmountable objection to the supposition that matter and the forces are original and eternal—the irresistible demonstration, in fact, that the forces at least had a beginning. We have already seen that, guided by geological science, we are able to go back over the line of all the effects which have transpired in the cosmos, up to the very dawn of cosmical phenomena! Chemical analysis takes us by the hand, and leads us back through other changes, until we are brought to discrete elements, behind which it is impossible there should have been any evolutions or changes of any kind. The whole history of the evolution of forces lies before us, therefore under our gaze, and falls within the limits of time. We have traced the river to its source; we have mounted the stream of consecutive effects until we have found the beginning, the fissure in the rock whence it bursts. Standing here at the top of the ages, and looking backward over the dreary wastes of an eventless eternity, we raise the question, how these forces, assuming them to have existed, which is the postulate of science, were employed during this immeasurable duration. They could not have existed, and yet have remained inactive; for science postulates that activity is their necessity. They were not active; for we have found them in the very act of their primal evolution. The demonstration is, therefore, that they were not at all. They are themselves creations, and so far from accounting for the cosmos, they are but an included part of it which needs to be accounted for.

The case is thus put by an American scientist of growing eminence and merited distinction. Having propounded the molecular condition of matter, he says: "This condition of matter is necessarily primordial. As matter could not have remained in such a condition—as, in fact, it did not remain in such a condition—the career of matter must have had a commencement. Its evolutions are not from eternity. As its earliest existence involves an evanescent condition, the *existence* of matter had a commencement. It began to exist only when it began to change."* However it may be with regard to the very substance of matter itself, the demonstration is complete and perfect, that what are called the inhering forces fall under the category of time; that they are not and can not be eternal; and if they are necessary quantities in the constituency of matter, as scientists declare, then by necessity matter itself is demonstrated to fall within the category of time; but whether it do or not, it is demonstrated to be no cause of the cosmos.

But, given matter and what are called inherent and eternal forces, we are still as far as ever from accounting for the cosmos. We have found a cause, but not *the cause.* A cause that is not *the* cause to the effect in question, is *no cause.* The cause carries in it the entire effect; for as the effect can have nothing which it does not derive from its cause, it must then have been

* Prof. Winchell, of the Michigan University.

in the cause. An unskilled laborer is a cause; but as to the production of a chronometer, or an oration of Æschines, or Leonardo Da Vinci's Last Supper, he is no cause. The forces are a cause, but not the cause, of the cosmos. They are cause to definite effects, but not cause to this culminated effect. There is that in this effect which is no more in them than Handel's Messiah is in the accidental rattle of the farmer's cart, or one of Mozart's great symphonies, or Haydn's Oratorio of the Judgment, in the jingle of sleigh-bells. For, observe, the completed cosmos is not simply a mass held by force of gravitation, massed by cohesive attraction, assorted by chemical affinity, magnetized by electro-galvanism, turned into globes by evolutions of force; it is more than all this: it is an arranged and adjusted unity, reached by taking the discrete forces and combining them into one great, universal whole, of ineffable ingenuity and skill; a plan in which each distinct part exists for a purpose, is controlled by a purpose, is subjugated to a purpose! We must find the home of this purpose—this factor that subjugates and makes slaves of all the other forces—if we would account for the cosmos. The purpose displayed is as veritable a fact, as well known and accredited a reality, as chemical affinity, or cohesive attraction, or electricity, and can no more be ignored in solving the problem than can gravitation. But while it is as much a reality as the other forces, it is discrete, is a force itself; not a mere resultant, not an accident. Nay, it is seen to be not only a force discrete, existing apart from the others in its own right, but seen to be the most masterful of all, taking the others and compelling them to do its behests. Now, this august power, this *causa causarum,* must be accounted for; this omnipotent purposing agent, forcing all forces to work out its design, to accomplish its will, nay, *his* will, for we are beyond things; he will insist that we notice him. Where shall we find his home? Is he, like gravitation, a discrete quantity of all matter? Science goes forth with its instruments of inquisitorial torture, and subjects all substances to the "*experimentum crucis,*" and each atom, even to the last, responds, It is not in me. All, with one accord, point backward, and declare with one voice, We know not of either our beginning or the cause that we are as we are. Each respondent says, I am not my own master; I am the slave of another whose bidding I do. This is the testimony of all nature extorted by science; nay, not extorted, though delivered in the processes which wrench atom from atom, but joyously uttered in the ear of reason. Thus it is discovered that a pre-existing will-force, guided by unerring intelligence, lies behind all so-called natural forces, giving them existence, or guiding them as it will to the accomplishment of its own imperial behests. No approach is made toward explaining cause until we reach the unific force in its transcendental home.

But we have only begun to intimate the insuperable difficulties which science herself interjects against the theory that inherent forces of matter account for the cosmos, without the aid of a personal cause. I will name one more. Starting with the protoplastic, or primordial, state of matter, we have the molecules in severance, each with its definite affinity; the whole lying disseminated over the infinite fields of space—wider than the boundaries where outermost suns now flame their glare upon the fields of ancient night. Forthwith, by a uniform necessity, atom rushes to the embrace of atom; the infinite abyss trembles into visible fiery forms; masses segregate and press inward toward their centers; each severed mass becomes the nucleus of a system of worlds. It is the splendid exordium of creation's pomp. Then follow ages—how long, science will only aid us to conjecture, but tells us, almost eternal—before the flaming vortices became orderly, quiet, globes of glowing homogeneous matter; myriads of ages more, and the molten masses have cooled, and their solid surfaces present the appearance of a crystal cosmos, each globe a radiant flaming crystal in itself; infinite ages more muster out to the drum-beat of the rolling spheres, and yet it is an azoic cosmos; ages how long since the morning broke, and yet no eye to behold the pomp; a universe without life! Whence shall life come? The universe says, It is not in me; each crystal world says, It is not in me; the mechanical and chemical forces cry out, It is not in us; we fashioned these worlds, but we have no power to make a tree, or even a seed, an embryo, or an animal. Thus, science again tells us, we must find help *ab extra*.

There is a curious problem right in this connection, which we would be pleased to have solved by that class of scientists who would explain all being by inherent laws of matter, or by inherent forces acting uniformly and necessarily; it is this: How, that is, in what order, did they, the forces, introduce life? Did they first evolve a seed, and from it grow a plant; or did they first make a plant without a seed? We are curious to know the answer. One of the two alternatives must have been the order at the beginning; for in no other way could life arise. But whichever alternative be taken, science presents a difficulty which is insurmountable. The thesis of science is, the forces act uniformly and necessarily; but now, it is known, no forces make a seed-life without a parent plant to produce it, and no forces make a plant-life without a seed to grow it. The necessary and eternal forces, if they be sole factors, it is thus seen, must have changed their method; and this is what science says can not be. Nothing is more settled, or scientifically certain, than that there was a time when there was no life on this planet, and that there was a time when it began; and no man is warranted in saying that any explanation has been given of its origin, except by absolute creation. To pretend the contrary is unscrupulous audacity, or unaccountable dullness.

I quote from Chadbourne another form of putting the same point: "Life is only manifested in connection with organization. Did the vital principle seize upon matter and organize it? This would imply that it resides somewhere free from matter. Is vitality a force accidental in its manifestation, correlated to some other force developed by the relationship of different kinds of matter; or was matter first organized by a creator, and then life joined to it? There are those who accept the second supposition, and believe in spontaneous generation, the production of life from matter and physical forces, and the evolution of higher types by development from lower. We pass, for the present, the geologic argument, which we believe to be conclusive against this theory, and ask its supporters how it comes to pass that the physical forces tend to originate an organism, when, the moment it is produced, they tend to destroy it. And it is a remarkable fact, that some authors who have expressed their belief in the production of life through chemical forces, have also expressed their belief in the antagonism of life and those forces. We leave to them the task of harmonizing their own views. The organic being struggles for existence, and lives only because the vital principle holds in abeyance the physical forces, and makes them its servants. In a certain sense, it is true that the physical forces build up all organic structures; but the moment vitality is gone, they tear down the structures which they have unwillingly labored to construct under its control, and they cease not their work until every particle has taken the inorganic form. In the perfectly adjusted steam-engine, moving the ship against wind and tide, or weaving finest fabrics with iron fingers, it seems to the thoughtful observer that the steam is a willing servant, bending its energies to the work. But the mission of the steam is to shatter and destroy. It rushes into the cylinder, not to move the machinery, but in the very hatred of itself, and struggles to escape. It is the genius of man that controls the struggling monster by bands of iron too strong for him to break, till, in his rage, he lifts the piston and moves the swift machinery as he darts howling into the air. Thus, also, does vitality control and use the adverse forces of the inorganic world. As well might we think that the steam which drives the piston originated the locomotive, or the locomotive the engineer that controls it, as to think that life is the offspring of electricity or any other physical force. It is latest born of all the forces, if it is proper to call it a force at all; and the time may come when it will vanish from our globe, and leave the physical forces victors on the field. But while it is here it holds its ground by warfare. It builds up only through the agency of the physical forces. They build organized beings only under its control. We have of late had the announcement made that we must expunge from our text-books the assertion that the vital principle overrides or controls the chemical forces. We may expunge it from the text-books; but we might as well expunge the satellites of Jupiter or the planet Neptune from our astronomies."

How the absurdity grows as our examination advances! Even yet we have not seen its utmost folly. Suppose, now, we could account for life, or if not account for its introduction, let us agree that in some way it did arise from the impersonal forces, or was itself, as the old Anaximandrian or Democritical speculatists conjecture, a primitive, plastic, or spermatic matter. In any event, when the time arrived for its achievements, it was here. It came in among the old forces as soon as they had made suitable arrangements for its advent. It was one of those ancient, beautiful mornings, when the crystal hills and valleys were all aglow, and the tepid rivers were running into the boiling seas, that it came. The older forces had completed their work. It had taken a great time; but there it was, a grand accomplished fact Gravitation had parceled out the ancient mass into suitable divisions; cohesive attraction had welded them into separate unities; chemical affinity had gone among the particles, and sorted them into homologous compounds; electro-galvanic force had magnetized the whole with its wizard spell; motion, resultant of all the forces, had rounded them into orbs; order had arisen out of chaos; the suns had taken their allotted stations, and, as became the dignity of such grave bodies, had adjusted themselves to fixedness; the secondaries and their satellites had come to know their orbits and seasons; the climatic and atmospheric conditions were balanced and orderly; the whole machine was finished and lubricated and running beautifully, without a creak or jar. Throughout the infinite system there was not a pin out of order, or a cord or pulley astray. It was a wonderful piece of mechanism, seeing that it was the blind forces that did it, without intending to do any thing of the kind. Could an infinite mind have done better? It was a beautiful morning, we said. The old forces had gathered together to hold a jubilee. Great was their joy over the works of their hands. But it soon became apparent that they were not content. This might seem unreasonable; but, then, they were mere forces of dull matter, how could they be expected to be reasonable? Gravitation broke the silence in an address, it may be, something like the following:

"Most noble peers! great and mighty potentates! I have called you together, as seemed to be most fitting, that we might rejoice together over the completed work of our hands. Was ever any thing more glorious? Your royal highness, Cohesive Attraction, could not have acted more admirably. You have consolidated your atomic subjects, and bound them up in bonds more indissoluble than steel or iron. And what shall I say of the perfection of skill and taste displayed by your majesty, Chemical Affinity? But, most worshipful peers, is there nothing more that we can do? Have our resources entirely failed, and must we now subside into inglorious indolence? You see, we have already used up all the atoms; and if we are not henceforth to content ourselves in listless inaction, we must hit upon some new device, which, by its ingenious contrivance, will give us permanent employment, and, by its kaleidoscopic changes, give us ever new delight."

The suggestions of the president were listened to with profound attention, and gave great satisfaction. They sat for many days in council, and were sore put about by the difficulty of devising how to proceed. Gravitation said: "I wish I could do something more; but your royal highnesses know that, though my power is very extended, embracing and holding all these worlds under my absolute authority, yet, in duty I confess it, this is the only thing that I can do; eternal necessity limits me. I can hold the vast system that we have built in harmonious movement forever; every atom is my slave; but 'directly as the mass, and inversely as the square of the distance,' is my necessity."

Cohesive Attraction expressed regrets also, but found it impossible to do more than he had already done. "I can not transcend my necessity, which is, to weld the mass into unity and solidarity."

Attention being turned to Chemical Affinity, he said: "Most worthy colleagues, you have proof of my industry, and also my skill; but I, too, am limited, as yourselves. I unite affinitive particles, and make curious compounds, but the stubborn atoms will obey me only according to definitive and ancient compacts. They have strange antipathies, as well as strong friendships; and I can neither coax nor drive them out of their prejudices."

They were in despair at this speech; for they had found their colleague so fecund of great and curious devices, that they had made much reckoning on his reserved power. There was yet one hope: Electricity might meet the emergency. All eyes were turned to this gay cavalier. What he said was not reported, and men have never been able to find out; but it suffices, by some strange device—a marriage of some kind—a sub-rosa, star-chamber, secret arrangement, whose mystery has never been lifted—they did, among them, hit upon a happy expedient. When the curtain was lifted, a new personage was discovered in the council—his imperial highness, Vital Force. Great was the joy of his welcome. For millions of ages the lifeless orbs had revolved through space untenanted, beauteous in crystal forms, and lustrous with the radiance of many suns, but empty of flower and plumage and song. The new artist entered at once upon his work. First he went out over the hills and valleys on a tour of observation, to see what it would be wise to do. He found that Atmospheric Action,

Force of Gravity, and Mechanical Attrition had broken off the crystals, and formed loose earth; and that Chemistry had prepared a transparent fluid, which often became vapor, and, rising up into the air, was drifted by the winds over the lands, until, condensing, it fell in showers, moistening the fragments, and spreading them out into soft and movable soils, and he said, "These singular conditions are just to my hand;" so Vital Force filled his apron full of seeds, and with the speed of wind he flew around the world, and planted it all over with most various and curious germs, and told them to grow; and when the earth had passed half-way through its annual orbit, it was coated with beautiful grasses, and many-colored and scented flowers and herbs; and Gravitation and Cohesive Attraction and Chemical Affinity and Magnetism clapped their hands, and shouted themselves hoarse, until the universe was filled with the resounding echo, "Eureka! Eureka!" Then they said: "It is a beautiful cosmos; but why should flowers bloom, and trees and herbage grow, purposeless? Go to, now, let us do something more wonderful still." Then they summoned their great captain again, and told him how delighted they were with his matchless work; but lest he might be proud and vain in his imagination, they gently reminded him that, whatever he was in greatness and skill, he was their offspring. But it occurred to Electro-Magnetism, who, somehow, seemed to have special pride in Vital Force, possibly because he had engendered him—be that as it may, it occurred to him to suggest whether it was not possible that some other kinds of living things might be made. Vital

Force said he would think about the suggestion, and put his head to work to see what might be done, and report at a future meeting; and all retired well pleased.

Vital Force went immediately to his study, and noted down the hint of Electro-Magnetism, and set apart a day for its consideration. The more he thought, the more interested he became. The curious things that came into his head, and mustered before his imagination, were almost suggestive of intelligence. Finally, after a long time—no doubt Electro-Magnetism had forgotten all about the hint dropped ages before—the whole matter opened with the clearness of sunrise upon the view of the unwearied student. Taking his hand from his aching head, and leaping into the air with a flash, he shouted, "Eureka!"—he had learned the word from the old forces. He had discovered how to make creatures, having power of locomotion, who should subsist on the very herbs which he had already set growing on the earth, and in the sea; creatures that could swim in the seas, and fly in the air, and run up and down the world on legs; creatures with stomachs and mouths and articulated frames; with eyes and ears and song; of many kinds, from the littleness of a mote to the largeness of a whale. So he went out one morning, when the trees were waving in the sunlight, and the grasses were growing thick along the brooks, and commenced his work. He never told any body the secret, so we know not how he began. But begin he did; and directly the seas and the air and the earth were swarming with all manner of fishes and birds and beasts. It seemed almost as if the old forces had some dim prophecy, and, in fact, as if they had worked with reference to this state of things; as if the soils were made on purpose for the seeds, and the herbs for the stomachs, and light for the eyes, and air for the lungs. It really looked like it; but of course it was not so. Blind forces do work so strangely sometimes!

But we have not reached the greatest puzzle yet. When the forces came together again to rejoice over the grand whole, the completed cosmos, they were in ecstasies; and then they bethought them, that a thing of such beauty and manifold purpose ought to have a sovereign; and they joined together on the spot, and made a man, and set him over it all. Then they stopped creation, and went into the trades. They became farmers and boss-carpenters, and workers in stone and brass and iron, and dealers in curious instruments, and projectors of great traffic; inventors and artists and authors; they built railroads and steam-ships, and wove a web of electric telegraph over the surface of the world; built cities, founded commonwealths, wrote laws; they made telescopes, and constructed astronomy; they speculated on their own doings, and wrote books about it, and laughed at the jokes they practiced on each other. Among their grand feats in authorship were Milton's matchless dream, and Shakspeare's witching tragedies. The world, in all its highways and byways, is full of their creations. In song, they composed Handel's Messiah; in color, they painted Raphael's Madonna. It is strange, is it not, what the blind forces did and what they still are doing! One can hardly credit what he sees and hears of them.

A bold attempt to reach unity of substance appears in a late number of the *North British Review*, and ingenious as bold. The writer says: "All true philosophy seeks to be universal, to contemplate the universe as a whole, possessed of an intrinsic unity. Hence, all true philosophy must assume that the dualism of mind and matter is only an apparent dualism, and that beneath lies a more comprehensive unity. . . There are two ways in which a philosopher may attempt, as far as he is able, to exhibit the unity of matter and mind, or, to use a better term, spirit. He may set down matter as an ultimate, and make spirit a function of matter; or he may set down spirit as ultimate, and make matter a function of spirit." For himself he says: "I hold, then, that all substratum or substance is of a spiritual nature; that the external world is definable as the perpetual interchange of impressions between spiritual beings. Body is strictly definable as the manifestation of spirit to spirit. Wherein does positive existence consist? I reply, in the spiritual basis of phenomena. Phenomena are the impressions which spirit makes upon spirit." Another late writer, an American, holds: "The inmost principle is the Divine life itself; not the Divine essence, as the pantheist would say, but an effluence from it, whence all the qualities of matter are but as leaves and blossoms from a stem. And is it not therefore true—not that he created it once out of nothing—but that he creates it every moment out of himself? And does not the great truth begin to dawn upon us, that the relation of creator and created subsists all the while, and if suspended for a single instant, the universe vanishes, like a bubble that breaks in air ?"

So far forth as these and similar utterances, which may be found interlarding the spiritual philosophy, so called, and the advanced theology of the times, simply mean to affirm that God is ultimate, we accept them ; but so far as they are pantheistic—deifying matter or materializing Divine essence—we discard them as unscientific, as puerile nescience.

Between God and all finite existence there is absolute otherness, and not identity. They have no attribute in common. Science finds God nowhere among things ; but it finds nothing that does not point onward to him. The telescope of the astronomer, sweeping the scope of sidereal heavens, nowhere gets a glimpse of their Maker ; but every shining orb proclaims his invisible presence and power. The microscope of the naturalist has no lens strong enough to take the tissue of his essence, but announces his sustaining agency under every infinitesimal life. The retort of the chemist decomposes all substances, without disclosing his essence ; but it finds no nicest grain of impalpable matter that bears not his impress. He hides behind the lightnings, and the luminiferous ether is but the sheen of his garment.

The wild dream of atheism and pantheism is as ancient as speculative thought. Long before Democritus and Leucippus, the elder atomists, it flourished in the East. No age has been without its advocates. The weird and marvelous developments of modern science furnished it a new opportunity to repair its broken fortunes, and, with amazing genius, it sought to suborn the new evangel. But it has signally failed. Science scorns the alliance. Against the profane attempt to merge the infinite and the created into unity, it is as loud and angry in its protest as its older-born and diviner sister, revelation. Equally they forbid the banns. Causation is scientifically, as well as Biblically, severed from matter. Its home is determined in the transcendental, metaphysical. Force comes to unity in spirit. As every invention first comes to reality in thought before it bodies in form ; as every end exists first in idea before it becomes incorporate, so it is a dictum of science, and a necessity of thought, that all material atoms, having affinities or ends, were first ideal, mental, existent simply in thought, and were evolved into reality by the fiat of the thinker. If any thing is demonstrated, it is, that personal cause is the necessity of the universe, and that the universe, existing by personal cause, is distinct from it.

I have not designed, of course, to give the argument, but only to indicate the relations of modern science to the question. While the heavens spread their starry arches above us, and the earth and the air and the sea pulsate with life and thought about us, God will not be without a witness. Every lane of science is finger-boarded, "*This way leads to God.*"

Lecture II.

ORIGIN OF LIFE:

An Examination of Huxley.

BY THE

REV. RANDOLPH S. FOSTER, D. D., LL. D.,

President of the Drew Theological Seminary,

Madison, New Jersey.

LECTURE II.

ORIGIN OF LIFE.

EXAMINATION OF HUXLEY.

HAVING established the existence of eternal, spiritual, intelligent *will-force,* as alone spontaneous, and as causative of all material forces, which have their evolutions in time, and which are necessitated in their evolutions, and which also are subordinated to the ends of ultimate and complex plans and arrangements, for a higher unity, we are prepared to advance to the discussion of the mode in which this great factor proceeded to construct living organisms.

There are two questions, not always separated in thought, but extremely distinct, lying in the embrace of this great problem. They need both to be dealt with, and in severance; the closing of neither, alone, ends the great debate. The first, relates to the origin of life; the second, to the origin of the diversified forms in which life shrines itself.

The first is treated by Professor Huxley, more specifically; while the second is the main subject of Darwin's elaborate dissertations. In the current parlance, they are jointly spoken of as Darwinism.

The conclusions of these noted, perhaps we should say eminent, scientists, are received by multitudes of admirers, as final on all questions with regard to which they express opinions. It is, indeed, deemed real impertinence, in some circles, to intimate a doubt, or raise a suspicion, that possibly they may not be quite infallible; and it would be a bold venture in even a specialist, to dissent from them on a scientific issue. But they are not the only eminent scientists who have uncovered a weak spot in attempting to prescribe mere conjectures for science. Even Achilles was vincible in his heel. Scientists, mighty in their special line, become like other men when they *dream*. We are bold to examine their conclusions, and declare non-concurrence, even without pretending to comparable scientific attainments, on the ground that they have abandoned Bacon, and fallen into a poor imitation of Bunyan.

It may be proper, before we proceed to the examination of their conclusions, and premises as well—but especially their conclusions, since it is assumed that they have quite retired the Bible, demonstrated it false and baseless in its teachings—to ascertain what its teachings are on the points in dispute; especially since we hope to show that they are neither baseless nor false, but the very truth, to which their science, rightly so called, does reverent homage.

The Scriptural theory is, that, primitively, there existed one only being; an Eternal Spirit, who, by the sole force of his will, in a manner ineffable and inconceivable to us, created the very essence of all other being; imparting to the essence so made all included forces and tendencies, insomuch that they are precisely what and as they are, in these respects, because he so determined; and so that there is nothing that he did not create and make. The product is not a part of himself, but a product of his power, which, as it was originated, may at any time be retired without affecting his being. It includes two distinct and easily differentiated substances, with discrete and conspicuously separate and separable classes of attributes. These are entities, and not merely mystical or ideal things. The creation is of solid and real being, but which has no other root except the infinite will which caused and continues it.

These substances are forever subject to his control, and under his government, but not in the same manner; the one existing and acting under direct and necessary impulses from him—mere slaves; the other invested with a power of spontaneous and perfectly free action, but held to limitation and responsibility by him.

Out of the created material substance, he fashioned the material cosmos, subordinating the included forces to that end, and making them the perpetual slaves of his purpose, so that, whatever they seem to do of themselves, they are really but modes of the manifestations of his power, visible expressions of his invisible will.

The *time* when this most primitive creative act occurred is called "the beginning;" but how remote it was from the present, as we count time, by the revolutions of the earth in its orbit, or the infinitely grander solar and sidereal cycles, is not anywhere intimated. There are Biblical as well as scientific reasons for placing it at an almost infinite distance in the remote past.

There is equal silence on the *method* of the Divine procedure. Whether the creative fiat struck the spheres, "full-orbed in all their round of rays complete," into being in one instant of time, and sent them on their magnificent circuits through the fields of space, as is the poet's brilliant dream, or rolled them up into solid resplendent balls, from a fire-mist of infinitesimal monads, disseminated over immensities of space, through eras of almost infinite length, as is the probable discovery of science—if true, the most sublime of its achievements—the record says not a syllable. What it declares, in words as concise as the event is majestic, is: "In the beginning, God created the heaven and the earth." With this statement it was content, and left it for the inquisitive wonder of adoring or irreverent men to search out the mystery of his ways, and develop the method of his power.

The *order* is not omitted. The declaration is express that in process of time, by a subsequent creative fiat, he who made the heavens and the earth, *created* life upon the earth; each of the kinds, vegetable and animal, in the order named, and their included kinds in an order of eminence specifically mentioned. But here again, as before, the precise method is left in obscurity, while the fact and order are incisively enunciated. Whether the differentiated species were discretely evolved by the creative fiat, in their several and perfect forms, at once, or simply germs of life were created, from which, starting at unity, all diversities of form have arisen by slow and tedious development, through almost infinite ages of time, as is the fascinating dream of Darwin, is nowhere stated. It is asserted by M'Cosh, and other not less eminent defenders of the Bible, that if science should establish the theory of evolution, it would not in the least conflict with the inspired text. Some even suppose that the text strongly hints the idea. It must be admitted that the language employed is very remarkable.

"And God said, Let the earth bring forth grass, the herb yielding seed, and the fruit-tree yielding fruit after his kind, whose seed is in itself, upon the earth: and it was so. And the earth brought forth grass, and herb yielding seed after his kind, and the tree yielding fruit, whose seed was in itself, after his kind." (Gen. i, 11, 12.) "And God said, Let the waters bring forth abundantly the moving creature that hath life, and fowl that may fly above the earth in the open firmament of heaven. And God created great whales, and every living creature that moveth, which the waters brought forth abundantly, after their kind, and every winged fowl after his kind: and God saw that it was good. And God blessed them, saying, Be fruitful, and multiply, and fill the waters in the seas, and let fowl multiply in the earth." (Gen. i, 20, 21, 22.) "And God said, Let the earth bring forth the living creature after his kind, cattle, and creeping thing, and beast of the earth after his kind: and it was so. And God made the beast of the earth after his kind, and cattle after their kind, and every thing that creepeth upon the earth after his kind: and God saw that it was good." (Gen. i, 24, 25.) This is the entire of what is said on the subject of the introduction of life upon the earth, except the particular account of the creation of man. Any after-references to the subject are such as simply allude to, or reiterate, the fact that God is the absolute creator of life in its various forms. Now, it is a remarkable fact that, in this account, the two things distinctly stated are, that God commanded life into being in a certain order of time, and in all the varieties of kind in which it is found to exist; indicating, also, the law of its propagation; but no statement is made as to how he fashioned the diverse organisms—whether he made each organism by a several creative act, or evolved them all, in their diverse kinds, from a primitive seed of life, which he made to contain them. The sum of the statement is, that he commanded the unliving elements of the earth and the sea to bring forth the *diverse kinds*, and his command was a creative fiat. The diverse kinds were contained in the fiat; but how, is not said.

That each several species was the product of a discrete creative act, we do not find reason to doubt; but the text is not shut up absolutely to this hypothesis. "Suppose it proved," says Doctor M'Cosh, "that there is such a thing as spontaneous generation; would religion thereby be overthrown, either in its evidences, its doctrines, or its precepts? I have doubts if it would. The great body of thinkers in ancient times—even those most inclined to theism—seem to have believed that lower creatures sprang out of the dust of the earth, without the need of a previous germ. Some of the profoundest theologians and ablest defenders of religion in the early Church, were believers in the doctrine of spontaneous generation; which may be consistently held in modern times by believers in natural and revealed religion." "Plants and animals," he goes on to say, "are now formed out of germs; or, if you can show it to be so, out of wisely endowed and carefully prepared matter. But how are they propagated? is the next question. By special acts of creation, or by development? I do not know that religion, natural or revealed, has any interest in holding by any particular view on the subject, any more than it has in maintaining any special theory as to the formation of strata of stone in the earth's surface. It is now admitted that Christians may hold, in perfect consistency with religion and Genesis, that certain layers of rocks were formed, not at once by a fiat of God, but mediately by water and fire, as the agents of God. And are they not at liberty to hold always, if evidence be produced, that higher plants have been developed from lower, and higher brutes from lower, according to certain laws of descent, known or unknown, working in favorable circumstances? There is nothing irreligious in the idea of development, properly understood.* It would not appall our faith, if it should be discovered that all the forms of life below man could be traced to a spontaneous generation from the unliving monads, and that from unity they were developed into diversity; given, that the spontaneous movement, from its inception to its ultimatum, emanated from, and was guided by, the Divine factor. We should still hold

* "Christianity and Positivism," pp. 36–8.

that the Bible story was the true and authentic account of creation, uncontradicted in a single syllable: more, we should find in the fact, if possible, additional support to our faith, because of the peculiar structure of the statement contained in the inspired text. We feel not the slightest alarm at the furor which has been awakened on the subject, and do not enter the arena to defend a faith, which has been put in peril by scientific discoveries, but only to aid in fixing the true status of the question, as between science and the Bible.

We advance with entire composure to the examination of the supposed scientific discoveries of "the origin of life," and the development of the organic forms in which it manifests itself "upon earth."

The origin of life is a subject which has interested the wisest and most thoughtful men, from the earliest ages. There have always been two, perhaps three, schools of thinkers in relation to it; materialists, who have accounted for it as either inherent in, or the product of, matter, by evolution; theists, who have believed it to be the immediate product of the gods; with, perhaps, an intermediate school, of pantheists, who blended the two. The doctrines which are just now awakening so wide attention, almost panic, are not new; in one phase or another, they date back to Anaximander, or the elder atomists. Several times they have invaded and disturbed Christian thought. Lamarck propounded them with great confidence, in the last century; and less than thirty years ago, within the memory of the present generation, they were reproduced with marvelous brilliancy, by an anonymous author, under the style of "The Vestiges of Creation;" a work not less widely read at the time, and producing a scarcely less profound agitation, than the books of Darwin, Huxley, Spencer, Tyndall, and others, to-day. The wave passed by, and left no ripple-marks. Professor Huxley, now, with, it may be, more learning, and many new facts—evidence of the progress of the times in which we live—renews the combat with brilliant promise, and is greeted with pæans of victory, before the ink is dry upon his pages. He has discovered the origin of life; the ages-old problem has finally reached a scientific solution. It is a bold venture.

What, then, is his solution? "The Physical Basis of Life," is the style of the essay in which he develops fully the theory which had been propounded, in part, in his discussion of "The Origin of Species," and other writings. The title suggests the idea of the treatise. He seeks, and professes to have found, the basis of life in matter, or, as his thesis requires, a composition of matter which underlies and originates life. In the unity of the composite substance he finds the unity of all life, as in the composition he finds the cause of all life; one invariable cause of one identical effect, manifesting itself in a variety of forms. He gives to the substance the name "protoplasm," or "matter of life." It is important to be remembered, especially as we shall not always find him consistent with himself, that the conditions of the problem are, not that he find the plasm, or matrix, in which life is cast, but that he find the origin of that which takes form in the mold. He advances not a step toward the origin of life, by discovering the components of the matter in which it invariably makes its home, if it were possible to do that. It is requisite that he should show, further, that the plasm, by virtue of its composition, is living, or that it becomes life; the protoplasm must be not simply the home of life, but it must originate, or in substance be, the occupant of the home; or the question remains, Whence the occupant? Precisely what Professor Huxley professes to do is, to identify life and protoplasm; to demonstrate that life is not something added to protoplasm, but is a component part.

This appears in many paragraphs of his writings, but in none more explicitly than the following:

"It will be observed that the existence of the matter of life depends on the pre-existence of certain compounds; namely, carbonic acid, water, and ammonia. Withdraw any one of these three from the world, and all vital phenomena come to an end. They are related to the protoplasm of the plant, as the protoplasm of the plant is to that of the animal. Carbon, hydrogen, oxygen, and nitrogen are all lifeless bodies. Of these, carbon and oxygen unite, in certain proportions and under certain conditions, to give rise to carbonic acid; hydrogen and oxygen produce water; nitrogen and hydrogen give rise to ammonia. These new compounds, like the elementary bodies of which they are composed, are lifeless. But when they are brought together, under certain conditions, they give rise to the still more complex body, protoplasm, and this protoplasm exhibits the phenomena of life."

This sentence is pregnant of significance. It is

true, that when he declares that protoplasm exhibits the phenomena of life, he introduces the qualifying phrase, "under certain conditions;" which might relieve him of the imputation of identifying protoplasm with life, or life with the matter of protoplasm; but what follows commits him inextricably. Says he:

"I see no break in this series of steps in molecular complication, and I am unable to understand why the language which is applicable to any one term of the series may not be used to any of the others. We think fit to call different kinds of matter carbon, oxygen, hydrogen, and nitrogen, and to speak of the various powers and activities of these substances as the properties of the matter of which they are composed. When hydrogen and oxygen are mixed, in a certain proportion, and the electric spark is passed through them, they disappear, and a quantity of water, equal in weight to the sum of their weights, appears in their place. There is not the slightest parity between the passive and active powers of the water and those of the oxygen and hydrogen, which have given rise to it. At 32° Fahrenheit, and far below that temperature, oxygen and hydrogen are elastic, gaseous bodies, whose particles tend to rush away from one another with great force. Water, at the same temperature, is a strong, though brittle solid, whose particles tend to cohere into definite geometrical shapes, and sometimes build up frosty imitations of the most complex forms of vegetable foliage."

Attend closely to the following sentence:

"Nevertheless, we call these, and many other strange phenomena, the properties of water; and we do not hesitate to believe that, in some way or another, they result from the properties of the component elements of the water."

Nothing can be more obvious than that he means to be understood as holding, that, even as the compound body, water, has nothing in it apart from the oxygen and hydrogen components; that, as the combination of these two gives rise to all the peculiar qualities of the resultant, without the addition of anything else; so the compound substance, resultant from the union of unliving water, ammonia, and carbonic acid, derives all its qualities, life included, from the combination; the life is not something apart from the component elements, but is of them, and but waits for the union for its manifestation. That that is precisely his meaning, the thesis, to account for the origin of life, requires, and his further statement still more expressly declares:

"We do not assume that a something called 'aquosity,' entered into, and took possession of, the oxide of hydrogen as soon as it was formed, and then guided the aqueous particles to their places in the facets of the crystal, or among the leaflets of the hoarfrost. On the contrary, we live in the hope and in the faith that, by the advance of molecular physics, we shall, by and by, be able to see our way as clearly from the constituents of water to the properties of water, as we are now able to deduce the operations of a watch from the form of its parts and the manner in which they are put together."

Note the words following:

"Is the case in any way changed when carbonic

acid, water, and ammonia disappear, and in their place, under the influence of pre-existing living protoplasm, an equivalent weight of the matter of life makes its appearance?

"It is true that there is no sort of parity between the properties of the components and the properties of the resultant, but neither was there in the case of the water. It is also true that what I have spoken of as the influence of pre-existing living matter, is something quite unintelligible; but does any body quite comprehend the *modus operandi* of an electric spark, which traverses a mixture of oxygen and hydrogen?"

Nothing could be more obvious than all this, and especially in connection with the question which is immediately added:

"What justification is there, then, for the assumption of the existence in the living matter of a something which has no representative, or correlative, in the not-living matter which gave rise to it? What better philosophical status has 'vitality' than 'aquosity?' . .

"If scientific language is to possess a definite and constant signification whenever it is employed, it seems to me that we are logically bound to apply to the protoplasm, or physical basis of life, the same conceptions as those which are held to be legitimate elsewhere. If the phenomena exhibited by water are its properties, so are those presented by protoplasm, living or dead, its properties.

"If the properties of water may be properly said to result from the nature and disposition of its component molecules, I can find no intelligible ground for refusing to say that the properties of protoplasm result from the nature and disposition of its molecules.

"But I bid you beware that, in accepting these conclusions, you are placing your feet on the first rung of a ladder which, in most people's estimation, is the reverse of Jacob's, and leads to the antipodes of heaven. It may seem a small thing to admit that the dull, vital actions of a fungus, or a foraminifer, are the properties of their protoplasm, and are the direct results of the nature of the matter of which they are composed."

Here we are told, in direct terms, that the vital action is a property of protoplasmic matter. And now follows the most remarkable and the most important sentence in the treatise:

"But if, as I have endeavored to prove to you, their protoplasm is essentially identical with, and most readily converted into, that of any animal, I can discover no logical halting-place between the admission that such is the case, and the further concession that all vital action may, with equal propriety, be said to be the result of the molecular forces of the protoplasm which displays it. And, if so, it must be true, in the same sense and to the same extent, that the thoughts to which I am now giving utterance, and your thoughts regarding them, are the expression of molecular changes in that matter of life which is the source of our other vital phenomena."*

This language, if terms have any meaning, convicts its author of teaching that all vital phenomena, mental as well as physical, sensation as well as respir-

* "The Physical Basis of Life:" in "Lay Sermons"—pp. 135-138—Appleton's edition.

ation, thought as well as digestion—all vital phenomena, from the contraction of a nerve to the highest flight of imagination or profoundest intuition of reason—are but the result of the molecular forces of protoplasm which displays them.

Tyndall, a name not less potent than either of the two distinguished masters already quoted, is, if possible, more bold. "Supposing, then," he says, "the molecules of the human body, instead of replacing others, and thus renewing a pre-existing form, to be gathered first-hand from nature, and put together in the same relative position which they occupy in the body; that they have the self-same forces and distribution of forces, the self-same motions and distribution of motions,—would this organized concourse of molecules stand before us as a sentient, thinking being? There seems no valid reason to believe that it would not. Or, supposing a planet came from the sun, and set spinning round its axis, and revolving round the sun at a distance from him equal to that of our earth, would one of the consequences of its refrigeration be the development of organic forms? I lean to the affirmative. Structural forces are certainly in the mass, whether or not these forces reach to the extent of forming a plant or an animal. In an amorphous drop of water lie latent all the marvels of crystalline force; and who will set limits to the possible play of molecules in a cooling planet? If these statements startle, it is because matter has been defined and maligned by philosophers and theologians, who were equally unaware that it is, at the bottom, essentially mystical and transcendental."*

Stebbing, one of the admiring adherents of the school, thus states his interpretation of the theory: "The problem upon which many thoughts and speculations of science are for the moment converging, is the origin of life. There are some who believe that, under certain chemical conditions, living creatures are continually coming into existence, ungenerated by any living parent; born, as it were, without birth; acquiring an animated existence, with powers of motion, feeding, and reproduction, from substances previously wanting in one or all of the capacities,—such creatures, in short, as, if asked for their parentage, would but answer each for itself, My father was an atom, and my mother a molecule. It should be remembered that the little animals, supposed to arise in the manner described, first become visible, if at all, as the tiniest objects that the microscope can detect. But whether there is or is not, in these days, a continual coming into existence of these infinitesimal pigmies, they are just such productions as the theory of development would suppose to have arisen originally, constituting the first outburst of life upon the globe, ancestral to the noblest forms of animated nature now extant, progenitors in an unbroken line of man himself."†

We have quoted thus extensively in our desire to do perfect justice by the eminent names whose opinions we combat, and that our readers may know the

*"Fragments of Science;" article, "Vitality," page 441.
†"Essay on Darwinism," page 94.

grounds upon which we interpret their theories; and especially because we shall soon find them taking back their own postulates and repudiating their own conclusions.

For a moment, before we advance to the rebuttal, we desire to present, free from all gloss, and nakedly, what we have found to be their teaching.

The basis of life is protoplasm. All the phenomena of life are resultant of protoplasm. All thoughts and feelings, as well as motions—all forms of activity, moral and mental, as well as physical—are properties of protoplasm; that is, of carbonic acid, ammonia, and water, chemically combined. Carbonic acid, water, and ammonia, apart, are lifeless bodies, subject to the common law of gravitation. Lying inert and dead in the common mass of matter, they enter into a copartnership, and go walking and flying, exhibiting all the phenomena of life. They were, when separate, involuntary and impassive and unintelligent; united, they think and will and feel. One parcel of carbonic acid, water, and ammonia, is cunning, shy, deceptive; another, dull, stupid, idiotic. One parcel, timid, hesitating, cowardly; another, bold, fearless, brave. One parcel, selfish, sinister, knavish; another, disinterested, magnanimous, cosmopolitan. One parcel, the slave of lust, of appetite, of passion, given to rapine, cruelty, and war; another yields to the sway of the ideas of the right, the beautiful, the true, and gives himself to the arts of peace and deeds of charity and love. One parcel loves song, and becomes a Handel, a Mozart, a Haydn; another is enamored of poetry, turns into a Homer, and writes the Iliad; into a Shakspeare, and composes the immortal tragedies; into a Milton, and creates the dream of heaven and hell. And yet another is imbued with the divine fervor of eloquence, and pours Ciceronian, Demosthenian, Websterian thunders down along the ages. Carbonic acid, water, and ammonia, that is all! One set of protoplasms indite laws, philosophies, religions, and set up governments, constitutions, and dynasties; another set invent steamships, printing-presses, electric telegraphs; and yet another hoard of brigand protoplasmic cells let loose the dogs of war, and, rushing with the frenzy of hate, fatten the fields of Marathon, Waterloo, Gettysburg, and Sedan, with their carbonic acid, water, and ammonia—protoplasmic dust!

Of this marvelous thesis, we are bold to say, you will search in vain, not only through all the pages of these eminent men, but no less fruitlessly through all science, and over the entire field of nature, for a particle of proof. Neither experiment nor observation has ever been able to point to a single instance of the origin of life from the mere union of carbonic acid, ammonia, and water. It is an assumption without the shadow of proof, and an assumption beset with the most trenchant difficulties that ever confronted any hypothesis.

The entire of what is known of life is, that it is a force which never, under any chemical or other conditions of matter, comes into existence or manifestation in unliving matter, except as it is propagated by living matter. Dead matter, organic or inorganic, has not now, and, so far as the proof extends, never did have power, under any conditions, to originate it; or, if so, the fact has never been made known to man, and rests upon no other foundation than unwarranted conjecture. The proof is positive that it can not be so; it is demonstrable that the hypothesis is false.* Thought is the topmost phenomenon of being—mentality. It as certainly antedates all cosmical wonders, from the primitive monad upward, as it pre-dates, in the inventor's brain, the mechanism he creates. "The physical basis" is too slender to support the superstructure. Protoplasm is a high compound, set apart and divinely designated to an honorable use; the palace of life, nothing more. The transcendental king comes to his palace and throne, beautifully and wondrously built up of the dead carbon, oxygen, hydrogen, and nitrogen, from afar, and sets light in its windows more lucent than diamonds, and makes all its telegraphic nerves dance and thrill with ecstasies of feeling and thought. But he was not born here; he is the bridegroom, coming with a shining train, to his waiting bride; his entrance wakes music and life in all the halls and along the corridors of his beautiful home.

We know nothing of final cause, we are told. Science ignores every such idea. Cause is transcendental; we know only what we touch and handle and feel,—that is science. Is it so? I see a graded way across a continent; the hills are leveled and tunneled; the rivers and streams arched with masonry and bridged with wood and iron; rails of

* For an exhaustive view of spontaneous generation, see Mivart and Figuier.

steel are laid upon ties of timber; a locomotive and train of cars, with strong wheels carefully fitted to the tram-ways, rush, with almost lightning speed, from one end of the land to the other; there are switches and turn-tables and tanks, and depots for men and merchandise. These things I see and know to exist. Do I know that the locomotive was made to draw the train; the trams made for the wheels; the cars for freight and passengers? I thought I did. It did seem to me that the purpose for which a thing was made might be known as well as the thing itself; that mind and thought were as really revealed, as the thing which they produced for a definite purpose; that even as I know there are eyes, I know they were for seeing; that the final cause, in innumerable cases, is as obvious to reason as matter bodying it is to sense. This, we are certain, is the common sense of mankind, which they will be slow to renounce at the bidding of pompous names. There is nothing better known to our experience and consciousness both, than that final cause, which is henceforth to be expunged from our knowledges, in the dream of the blatant experimentalists and positivists of modern notoriety.

Will it surprise you when I say that, after all, Professor Huxley himself acknowledges that he has failed; and, in concluding his elaborate researches, admits that the life which he sought in, and declared to be of, matter, has a metaphysical source? He shall confess for himself:

"In seeking for the origin of protoplasm, we must eventually turn to the vegetable world. The fluid containing carbonic acid, water, and ammonia, which offers such a Barmecide feast to the animal, is a table richly spread to multitudes of plants; and, with a due supply of only such materials, many a plant will not only maintain itself in vigor, but grow and multiply until it has increased a million-fold, or a million million-fold, the quantity of protoplasm which it originally possessed; in this way building up the matter of life, to an indefinite extent, from the common matter of the universe. Thus, the animal can only raise the complex substance of dead protoplasm to the higher power, as one may say, of living protoplasm; while the plant can raise the less complex substances—carbonic acid, water, and ammonia—to the same stage of living protoplasm, if not to the same level."*

The plant, then, a living being, is factor of protoplasm; so protoplasm, in place of originating life, is elaborated only by life. To the same effect are these words, taken from another work by the same writer:

"The horse makes up its wastes by feeding; and its food is grass or oats, or perhaps other vegetable products. Therefore, in the long run, the source of all this complex machinery lies in the vegetable kingdom. But where does the grass or oats, or any other plant, obtain this nourishing, food-producing material? At first it is a little seed, which soon begins to draw into itself, from the earth and the surrounding air, matters which, in themselves, contain no vital properties whatever; it absorbs into its own substance, water, an inorganic body; it draws into its substance,

* "The Physical Basis of Life," "Lay Sermons," p. 134, Appleton's edition.

carbonic acid, an inorganic matter; and ammonia, another inorganic matter, found in the air; and then, by some wonderful chemical process, the details of which the chemists do not yet understand, though they are near foreshadowing them, it (the living seed) combines them into one substance which is known as 'proteine,' a complex compound of carbon, hydrogen, oxygen, and nitrogen, which alone possesses the property of manifesting vitality, and permanently supporting animal life. So that you see that the waste products of the animal economy, the effete materials, which are continually being thrown off by all living beings, in the form of inorganic matters, are constantly replaced by supplies of the necessary repairing and rebuilding materials drawn from the plants; which, in their turn, manufacture them, so to speak, by a mysterious combination of those same inorganic materials. Thus we come to the conclusion, strange at first sight, that the matter constituting the living world is identical with that which forms the inorganic world."*

"Notwithstanding all the fundamental resemblances which exist between the powers of the protoplasm in plants and in animals, they present a striking difference in the fact that plants can manufacture fresh protoplasm out of mineral compounds; whereas animals are obliged to procure it ready made, and hence, in the long-run, depend upon plants. Upon what condition this difference in the power of the two great divisions of the world of life depends, nothing is at present known."†

* Huxley: "Origin of Species," pp. 15–17.

† "The Physical Basis of Life:" "Lay Sermons," p. 126.

Finally, he says of these teachings of his:

"I should not wonder if 'gross and brutal materialism' were the mildest phrase applied to them in certain quarters. And, most undoubtedly, the terms of the propositions are distinctly materialistic. Nevertheless, two things are certain: the one, that I hold the statements to be substantially true; the other, that I, individually, am no materialist, but, on the contrary, believe materialism to involve grave philosophical error.

"This union of materialistic terminology with the repudiation of materialistic philosophy, I share with some of the most thoughtful men with whom I am acquainted. And, when I first undertook to deliver the present discourse, it appeared to me to be a fitting opportunity to explain how such a union is not only consistent with, but necessitated by, sound logic. I purposed to lead you through the territory of vital phenomena to the materialistic slough in which you find yourselves now plunged, and then to point out to you the sole path by which, in my judgment, extrication is possible."*

This is very remarkable language, as disclosing the fact that, after all, Huxley does not believe that he accounts for life without a metaphysical cause. He employs materialistic language, but only for convenience of terminology, while he has a reserved metaphysical sense; he plunges us into the slough of materialism by its use, but tells us in the end, it is only a trick of logic, in which he, personally, has no faith at all; indeed, knows to be misleading and false,

* "Physical Basis of Life:" "Lay Sermons," p. 139.

but from which the only escape is to continue to employ the misleading terms.

"If we find that the ascertainment of the order of nature is facilitated by using one terminology, or one set of symbols, rather than another, it is our clear duty to use the former; and no harm can accrue, so long as we bear in mind that we are dealing merely with terms and symbols. In itself, it is of little moment whether we express the phenomena of matter in terms of spirit, or the phenomena of spirit in terms of matter; matter may be regarded as a form of thought, thought may be regarded as a property of matter,—each statement has a certain relative truth. But with a view to the progress of science, the materialistic terminology is in every way to be preferred; for it connects thought with the other phenomena of the universe, and suggests inquiry into the nature of those physical conditions, or concomitants of thought, which are more or less accessible to us, and a knowledge of which may, in future, help us to exercise the same kind of control over the world of thought as we already possess in respect of the material world; whereas, the alternative, or spiritualistic, terminology is utterly barren, and leads to nothing but obscurity and confusion of ideas.

"Thus, there can be little doubt that the further science advances, the more extensively and consistently will all the phenomena of nature be represented by materialistic formulæ and symbols.

"But the man of science, who, forgetting the limits of philosophical inquiry, slides from these formulæ and symbols into what is commonly understood by materialism, seems to me to place himself on a level with the mathematician who should mistake the *x's* and *y's*, with which he works his problems, for real entities—and with this further disadvantage, as compared with the mathematician, that the blunders of the latter are of no practical consequence, while the errors of systematic materialism may paralyze the energies and destroy the beauty of a life."*

The question comes back with all its original difficulty, therefore, as is here confessed: Whence did the vegetable world get its original protoplasm, the matter of life in which it started as a factor of protoplasm? As living, it is able to extract the nutriment of its life, by a chemistry peculiar to itself, from inorganic substances, to make its protoplasm; but this is no account of its origin, but only of the mode of its sustentation. It in turn becomes transmuted into the tissues of the living animal; but the fact that it becomes nutriment to the animal life, does not account for the origin of that which it nourishes. The substance of all which is, that there is matter without life and matter with life, the only differentiation being life; the one dead protoplasm, the other living protoplasm. Whence the life is, remains unexplained by science, and has no solution except that, like matter in which it dwells, it was created—not evolved from unliving forces.

If, then, all should be granted that is claimed as known by these savans, what disquietude ought it give to our faith? None at all. What warrant does it give for their boast that life is a phenomenon, evolved from the forces of unliving matter? None at

* "Physical Basis of Life:" "Lay Sermons," pp. 145, 6.

all. This appears, and it is no great addition to former knowledge: there is a composition of matter which is the basis of life, as being a form of matter in which life manifests itself; let it be called protoplasm, the name is harmless. This protoplasm is formed from unliving matter; its chemical constituents are water, ammonia, carbonic acid; it is the same in fungus and man, or nearly so; the plant derives it from the unliving elements, hydrogen, nitrogen, oxygen, carbon; the animal takes it from the plant; when plant or animal dies, the protoplasm returns to unliving dust; each vegetable elaborates its own protoplasm, and never that of some other vegetable; each seed has a chemistry of its own; each animal, in turn, devours the protoplasmic plant, or some other protoplasmic animal, and restores its own wastes, or propagates its own protoplasm. That is all, and it is not new. How these living beings got their first protoplasmic capital, or how the chemically prepared proteine got its indwelling life, does not appear at all; the solution is not touched, and, we hesitate not to say, never can be, until we go behind matter, and find its cause in the only cause, ultimate spontaneous will. It is a quantity—life is—alien from, and unknown to, matter; no chemistry detects it; no microscope discovers its advent. Chemically and atomically, the protoplasm in which it shrines is precisely the same before and after its advent. It comes from abroad, *ab extra,* and seizes a protoplasmic cell, and from it, builds itself a body—it may be this or that—but each seed or ovum, its own body. This is acknowledged by both Darwin and Huxley, and is contradicted by no fact as yet known to any scientist. Here, then, we rest as to the origin of life, in transcendental cause. The force of the argument is, confessedly, with theism; all the phenomena of life emanate from an extra material fountain; wherever found, in rudimental cell or archangel, it acknowledges one Fatherhood; and with every tongue of its million million mouths, proclaims the Godhead of its source.*

Sir William Thomson, President of "the British Association for the Advancement of Science," in his late inaugural, reflected the very latest phase of scientific thought on the subject; and his words are of so much value that we give them a place here:

"A very ancient speculation, still clung to by many naturalists—so much so that I have a choice of modern terms to quote in expressing it—supposes that, under meteorological conditions very different from the present, dead matter may have run together or crystallized, or fermented into 'germs of life,' or 'organic cells,' or 'protoplasm.' But science brings a vast mass of inductive evidence against this hypothesis of spontaneous generation, as you have heard from my predecessor in the president's chair.† Careful enough scrutiny has, in every case up to the present day, discovered life as antecedent to life. Dead matter can not become living without coming under the influence of matter previously alive. This seems to me as sure a teaching of science as the law of gravitation. I utterly repudiate, as opposed to all philosophical uniformitarianism, the assumption

*See Stirling's "As Regards Protoplasm;" and M'Cosh's "Positivism," pp. 24, 25, 26. †Professor Huxley, 1870.

of 'different meteorological condition'—that is to say, somewhat different vicissitudes of temperature, pressure, moisture, gaseous atmosphere—to produce or to permit that to take place, by force or motion of dead matter alone, which is a direct contravention of what seems to us biological law. I am prepared for the answer, 'Our code of biological law is an expression of our ignorance as well as of our knowledge.' And I say, Yes; search for spontaneous generation out of inorganic materials. Let any one not satisfied with the purely negative testimony, of which we have now so much against it, throw himself into the inquiry. Such investigations as those of Pasteur, Pouchet, and Bastian, are among the most interesting and momentous in the whole range of natural history; and their results, whether positive or negative, must richly reward the most careful and laborious experimenting. I confessed to being deeply impressed by the evidence put before us by Professor Huxley; and I am ready to adopt, as an article of scientific faith, true through all space and through all time, that life proceeds from life, and from nothing but life.*

"I feel profoundly convinced that the argument of design has been greatly too much lost sight of in

*In the inaugural address here referred to, after an immense array of facts and experiments, *all* pointing in the same direction, Professor Huxley concedes that "the *evidence*, direct and indirect, in favor of Biogenesis ['life from life, and from nothing but life'], for *all known forms of life*, must be admitted to be of great weight." But that is no reason why the great *inductive philosopher* should abandon his *theory!* He proceeds: "But though I can not express this conviction of mine too strongly, I must carefully guard myself against the supposition that I intend to suggest that no such thing as Abiogenesis [spontaneous generation] has ever taken place in the past, or will take place recent zoölogical speculations. Reaction against the frivolities of teleology, such as are to be found, not rarely, in the notes of the learned commentators on Paley's 'Natural Theology,' has, I believe, had a temporary effect in turning attention from the solid and irrefragable argument so well put forward in that excellent old book. But overwhelmingly strong proofs of intelligent and benevolent design lie all around us, and if ever perplexities, whether metaphysical or scientific, turn us away from them for a time, they come back upon us with irresistible force, showing to us through nature the influence of a free will, and teaching us that all living beings depend on one ever-acting Creator and Ruler."

in the future. . . . If it were given me to look beyond the abyss of geologically recorded time to the still more remote period when the earth was passing through physical and chemical conditions, which it can no more see again than a man can recall his infancy, *I should expect to be a witness of the evolution of living protoplasm from not living matter.* . . . That is the expectation to which analogical reasoning leads me; but I beg you once more to recollect that I *have no right* to call my opinion any thing but an *act of philosophic faith.*" (Spontaneous Generation: Lay Sermons, pp. 364–366.)

LECTURE III.

ORIGIN OF SPECIES:

An Examination of Darwinism.

BY THE

REV. RANDOLPH S. FOSTER, D. D., LL. D.,

President of the Drew Theological Seminary,

MADISON, NEW JERSEY.

LECTURE III.

ORIGIN OF SPECIES.

EXAMINATION OF DARWINISM.

WE have seen that the Bible, as to the origin of life, finds no foe in, and has no litigations with, science. On this point they are at one.

The next question to be discussed relates to the origin of the diverse organisms in which life appears, called, in the terminology of science, *Species*.

This is the special subject to the elucidation of which Darwin devotes himself. Starting with the concession that life is transcendental or metaphysical in its source, he confines himself to the subject of its evolutions in matter; more specifically he seeks to show that, and how, all organic forms have arisen by the sole agency of this factor. The idea, as we have already seen, is not original to him. It has cropped out many times and in many places along the ages. He has the merit of giving it the most elaborate expression and impressive defense it has yet received. It takes his name, not so much because it is his as that he is its most eminent expounder.

His theory, in brief, is, that all the *organized living*

forms, now, or at any past time, peopling the earth, were evolved from a simple primitive mass of living matter. This substance, impregnated of life, was the most rudimental possible. It was disseminated over the whole surface of the earth. Each infinitesimal part was a factor, containing in itself, potentially, all possible organisms; and from these atomic centers, in fact, all organisms have emanated.

He thus states it: "There is a grandeur in this view of life, with its several powers, having been originally breathed by the Creator into a few forms, or into one; and that, while this planet has gone cycling on, according to the fixed law of gravity, from so simple a beginning, endless forms, most beautiful and most wonderful, have been, and are being evolved."* At the time of this utterance, Darwin had not reached the real point of departure for his theory. He evidently saw it dimly, but hesitated. He had traced the beginning of life to a few forms—primitive, created organisms; he saw the foreshadowing of a possible unity; but the venture was too bold. Later, all uncertainty seems to have disappeared, and the few forms were surrendered, and one only remained. The final utterance is in a note, supplemental to the treatise, and in these words: "I should infer, therefore, that probably all the organic beings, which have ever lived on this earth, have descended from some one primordial form into which life was first breathed by the Creator."

It is fair to say, that, among the numerous expounders of this hypothesis, there is not perfect

* "Origin of Species," chap. xiv, *in fine*.

harmony along the entire line of its assumptions, reasonings, and conclusions. At bottom, there are at least three fundamentally distinct schools: one of which is sheerly materialistic; another, semi-materialistic; the third, theistic, and, with a liberal construction, Christian,—all agreeing in the general theory of evolutionism.

The former knows only of matter. It finds it existing, with its inherent constituent forces, among which is life. From the co-action of the forces, it evolves the entire cosmos; the life-force coming in as the last factor, and acting from the others as fulcrum.

The theory knows no such being as a creator, and no such idea as creation. It is baldly *atheistic*. That one organism, or what seems to be one system of related organisms, exists rather than another, is the result of no purpose resident anywhere, but the accident, merely, of blind forces, which act from a necessity internal to themselves.

This was, in a former lecture, shown to be not simply the height of unreason, but absolutely unthinkable and impossible. The attempt to unify substance by locating intelligence in matter, does not relieve the difficulty. For the characteristic of the newly supposed force is, that it is a force which acts not from necessity, but intelligently; that is, from a perception of ends to be reached, and in order to the perceived ends; therefore, spontaneously. Now, this new will-factor must be supposed to be primitive, and always masterful, in the substance of which it is integral; subordinating other forces to its ends; or, otherwise, resultant of the action of the more ancient forces.

If the former case be supposed, then we have a spontaneous worker originating the cosmos; which is the theistic idea, and the very thing denied by the theory under consideration. If the latter, then we have the double difficulty of accounting for the order or adaptation of means to ends, which preceded the advent of the factor, by which alone the adaptation could exist; and, what is more serious, we have the difficulty of supposing a cause, which, as to the effect, is no cause; since that which is not intelligent, can not be cause to intelligence; and, what is yet more serious still, we have the difficulty of supposing that all the intelligence in the universe, that which organized all order, and that which we are conscious we possess ourselves, came out of non-intelligence, sheer and utter; and, yet still more, we are beset with the necessity of denying action from will, or spontaneity, against our consciousness of voluntary activity.

What I would call the second school of evolutionists, must be ranked as theistic. It differs fundamentally from the school just described, in that it holds that both matter and life are created; matter, as a substance possessing definite forces; life, as an extraordinary and superadded force. But the life-force, thus lodged, by a new creative fiat, in matter, was not primitively placed in definite and discrete organisms, such as it afterward appeared in; but was at first placed in mere formless protoplasm, or particles of matter, from which, as so many innumerable centers, it unintelligently elaborated diversified forms for itself. Thus, the life-force was theistic in its origin, but atheistic in its evolutions. God placed it in formless matter, as a power to elaborate forms, but left it to itself to work out such forms as might come from the blind operation of an unguided force; so that the actual result of all existing organisms is expressive of the action of no final, intelligent will-factor. This is certainly the hypothesis of Darwin, and indicates the ground of the charge, made against him by one class of his critics, of undiguised atheism; at the same time that another class of his admirers pronounce him a devout theist. In fact, as tried by his scientific writings, he is both, and neither.

The third school of evolutionists—horrified by the gross materialism of the first, and unsatisfied with the equivocalness of the second, and yet fascinated by the glittering generalizations of both, and confused by the array of indubitable facts which seem to support their conclusions—attempts a consistent theistic hypothesis; a theory of evolutionism, which, at the same time that it meets the demands of science, is uncontradicted by revelation.

They assert the direct agency of final cause, both in the origin and method of matter, and all the evolutions of its contained forces. Every phenomenon of being is traced to natural law, but all natural law has its home and forth-putting in God. The grand structure of the universe was evolved and fashioned to precisely what it is, both as to the vast masses of inanimate matter and each of the innumerable myriads of living forms, by the necessary evolution of natural forces; but these forces, each and all alike, were, and are, simply the fixed methods in which the Divine factor carries out his plan. He is the ultimate worker, but forever conceals himself behind these visible sub-agents. He created the primitive monads, and shrined in them certain definite forces, which tended, as to themselves, to necessary evolution along predetermined lines, ultimating in a foreseen, perfectly adjusted cosmos. Among the forces thus set at work, but appearing later in the plan, when the atmospheric, climatic, and electrical conditions were suitably adjusted, he introduced, by a final creative fiat, the new transcendental force, called life—transcendental, metaphysical, mystical—as not included in the original forces constituent of matter. This new factor—clothing itself in matter, as the electric force robes itself in iron mail when it rushes from hemisphere to hemisphere of the globe, but more spiritual than its magnetic kinsman—was endowed with a potency peculiar to itself, and commissioned to perform manifold mysterious functions; among which were these: It had the power of self-perpetuation, translation, and indefinite increase; it could pass out of the particles of its original investiture into other particles where it was not, but which, by the alchemy of its contact, became at once impregnated; it could also organize these impregnated atoms into unity, and thus, from infinitesimal centers, by annexation and organization, concentrate and subordinate their aggregate force to one end; thus evolving forms of wondrous beauty and strength and activity, to fill the earth, the air, and the sea. But, in all these weird and marvelous functions, it was itself the slave of law, imposed by its creator, and worked along lines preordained by him, to the accomplishment of his purpose, and not its own; whatsoever it did, it did for him, and by him; it was, in fact, the infinite creative force and intelligence polarized or concreted in certain atoms of matter, from which it manifested itself in all possible forms of life. This is the theory of some evolutionists, who are both devout theists and believers in revelation. They see no contradiction, in this view, to the statements of the Bible. We are not entirely sure that there is any necessary conflict. It is, certainly, a wonderfully brilliant and beautiful conception. Its boldness fascinates us. It appears to lessen the mystery of the phenomena of life, and to find favor in many of the facts connected therewith; but, after all, we are convinced that it is a speculation, of which the utmost that can be said is, that the creator might conceivably have laid the foundation of life in this way. The vanity which attempts to dogmatize it as science, is only equaled by the vanity which asserts that it certainly could not be. We neither reject nor accept it, but accord to it hearty admiration, as an ingenious speculation on a point which must forever be clothed in mystery—the *modus operandi* of the creative act. Neither its truthfulness nor falsity is of consequence to our Christian faith; and as neither can be ascertained, we are content to leave it undisputed and unaccepted.

The second theory is that which we propose to discuss, and which we reject, as utterly at variance with all known facts. The thesis is, that life in its most primitive form appeared, by a creative fiat, in minute particles of matter, each particle being an egg, or seed (so far we have no controversy with it—it may have been so); that these quickened seeds, or infinitesimal cells, had a tendency to increase and grow into indefinite organisms; and that from them, as so many centers, life's tree grew to its topmost flower, man; all the diverse organisms growing from the same primitive root, by almost imperceptible variations, until they reached their utmost difference. Specific organisms were not contained in specific seeds; but each quickened atom contained potentially, all possible organisms—was the seed of whatever type might happen to result from its accidental evolution; and that the development has been as it has been, implies nothing of special provision or endowment or direction in the several life-centers. Nevertheless, there was, in fact, for some reason or by a strange accident, a seeming method in the simultaneous movements of the blind factors.

We are left to infer the actual progress, but not without hints to guide us. It is probable that it was thus: At the first essay, the cell-factors, with marvelous unanimity, considering that there was no plan or guidance, evolved the minutest and most rudimental fungus—a kind of mildew of vegetation—microscopic mushrooms, toad-stools, and lichens, over the shallow pools and marshy surfaces of the earth. These, by slow process, transformed themselves into mosses, liverworts, and various kinds of algæ. In due time, and by force of persistent effort, these grew into the endless variety of those ancient cryptogams, the great flowerless ferns of the coal period, from whose primeval forests were corded away the carbon which furnishes our homes and workshops with the thermal agents necessary to our modern civilization. Then followed flowering and fruit-bearing shrubs and trees and plants, by easy and natural transformation, in the abundance and diversity in which they have flourished along the millenniads even to this day.

At some point, along the infinite ages, the animal variety mysteriously appeared. Whether it was a transformed plant, or fruit of some ancient tree, or exalted diatom, or evolution of a primitive cell-factor, science has not yet been able to find out with entire certainty; but, in either case, its first form was the most rudimental and microscopic possible. Whatever its origin, it immediately displayed marked difference from its congeners of the vegetable variety; not a difference of form alone, but of fundamental law of life. The vegetable cell-factors set up life on a modest scale, and extracted their humble fare from the unsavory particles of water, carbonic acid, and ammonia, in the crude state, building up thus their delicate and luscious tissues into shapely and beautiful forms. The animal pigmies were both more dainty and more ambitious. They scorned the unsavory elements, and went foraging remorselessly on the succulent protoplasmic plants and fatty joints of their less robust kinsmen. When they first appeared, they were an exceedingly low, and altogether ungainly, mob of extremely minute but murderous marauders: protozoans they are called by their learned descendants; rhizopods and foraminifers, in some of their varieties. In process of time, the more prosperous and robust members of this most ancient house, by a succession of intermarriages, established a new order, known in palæontological heraldry as radiates, the old and honorable house of echinoderms, polyps, and acalephs. There were adventurers among these also, who, discontented with the pre-eminence of their family name and hereditary condition, and becoming, by imperceptible changes, extremely unlike their brother zoophytes, ceased to marry with them. These swells, confining their amours among themselves, determined to set up a third house—the well-known molluscan family, which still flourishes, in almost infinite varieties, of marvelous beauty and strength, in all the seas of the globe.

Up to this period, our ancient kinsmen were content to dwell in the waters; but the oldest and most primitive branch of all—the vegetable cells—had extended themselves over the lands, spreading out a table of rich and abundant protoplasm along the shores of the rivers, and up among the hills and valleys, which, some of these rowdy and voracious molluscans perceiving, their cupidity became inflamed, and they determined to make incursions on the inviting pastures of their prosperous and unsuspecting neighbors. These pioneers of land-life soon became a community among themselves; and, under the new conditions in which they found themselves, thought it wise to establish a fourth dynasty—the respectable order of articulata, of which are the illustrious branches, trilobites, lobsters, insects, decapods, tetradecapods, entomostracans, and a great variety of descendants, living in respectability, both on land and in the seas, even to our day.

The infinite ages rolled on. The struggle for existence among these old empires waxed more and more fierce. Great warriors arose under the pressure of the feuds and necessary strife for victory. Internecine wars divided and developed the bands of contending articulates. The result was, that, growing, by dint of need and effort and improved air and other altered conditions, some of the victorious households became proud, sloughed their articulated shells, made themselves back-bones, and declared a fifth dynasty—vertebrata.

This was a grand advance in the realm of life. It was, in fact, in its possibilities, a new departure; a splendid affair altogether; the founding of a magnificent empire of cosmopolitan life and enterprise. Some individuals of the new order inherited the seafaring propensities of their early ancestors. These betook themselves to the deep, and from them have descended all the piscine, saurian, and reptilian branches of the family, from the smelt to the whale and plesiosaurus. Some were fond of aerial sports, and they grew wings to themselves, and propagated ornithological varieties, from the humming-bird to the eagle. Other some neither cared to fly nor yet to swim: they feared things that are high, and they were troubled with a malformation of the respiratory organ, which made it difficult for them to remain long in the water; they betook themselves to the woods, and turned themselves into mammals, from the mouse to man. Thus it all came about; and this is the simple story of how we all got to be. Topsy explained it all in a single sentence: "I 'spects I growed."

This is the genealogy which Darwin and the evolutionists of all schools furnish us. It must be confessed that it is not flattering to our pride; that, as a matter of fact, it requires the surrender of time-honored prejudices, of boasted titles, and heraldic emblazonry; and, more than all these, the surrender of the pre-eminent distinction of a differentiated spiritual and immortal life. Is there need for the sacrifice? Has science traced our pedigree to the spore of the "polliwog" so certainly that we are absolutely shut up to the fact; or are we only mocked, insulted, and traduced by the effrontery of base and scurrilous nescience?

What are the facts from which Darwin deduces these strange conclusions? If the theory is really scientific, it rests on no uncertain data; it is not wanting in proof. Science wastes no time in stammering and muttering of conjectures and possibilities; that is the method of doubt, not of knowledge. Its sanctions are imperative. It proudly points to the facts, and enforces faith.

What are the facts upon which it is demanded that we accept the conclusion that our most primitive ancestor was a polliwog? our most modern progenitor an ape?—our genealogical line including all the intermediate species between these odious extremes? Has he discovered the family record, and traced the flower of humanity to this ancient root? Has he discovered, by experiment, or authentic observation any where, that it is so? The facts alleged to support the thesis are these: First, he posits the well-known fact that there is a tendency in the offspring of all living beings to depart from an exact resemblance to their progenitors. This he styles "the law of variability of species." He asserts, and it is not disputed, that any offspring may vary, in any conceivable direction, in a minute degree from its parent, and, by consequence, that all the descendants of any progenitor will, and do, differ minutely among themselves. This position is sustained by a brilliant array of exceedingly interesting illustrations. It is established beyond the possibility of dispute. It is fairly a fact of science; but his arguments were wholly unnecessary; for nobody ever doubted it. He gives rich interest to the subject, and introduces many new facts; but he furnishes no data for new conclusions.

His next position in logical order is, that, where the offspring is numerous and the ratio of increase great, a struggle for existence must immediately ensue, in which many must perish. This, as his first position, is perfectly obvious, and is never questioned. The point, it has long been known, was early reached in the history of developing life, where but the millionth seed could find a foot-hold for existence on the soil that gave it birth. The prodigality of life, in all its forms, and especially the lowest, has been a theme for poets and moralists, as well as naturalists, from immemorial ages. The earth is a greedy mother, devouring most of her children as soon as they are laid upon her bosom; or perhaps it were better to say, she has a passion for maternity, and her fecund womb is more prolific than her means for sustenance; her matrix larger than her breasts; her mouths more numerous than her pap. Where few can survive and the million must perish without gaining a permanent hold on life, it becomes a question which will have the fairest chance of success, and which must probably succumb. Only the successful can establish dynasties. This gives rise to what Darwin names his third law, or, what is the third in logical order, the law of "natural selection," called by Herbert Spencer, more happily, "survival of the fittest;" which means, simply, that certain facts of nature determine which of her offspring shall survive and which perish. Selection seems to imply intelligence, deliberation, comparison, and election; natural selection, if this were the meaning, would imply that nature, which is another name for matter and its phenomena, as used by these authors, is intelligent, and works to rational lines. This is not their meaning. By selection is not meant intelligently choosing, but only this, that the nature of the case determines that seeds of life will thrive in suitable conditions, and perish in unfavorable conditions; that the strong will have a better chance than the weak; that the probabilities of permanence to a given seed will be according to the ratio of its inherent vigor, and the favorableness of the circumstances in which it is found to exist, and *vice versa.* Darwin has many curious remarks on the subject of sexual selection, which he treats as a branch of natural selection; of the amours of plants and of microscopic insects, monads indeed; with the courtships, coquetry, and embraces of birds and beasts; the fastidiousness of their tastes as to color, form, and motion, and the strange arts by which they conduct their wooing and reach their winning,—which are either mere imaginings, or indicate that he has consumed a great deal of time and been extremely minute in his observations. We are quite willing to accept all his facts, and therefore need raise no questions on this branch of his elaborate researches. It suffices that nature, in one way and another, determines which of her offspring shall survive in the struggle for existence, and which shall come to grief, or extinction. The best-conditioned varieties gain the ascendency, and the earth becomes full of their children, who inherit their victorious qualities; and so, on the whole, the tendency is upward. Let it be so; what then?

The answer is obvious, and it expresses Darwin's fourth law; namely, that, where divergence or variation is perpetual, it only requires time to reach the utmost extreme of difference possible. Given infinite ages, the polliwog, by a series of minute changes in each successive generation, will ultimately reach the form of man, or, possibly, in some remote future, a type so transcendently superior to the lordly human, that our unborn descendants will redden as deeply with shame and scorn at the imputation of Adamic kinship, as we do at the supposition of ancestral unity with the toads and lizards of the long-vanished past. To these laws Darwin adds a number of facts, which he finds supporting his conclusion.

First. He names what he calls atavism, or reversion. He means by this, the appearance, occasionally, in every family, of an individual who reproduces a remote ancestor in typical form, and whose extreme unlikeness to the present generation marks the progress of the change which has been imperceptibly going on.

Second. Rudimental structure, or the appearance, in the lower forms, of rudimental members, which, in process of time, might develop into the perfectly formed corresponding members of developed species; or, in some instances, precisely the reverse, rudiments of what were once perfect members, but, by reason of altered circumstances and disuse, lapsed into mere rudiments; the fact, in both cases, showing the marvelous power of the organism to advance or retreat, and take upon itself extreme modifications.

Third. Embryonic phenomena, which prove that the primary embryonic condition of all living beings is identical; and that the embryonic changes are so similar that, at any given periods, all creatures have a precise resemblance; from which it is inferred that any embryonic being might, under favorable or unfavorable circumstances, develop upward or downward into any living form.

Fourth. General resemblances among all orders, as they appear in living species, showing a closely articulated chain of fundamentally similar links, consecutively differentiated by almost imperceptible diversities; so that, beginning at the inferior extreme, we are enabled to see how, by a slight departure, each successive modification arose, until the superior extreme was reached.

Fifth. The fact that is now made certain by geological research, as revealed in the rocky strata of the earth, that most anciently the crudest and lowest typical forms alone existed; and that the actual order of the appearance of life has been that of an ascending scale from the beginning until now.

These are the supposed laws and ground-facts upon which the theory is assumed securely to rest. It must be admitted that they not only have the appearance of great plausibility, but that they give the hypothesis the semblance of solidity and strength, in a very high degree. It is not to be wondered at, that, to many minds, the fascinating dream seems to be demonstrated reality; that, yielding themselves to what appears to be irresistible argument, they account resistance and hesitation in others the result of blind prejudice or willful ignorance.

The theory stands upon this high vantage-ground, that its facts are, indisputably, substantially as posited, and they appear to go directly to the conclusion.

Why are we not convinced? The question is a reasonable one. The assault upon hereditary opinions is so far effective that the demand is fully made out, that we attend to the case and put in an answer, or allow judgment to be entered up against us by default.

We have already stated, that of the first two of these positions there can be no dispute; they rise above mere conjecture into the region of assured certainty. The third is probably true. Species are not confined to one variety. They have wide margins, of considerable possible and actual difference. From the same primitive root-stock, it is safe to infer, have proceeded many quite unresembling but fundamentally resembling varieties. Individual peculiarities propagated, and peculiarities created by circumstances, have been perpetuated along wide and far-extended lines, and become, in some instances, so great a departure from the stock-pattern as almost to obliterate the genealogy. The human species is an example, but not by any means the strongest.

It is in the fourth predicate that we find the fatal fallacy, which breaks the chain in the midst; namely, where divergence is perpetual, it only requires time to reach the utmost variation possible. Hence, given infinite time—which means no more than geological time, which is practically infinite—the divergence might, nay, certainly would, reach from the polliwog to man; one minute change following another, such as we observe taking place, would ultimately traverse the whole distance, and reach the end. This looks like a statement which expresses a necessary truth; but a little examination will suffice to show that it contains a fundamental fallacy. The variation in the individuals of a species from the stock-pattern is not a longitudinal one, which carries them further and further away from the stock-pattern into fundamentally new types, which is the assumption here, but it is variation of a fundamentally permanent pattern. The law of disresemblance among living beings of the same stock is not that of the disresemblance of beings of diverse stocks. The change or variation perpetuated through infinite ages, is variation within a circle, not along a line. This is a most important fact; so trenchant that, if it be a fact, it is absolutely fatal to the whole hypothesis of evolutionism. All the elaborate and learned dissertations that have been written on the subject, dash into foam and spray upon this rock.

That it is a fact, we allege, is in positive proof, in

that not a single instance has been found, in the entire history of life, of the offspring of one stock-pattern taking upon it the form of a fundamentally different type. No man has ever observed a single instance of the kind. Geology declares unequivocally, as is the testimony of all the masters in that science, that it knows of no such event in all the ages of life. Numerous attempts have been set on foot, by means of artificial selection, breed-crossing, change of condition, and all other possible artifices, to divert nature from her established order, but utterly without success. Minute variations have been produced, but no fundamental departure has been attained, either *per saltum* or by long and tedious processes. Some species, as man, dog, horse, pigeon, have shown remarkable facility of variation, capacity to take on new and marked peculiarities, which come to comparative permanence, under changes of condition, place, habit, food, and matters of this kind; but they have never been known to become something else than man, dog, horse, pigeon. Neither accident nor methodical effort has developed a new species, so far as has become known to man.

In some instances, two neighboring species of close general resemblance have married, and progeny has been the result; the offspring taking on some resemblances to each of the progenitors. But in every such case the hybrid has been infertile; so that, even when the stock-patterns of life have run so close together as to be almost identical, it has been impossible to break over the fixed bounds. This is admitted by Darwin, and, indeed, can be disputed by none.

All known facts, thus, we positively aver, stand

solidly against the hypothesis. How, it will be asked, does Darwin reply to this damaging allegation? In the easiest manner possible, by manufacturing another assumption; namely, that the confessed absence of proof is not because there is no proof; not because the case is not as supposed; but because, in the first place, we have not lived long enough to note the changes which have taken place in infinite ages; and, in the second place, the geological record has only been discovered in scraps and fragments. If we could but find a witness of sufficiently broad experience, or an unbroken record of the facts, we should find them supporting his hypothesis. And yet, further, that the absence of positive proof is not the absence of proof; that though it be admitted as true that no instance is known of a translation of species, yet it must be allowed that such remarkable variations do often take place as to make it probable. What are the cases? Darwin devotes many pages to this particular point, and it may be presumed that he brings the most forcible facts known for its maintenance. He has himself, in a brief period, by crossing the breeds of pigeons, produced new varieties, with shorter beaks, gayer plumage, and a few more feathers in the tail; therefore, he infers that, if he could carry on the process for a great number of ages, he could certainly turn a pigeon into a man; and as the variability of sheep has been shown to be fully as great as that of pigeons, the argument is just as clear that a Southdown might, nay, certainly would, in an endless succession of generations, become bimanous, erect of posture, rational, and employ the tailor to make his clothes; and as florists have been able to variegate roses and geraniums, both as to bloom and fragrance, there is reason to believe that a time might come, far along the eternities, when they would compose oratorios, wear silks and satins, and take their protoplasm with knives and forks.

The argument from resemblance of structure is considered of great value by Darwin. He thus puts it in his "Descent of Man:"

"The homological construction of the whole frame in the members of the same class, is intelligible, if we admit their descent from a common progenitor, together with their subsequent adaptation to diversified conditions. On any other view, the similarity of pattern between the hand of a man or monkey, the foot of a horse, the flipper of a seal, the wing of a bat, etc., is utterly inexplicable. It is no scientific explanation to assert that they have all been formed on the same ideal plan. With respect to development, we can clearly understand, on the principle of variations supervening at a rather late embryonic period, and being inherited at a corresponding period, how it is that the embryos of wonderfully different forms should still retain, more or less perfectly, the structure of their common progenitor. No other explanation has ever been given of the marvelous fact, that the embryos of man, dog, seal, bat, reptile, etc., can, at first, hardly be distinguished from each other. In order to understand the existence of rudimentary organs, we have only to suppose that a former progenitor possessed the parts in question in a perfect state, and that under changed habits of life, they become greatlv reduced, either from simple disuse, or through the natural selection of those individuals which were least incumbered with a superfluous part, aided by the other means previously indicated.

"Thus, we can understand how it has come to pass, that man, and all other vertebrate animals, have been constructed on the same general model, why they pass through the same early stages of development, and why they retain certain rudiments in common. Consequently, we ought frankly to admit their community of descent; to take any other view, is to admit that our structure, and that of all animals around us, is a mere snare, laid to entrap our judgment.

"The conclusion is greatly strengthened, if we look to the members of the whole animal series, and consider the evidence derived from their affinities or classification, their geographical distribution and geological succession. It is only our natural prejudice, and that arrogance which made our forefathers declare that they were descended from the demi-gods, which lead us to demur to this conclusion. But the time will come, before long, when it will be thought wonderful that naturalists, who were well acquainted with the comparative structure and development of man and other mammals, should have believed that each was the work of a separate act of creation."

It is not merely in the physical organism that he traces a minute resemblance between all living beings, from a mushroom to a man; but it is no less striking in what are called the mental and ethical powers. If a giraffe or an alligator is a close physical copy of the Apollo Belvidere, the perfect human type, so the mental resemblances are equally strong. Carlo barks in his sleep; therefore Carlo has the power of imagination; therefore he resembles Milton; therefore some future pup, Newfoundland or terrier, in the infinite ages, may write the "Paradise Lost." Carlo has a hang-dog look when he is chided; therefore he feels the sentiment of shame; therefore he is a moral being; therefore the time will come when his descendants will write books, like Hopkins's "Law of Love," build temples, and quarrel on questions in ethics and casuistry. The ape uses a stone to crack the shell of a cocoa-nut; therefore he is an inventor; therefore he will, in the ages to come, build steam-ships, railroads, and printing-presses. In a word, every living thing is an incipient man, and has a close physical, mental, and moral resemblance to man, and, in infinite time, will come to the estate of man. Is it absurd? Do not imagine that I misrepresent Darwin when I assert it is precisely his argument, stripped of disguises, and carried to its legitimate end. His position is, that there is a fundamental unity among all things living, and a diversity, which, in infinite ages, returns to unity; each living thing containing in itself, incipiently, all the possibility of every other living thing, and only requiring time and conditions to attain the topmost possibility. A pig, taken miles away from home, will return on a mathematical line; therefore he is an incipient mathematician, knows astronomy, and understands the axiom, "A straight line is the shortest distance between two points;" and, some millenniads hence, one of his descendants will write the "Principia," or project a geometry of the heavens. In on-coming ages, the progeny of mice and men, quarrelsome landlord and tenant now, will worship in the same pew, preach over the same pulpit, and give their sons and daughters in wedlock. It is only a question of time.

We confess that we are not convinced. Even at the hazard of appearing dull and obstinate and unscientific, we must profess disability to see the point. It may be a natural defect, or an acquired infirmity; but whether from one cause or the other, it is a fact that we are unable to discern the remarkable resemblance alleged in the case. To our strangely distorted powers of discernment and perception, there does seem to be a difference, quite noticeable, between a flea and a mastodon, a mosquito and a finner-whale, a maggot and a man. The resemblance between Sir Isaac Newton and a kangaroo does not, to our thought, necessitate a common parentage. In fact, we labor under the strange hallucination that, given the design, in a creative mind of infinite power, to people the world with life in the greatest possible physiological variety, embracing the widest conceivable extremes, he could not have either multiplied or intensified the disresemblances. Neither unity of type nor poverty of invention appears to be a fact noticeable in the scheme of creation. Certain stock features must characterize all life; as, arrangements for gestation, locomotion, alimentation, sensation, and propagation. To accomplish these ends, amid whatever diversity, there must be remote similarity of plan. For locomotion, for instance, the arrangement must be for propulsion either in the air, or in water, or on the solid earth; and for these, all diversities must include either wings, fins, sails, legs, or sinuosities, or something of the kind. Is there not variety enough in the kinds, number, and fashion of these, from the gossamer wing of the butterfly to the double-braced pinion of the eagle; from the hair-like leg of the centipede to the mill-post limb of the elephant? Is it a fact that a human hand, the antennæ of a spider, a bat's wing, and a tiger's claw, are so fashioned after one model, that I must suppose them originally one, or slur the Architect of the universe with charges of sterility of contrivance?

The argument from embryonic phenomena is no more convincing. We accept the very questionable facts as posited: most primitively of all, every life, of every species, to all appearance, is identical; in the germ there is no sign of difference. What of it? Why not? Each higher development passes through all the embryonic changes of all lower forms in reaching maturity; is successively polyp, tadpole, fish, bird, quadruped, man. Be it so; what then? Are there not marked differences and invariable peculiarities enough? Who ever heard of an embryo of one species stopping short of its type, or transcending it? Is it so that there is really such a correspondence between the act of a shad in spawning its young, an eagle in incubating and breeding young eaglets, an English rabbit and other animal varieties in propagating their kinds, and a daughter of Eve in giving birth to her human children, that we can see no difference, or at most only a slight modification, which time and circumstances will account for? Allow that the young Adam takes on all known embryonic stages in reaching his superior perfection of organism ; that he is, when mature, microcosmic, the embodiment of all types; does that fact show community of root? Where is the proof? To infer it is an instance of hasty generalization, which savors more of presumption than wise induction. No more convincing is the fact that life did certainly begin with the lowest organisms, and progress in an order of eminence till it reached man. And why not? Can any one show a reason why these diverse orders should not exist, or why they should not be introduced in the precise order that has actually obtained? We are not able to see it. Is their presence in the time and place so manifest a blunder that we must find folly in the cause? or is the ever-improving type a reason for dispensing with a creator? Is not progress, climax, the most fitting conception of a great drama? How could the Infinite, who has eternal ages for his evolutions, and immensities of space for the theater of his operations, and immeasurable resources of power and invention with which to diversify his wonderful cosmos, and no need of haste to the conclusion of his manifold creations,—how could he more fittingly proceed to inaugurate, and lead on to its culmination, creation's pomp, than by the adoption of the method actually pursued? Most primitively of all, he laid the foundations of his magnificent temple in the atomic stones, out of which he was to beautify its walls and hang its dome with diamonds. He was in no haste, so he took ages to bring forth the top-stone of the material structure, with shouting of Grace, Grace, unto it! It was worthy of God as it hung, blazing with the radiance of its thousand suns, above the brow of ancient night; more worthy yet, as it swept in sublime circuits, orb wheeling in concert with lucent orb, to the fraction of a moment in the completion of a revolution, which light only would trace in millions of years. Then opened the drama of life. Why should not the algæ, humblest of its kind, lead out the floral pomp of endless Springs? Why not verdure first fringe the golden streams with banks of moss, and then cover the hills and valleys with the woody fiber of stalwart oaks and cone-bearing pines? Why should not protozoa come forth, with their headless train, and mustering after them, adown the long-drawn ages, fishes of every fin, birds of every plumage, mammals of every spot and form, until—grandest of all, and that for which the rest were made—the Adam should march through opening ranks to his palace and his throne?

To our conception, there is infinite harmony and beauty in the successive acts from protozoa to the human age. Each lifting of the curtain thrills us with fresh pageants more brilliant than the last. The great artist, in the unity of his plan, but inexhaustible diversity of the figures, and ever-increasing impressiveness of the growing drama, more and more holds us breathless in expectation of the coming act. When the curtain of the grave drops, is that the end? So says Darwin and all his worshipers. So we should say, had we no light but the feeble flicker of earth-born science. It quenches its torch in the tears and darkness of the grave. So says not faith.

With an eye undimmed by death, it pierces the darkness of the tomb, and reveals a realm of more transcendent beauty than the drama of life has yet unfolded. Upon its gaze there rise invisible splendors; and the great God and maker of all walks among his rejoicing children, "wiping away tears from all faces; and there is no more death, nor pain, nor sorrow; for the former things are fled away."

After all human efforts, and as the sum total of the results of human endeavor, to fathom the mystery of life, we have these facts, and no more: First, that life exists in connection with matter; second, so far as known, it, in no case, has appeared in unliving matter except by transmission; third, it appears, in the first stages of an organism, as a minute germ; fourth, the germ invariably emanates from an organism previously matured; fifth, the germ advances by growth and several stages of development to a substantial resemblance to the organism which produced it, and in no case to one substantially different; sixth, it has appeared on the earth in an order, as to time, of progressive perfection of organic structure and vital power; finally, while each individual differs from every other of its kind, and is subject to modifications, in some instances in a remarkable degree, from the stock pattern, the difference, in no case, is fundamental. These are the things that are known, and they are also the things that are revealed. What life is, whence it came, and how it arose, no solution has been furnished, though many times attempted, other than that which is given in revelation.

In the absence of positive proof that our immediate ancestor was an ape, we confess to the weakness of tempered zeal in pushing the claim to kinship. The advantages do not appear so great as to make us anxious to strain the argument, or desirous to enter upon the proffered honors before our claim is fully established. The Adam, whatever our prejudices might dictate, we are constrained to admit, seems to have a tolerably clear title to our allegiance. In any event, we must be allowed time to look about before we make a final surrender of the venerable faith which has become sacred by so many memories, and which, even to this hour, makes so brave a fight for the life which others would take away.

We have said nothing in this discussion of the positive argument, which buttresses the citadel of revelation, and which for ages has made it invincible to its assailants, and which becomes more and more impregnable by each successive assault. We have been content to take the new enemy upon his chosen ground, and upon his own facts have shown that, however proficient in science, in this case, by departing from science, he becomes a mere bastard pretender, without claim to the ambitious title which he assumes. Science disowns him, and throws its protecting arms around the Bible he asperses and seeks to slay.

Let scientists proceed with their investigations; let them, by patient observation and tentative experiment, educe all possible laws and facts, and they may be assured of rich rewards of gratitude and praise from their fellow-men. Every true advance they make enriches the present and future ages; exhumes wealth and blessing from the earth; extracts health and power from the atmosphere, and draws down culture and benediction from stars and globes above us. Let them go on with their brave and humanizing work; but let them not, becoming bewildered by their brilliant vocation and almost miraculous achievements, transcend their calling, and undertake to palm off mere conceits for knowledge. As often as they have undertaken to do this—and the instances are not few—from being justly admired for their discoveries they have come to be pitied for their empty boastings. The good they have done has been made the instrument of injury; and from being the friends, they have come to be the enemies, of mankind. Physical science is a magnificent department, and, to him who has the skill and patience to pursue it well, is ordained a high vocation; but it is a department only, not the whole. Its earnest culture calls into requisition talents of a peculiar kind; and these it absorbs so completely and employs so exclusively, that but little time or occasion is left for the development of other and not less noble powers. So long as the scientist remains in his realm of material laws and facts, he is a king; but when he attempts to extend his scepter over the departments of mind and ethics and faith, he becomes illegitimate, a vain braggart and pretender, and his power departs from him; his voice, that was as the voice of God, becomes as the unmusical croakings of odious things. Let him not imagine, because we listen with delight, and behold with rapture, when he discourses to us, with tongue or apparatus, of the wonders of chemistry, astronomy, geology, or other of his arts, that we therefore will obsequiously accept him as master when he promulgates his crudities on subjects of which, if he were modest, he would confess that he knows nothing. The highest proof of his unfitness and incapacity is, that he presumes to dominate when he ought to be silent; to impugn powers and authorities, which, in their department, are not less regal than he is in his own.

Two things, rest assured, science can never do: it can not employ nature to expunge God; it can not suborn matter to displace mind. Rightly pursued, it will go forward with its retorts and pick and reagents, lifting the cloud of ignorance from the face of nature, and pouring light into every dark recess of being; but the further it goes, and the more profound its discoveries, the more resplendently shall it find shining the glory of His power and wisdom, who made all. And even as it discovers him, so, it is our firm belief, it will discover, in the future as in the past, the exact and beautiful conformity of his revelation to the facts and wonders of his creation—a harmony as complete as the author is glorious. Certain it is that, up to this hour, every advance of knowledge into the realm of nature; the lifting of the veil from each secret that has yet been discovered; the exposure of all the mistakes that have yet been made; the detection of every previously unknown law and force,—has only brought into more brilliant manifestation the reality and regality of mind, the glory and eternity and infinite majesty of transcendental cause. Each new knowledge has come, like the pilgrim magi, bearing in its arms precious gifts and kingly trophies, to crown and do reverent homage to noble faith. No; it is not science that has been an enemy to faith, that has put in peril the idea of mind as a reality distinct from matter, and final, personal cause of all that is;—but idle conjecture only, and a brazen-faced presumption, which deserves only rebuke for its profanity, and horror for its blasphemy. It is a slander against science, which we resent; and a protest against the dishonor of its name, which we make.

The instance in hand comes with more boldness than usual, and parades, with measured pomp, august names and sounding titles; but it is not an exception, either as to the grounds or measure of its presumption.

That were a bold conjecture, indeed, which pertinaciously insists upon its right to be respected, when it stands rebuked before the best-known facts of science, and finds not a single voice of nature or reason raised in its support, from the beginning of the world until now; but only a wild acclaim of angry protest from every mouth of animated being.

Given all the facts claimed by evolutionists, we make no approach to the conclusion adduced. The blasphemous theory fails at its own venue. When its witnesses come to the tribunal, they rebel against the indictment, and glow with rage against the prostitution attempted. As they come mustering down the ages at the summons, and answer to the call, each fact, with loud and sonorous voice, declares against the profane thesis which implores its support. The rocks cry out, and the grave-yards of a million generations rattle their bones in anger; and not a single recusant, from protozoa downward, comes to the rescue of the infamous cause.

No; it is a brilliant conjecture, but it is not true. Scientists babble when they count out God. They seek in vain to explain either the origin or the ordering of the universe, without him. In their folly, they have endeavored, time and again, to eliminate faith from the world, and dethrone the Infinite from the universe he had built for himself; but as often, they have lost their way, and become confused and confusing. Great and grand, almost divine as religion itself, when it is content to interpret him, their science staggers and stammers the pitiable jargon of gibbering idiocy itself, when it attempts to supplant him.

The granite facts stand brawn and bold, when the silly dream and sillier dreamer come, and vanish away. Each dead and living thing, from mite to archangel and from atom to sun, lifts up its voice against the folly and the wrong; and ever, louder and louder still, from all worlds and all orders of life, comes the resounding confession, "The Hand that made us is divine."

The forces, which play so conspicuous a part in naturalism, by which all phenomena of change are accounted for, which build worlds and round dewdrops, and, more mysteriously still, form the facets of minutest crystals and the tissues of all life,—the forces themselves declare that they are not many, but one; not perishable, but permanent; not material, but transcendental; not necessary, but spontaneous; that their home is the bosom of the Eternal Will-factor, who speaks, and it is done; who *commands*, and the foundations of the universe stand fast forever; out of whom there is nothing, and by whom all things consist; of whose invisible and intangible substance the whole frame of the material cosmos is but projected shadow; who only has being in himself, and in whose will alone all else that is has root and hold of existence; who, if the thought of his non-existence could become reality but for a moment, would carry down with him, in his fall, the universe itself, and leave but the dark and dreary pall of utter nothing over all the regions where suns flame and angels utter forth their ecstasies; and in whom, because he is, from eternity to eternity, unchangeable—a God of infinite love and power—we may rejoice for evermore; to whom be glory and majesty and dominion, as it was in the beginning, is now, and ever shall be, world without end!*

* The isms exposed in these brief lectures are already receding, and, from having alarmed, even now only amuse; but to any one who may be curious to see how they unfolded, with pomp of promise, and how they withered in a day, we would suggest the careful perusal of such books as "Vestiges of Creation," Darwin's several treatises, Huxley's, Argyle, Mivart, Stebbing, Wallace, Mill, Spencer, Figuier, and Tyndall. Lubbock, Lesley, and Büchner will not pay for the reading. These authors comprise the ablest, on both sides, and will richly repay the study. They exhaust the subject, and, to a candid reader, will not fail to suggest profitable lines of reflection; and, I am persuaded, will not fail to produce the conviction that human research furnishes neither the refutal of, nor substitutes for, the simple statement of revelation.

LECTURE IV.

THEISM AND ANTI-THEISM

IN

THEIR RELATIONS TO SCIENCE.

BY THE

REV. ASA MAHAN, D. D.,
President of Adrian College,

ADRIAN, MICHIGAN.

LECTURE IV.

THEISM AND ANTI-THEISM IN THEIR RELATIONS TO SCIENCE.

THE *Claim set up.*—All are aware that anti-theists, in all ages, the present and the past, have claimed for themselves an exclusive abode in the high realm of pure science, and have represented religionists of all schools as having their dwelling-place in the lower sphere of superstition and credulity. "Religion," says Mr. Emerson, "is a system which the people passively receive from the priest." "The Churches," he accordingly assures us, "are in the service of the devil;" while "vice and crime are normal states of human nature." In the great anti-theistic work of the age it is affirmed, that when the mind ascends to the realm of pure science, religious ideas and sentiments will forever drop out from the sphere of human thought and regard. The teachings of leading thinkers in the service of skeptical thought are set forth, by themselves and their disciples, as immutable truths of science. Science, they claim, is "all their own." As introductory to the argument which we design to present, we will stop right here, and inquire into the validity of these high claims.

Facts as they are.—We here announce, as an undeniable and undenied historic verity, that, without exception, all thinkers of past ages, who have, in the united judgment of mankind, vindicated for themselves permanent places as fixed stars in the firmament of science, have been openly avowed and uncompromising theists; while the most eminent of all anti-theistic thinkers are known and designated, not as sages or philosophers, but exclusively as sophists. Just as soon, also, as the most eminent unbelievers and skeptics of modern times drop into a past age, they, too, in the judgment of mankind, fall from the firmament of science, lose forever the designation of philosopher and sage, and descend to the low sphere occupied by ancient sophists. Where, for example, in human regard, are now the great thinkers of France, who laid the foundation of modern material atheism? Not one of them is, by any class of men, believers or unbelievers, thought or spoken of as a philosopher, and hardly as a sophist. They are simply known as a class of bewildered thinkers, who reared up proud and imposing systems upon "airy nothing." A similar verdict has, in fact, been passed by the German mind upon the founders of the various systems of modern rationalism. A few years ago, those systems were the great theme of thought and study throughout that country. Now, among the tens of thousands who crowd those great universities, no lecturer, whose object is to expound and verify the system of Kant, Fichte, Schelling, or Hegel, can command a class of twenty hearers. These men, who were once regarded as central suns in the firmament of science, have already practically taken rank among the sophists of old. Long before the year 1900 shall roll round, will the great unbelievers of the present era—unbelievers such as Parker, Emerson, Mill, Spencer, and Huxley—be known only as the bewildered sophists of the nineteenth century.

Science and Sophistry distinguished.—A clear exposition of the real distinction between science and sophistry, will evince the strict justice of the discrimination which mankind ever have made, and ever must make, between the two classes of thinkers under consideration. *Science is knowledge systematized.* Into a scientific process, nothing but what is *absolutely known* can enter. Any opinions, beliefs, instinctive or otherwise, any conjectures or assumptions introduced into a scientific process, would utterly vitiate the whole procedure. Science has to do with principles known to be necessarily true, with facts known with equal absoluteness to be real, and with such deductions only as are necessarily implied by such principles and facts. Here, and here only, do we have real science. Whatever else, outside of this, is given forth as scientific truth, is sophistry, having no other foundation than mere opinion, belief, conjecture, or assumption. *Sophistry*, you will bear in mind, *is a plausible show of reasoning, in which deductions having no other basis than such opinions, beliefs, assumptions, or a partial induction of facts, are imposed upon the public mind as truths of science.*

Knowledge and Opinions, Beliefs and Assumptions, distinguished.—Here a question of fundamental importance arises, to wit: What is the real distinction between knowledge on the one hand, and opinions, assumptions, and beliefs on the other? Opinions, beliefs, etc., we answer, may and do change, and vary their character. An individual may hold one opinion on a given subject at one time, and the opposite at another. Science may forever displace from the sphere of thought and belief an opinion which was once universally held as valid. Real knowledge, on the other hand, *never changes*. When you know an object, your apprehension of it, just so far as you do know it, becomes permanently fixed. Any change would imply, enlargement excepted, that the object was not known.

Matter and Spirit KNOWN *Substances*.—The question of questions arises here. When we reason from the apprehended facts of matter and mind to the ultimate cause of these facts, are we reasoning from mere opinions, assumptions, or beliefs, which happen to be universal in the mind, or are our deductions based upon real knowledge? All admit that if our deductions are based upon real knowlege, then we have demonstrative proof of the doctrine of God. Antitheism affirms that these deductions are not based upon real knowledge, but upon mere opinions, assumptions, beliefs, which happen to be universal, and are, therefore, void of validity. We are now prepared for a final determination of this question. It will be universally admitted that, in all minds in common, there exists one and the same apprehension of mind on the one hand, and of matter on the other. Mind, as apprehended by the universal consciousness, is a power possessed of, and exercising the functions of, thought, feeling, and willing. Matter, on the other hand, is given with the same distinctness and absoluteness as an exterior substance, possessed of the fixed and essential qualities, among others, of extension and form. Now, our apprehension of these substances can no more be changed or modified than can our ideas of a circle or a square. We may question or deny the reality of either or both of these substances, or the validity of our knowledge of the same; yet they are, to our apprehensions, the same identical substances that they were before, and are known with the same absoluteness that we know a circle or a square.

Here, then, we find ourselves standing in the presence of real knowledge; or knowledge in no form has a dwelling-place in the mind. Do you ask how we became possessed of this knowledge? The answer is this: When the proper conditions are fulfilled, we have a direct and immediate perception or knowledge of the fundamental qualities of each of those substances. To deny the validity of such knowledge, is simply to affirm the universal intelligence to be a lie. In reasoning, then, from the great leading facts of mind and matter to their ultimate cause, we are not reasoning from mere opinions, assumptions, or beliefs, but from absolute knowledge, facts absolutely known, to what is implied by the same.

Grounds of the Distinction ultimately made by all Men between Theistic and Anti-Theistic Thinkers.— Such is science on the one hand, and sophistry on the other. The reason why the great theistic thinkers of past ages do and ever will occupy their places as fixed stars in the firmament of science; and why all unbelievers and skeptics do and must, in the just judgment of the race, take rank as sophists, now becomes perfectly obvious. Thinkers of the former class base all their deductions upon principles and facts, which are given in the universal intelligence as absolutely known *verities*. Whatever is thus given, they accept and reason upon as real, and as being in itself just what the intelligence shows it as being. They never perpetrate the absurdity of assuming that the intelligence, by one procedure, can know an object as a fixed reality, possessed of certain immutably essential qualities—extension and form, for example—and then, by another procedure, know that same object as a mere shadowy appearance, and no reality at all. All their deductions are strictly within the sphere of the knowable and known. Hence, said deductions legitimately take rank as truths of science, and the great thinkers who reason thus will ever, in the judgment of mankind, retain their places as fixed stars in the firmament of science. It was on the authority of principles and facts thus known, that La Place affirmed that the evidence stood as infinity to unity, in favor of the being and creative agency of a personal God, as opposed to any other hypothesis of ultimate causation. It was on the same authority that Cicero affirmed that the idea was infinitely more reasonable that the throwing down at random, on a piece of parchment, of a mass of writing instruments, would be the production of such a poem as Homer's Iliad, than that creation, as now constituted, was originated by any other cause than that referred to.

Wherein, then, lies the sophistry of anti-theistic thinkers, of all schools? It lies here: All their systems are based upon *a denial of the validity of what is given in the universal consciousness as absolute knowledge.* Anti-theism now takes on, and ever has taken on, one of three forms—materialism, idealism, or skepticism. Materialism affirms the validity of our knowledge of matter, and denies that of mind; idealism affirms the validity of our knowledge of mind, or its operations, and denies that of matter, and all this while our knowledge of each is given in the universal consciousness as equally absolute. Both systems rest upon the common assumption, an assumption for the validity of which no reasons whatever can be assigned, that what is given in the universal consciousness as absolute knowledge is no real knowledge at all. Skepticism denies absolutely the validity of our knowledge of both these substances in common, and thus bases its claims wholly upon a universal impeachment of the intelligence as a faculty of knowledge.

Take another view of this subject. In every act of external perception, two factors are always given—the subject and the object, mind and matter; the subject as endowed with the powers of thought, feeling, and willing, and the object as possessed of the fixed and immutable qualities, among others, of extension and form. No affirmations of the intelligence are, or can be, more absolute than the distinction under consideration. Now, while the intelligence never does, and never can, confound these two substances, the one with the other, materialism, in resolving all substances into matter, confounds the subject with the object; while idealism, in resolving realities into mind, confounds the object with the subject. Thus, these two systems rest upon one common assumption, to wit: that, in the language of Sir William Hamilton, the universal "consciousness is a liar from the beginning." Skepticism, basing its claims upon a denial of the validity of what is given in the universal consciousness as absolute knowledge, must stand or fall upon the assumption that the universal intelligence is itself a lie. Here, undeniably, is all the science that can be found in the sphere of anti-theistic thought; and here, as undeniably, sophistry reaches its consummation.

Suppose, now, that an advocate of one of these theories attempts to convince you that your knowledge of one or both of these substances is invalid. On what conditions can he escape the just charge of acting the sophist? On this only, that he makes it more manifest to your mind that his reasoning has absolute validity, than is the fact that you yourself exist, as possessed of the powers of thought, feeling, and willing, and that matter is before you, as possessed of the qualities of extension and form. This no anti-theist professes to be able to accomplish. Kant, for example, affirms, and all anti-theists agree with him, that no form of reasoning, no deductions of science, can displace from the human intelligence the conviction of the absolute validity of our knowledge of nature. This is an open acknowledgment that he, and all other anti-theists, are doing nothing but acting the sophist in all their attempts to subvert that conviction.

The reasoning of the anti-theist to induce the results he desires, may have the appearance of conclusiveness ; yet if his deductions are not more manifestly absolute than is the knowledge referred to, his argument must, upon scientific grounds, be regarded as nothing but sophistry. I once, for example, saw a mother very much perplex her little child with this form of sophistry : Every creature which has two feet is a biped. You are a biped. A goose is a biped ; therefore, you are a goose. The child was perplexed ; yet it absolutely knew that it was not a goose. Suppose it had replied thus : Your argument appears valid, and I can't meet it ; yet I KNOW that I am not the animal referred to. I, therefore, conclude, not that I am a goose, but that you are acting the sophist. The reply would have entirely accorded with the principles of perfect science. So, when individuals attempt to convince you that your knowledge of the great leading facts of matter or mind, or of both in common, is invalid, your proper reply is this : Your reasoning is quite plausible. It utterly fails, however, to induce that absolute assurance that I have, that I, myself, exist as endowed with the powers of thought, feeling, and willing, and that matter is before me as possessed of the qualities of extension and form. I conclude, therefore, that you are acting the sophist with me ; and I know well that I should make a goose of myself if I should judge otherwise. Science affirms absolutely the validity of such a reply. The sophistry of the anti-theist, in all such cases, is perfectly obvious. On the authority of deductions which have nothing but assumptions for their validity, he professedly invalidates that of original, immediate, and absolute knowledge.

Reason why Anti-Theists regard each other as Sophists.—The reason why every anti-theist is to every other, as well as to the rest of mankind, a sophist, and especially why each class of anti-theists is to every other a mass of unqualified sophists, now becomes perfectly obvious. Each anti-theist bases his theory upon a denial of the validity of what every individual of the race, whatever his views may be, does and must distinctly recognize as absolute knowledge. For this reason, while any two individuals may perfectly harmonize in their skeptical views, each does and must intuitively recognize the other as a sophist. In Germany, for example, unbelievers all take rank in different schools, and each school is charged by all the others with teaching nothing but sophistry; each school, with every other, laying down absolute ignorance of all realities as the basis of a scientific exposition of the unknown and unknowable secrets of universal existence and its laws. The light in which each French skeptic regards every other, is thus very impressively set forth by Rousseau: "I have consulted our philosophers, I have perused their books, I have examined their several opinions. I have found them all proud and dogmatizing, even in their pretended skepticism; knowing every thing, proving nothing, and ridiculing one another. If you consider their number, each one is reduced to himself; they never unite but to dispute." Upwards of two years since, a national, or world's, convention of unbelievers was held in Boston. Each member was permitted a free utterance of his own views. Every speech was taken down at the time, and afterwards published. The character of the utterances of that confused assemblage is perfectly represented in the picture given above. Each speaker was literally "reduced to himself," uttered little, or nothing, but what was regarded as the consummation of sophistry by the rest of the assembly. The only form of unity that has been claimed, even by skeptics, for the convention, is that of perfect *toleration*. The convention, as all such assemblages must do, presents to the world the most impressive and edifying spectacle of Chaos and Old Night dwelling with great quietness and full fellowship with Anarchy. Nor is any other form of unity possible among this class of scientists, starting, as they do, with the assertion of absolute ignorance of all realities, and then attempting a scientific elucidation of the secrets of the world, nature, and its laws. To attain to concurrent thought in such circumstances, is as impossible as it would be for a thousand blind men to start from a given point, and then walk a thousand miles on the same straight line.

The Basis Principle of Anti-Theism renders Scientific Thought Impossible.—If we recur to the principle that lies at the foundation of modern skepticism, we shall perceive at once the utter sophistry of all the professed scientific teaching of this class of thinkers. Mr. Herbert Spencer, for example, the great leader of the sect, after affirming that all objects of thought and perception in the universe are mere shadowy appearances, and no realities at all, adds that "the reality existing behind all appearance is, and ever must be, unknown." This principle lies at the foundation of ancient anti-theism. The wisest among their thinkers, as Milton says, "professed to know this only, that they nothing knew." The same holds true of modern anti-theism. No objects of thought or perception in the universe, says Kant, "are that in themselves for which we take them. Neither are their relationships so constituted as they appear to us." Again, he adds, "We know nothing of these objects but our manner of perceiving them, which is peculiar to us, and may not be the same in any other class of beings." Here, as we perceive, absolute ignorance is affirmed of all realities of every kind, realities material and mental, finite and infinite; and here we should suppose that the mission of science is ended. How can we reason but from what we know? Anti-theists, on the other hand, make this infinite and acknowledged ignorance the basis of a scientific exposition of the secrets of universal existence and its laws. Mr. Spencer, for example, on account of his science of the unknowable and unknown, has been called by his disciples the Sir Isaac Newton of this age.

I here affirm, without fear of contradiction, that not a proposition or deduction can be found in Kant's "Critic of Pure Reason," or in the multitudinous philosophical works of Herbert Spencer, that does not bear upon its face the clearest indications of gross sophistry. When you have affirmed absolute ignorance of any object, you have undeniably placed that object wholly out of the sphere of true science. This is just what these authors have done in respect to all realities of every kind. Any propositions or deductions, consequently, which they may put forth in respect to such objects, and put forth especially as truths of science, can have no other foundation than mere baseless conjectures and assumptions, for the validity of which no reasons whatever can be assigned. Kant, for example, after affirming an absolute ignorance of mind, professedly determines, from a stand-point purely scientific, the number and character of the mental faculties, and the precise laws which govern their activities. If he knows nothing, as he affirms he does, of the mind itself, what can he know of its faculties? Mr. Spencer, after affirming an absolute ignorance of all realities, mental and physical, finite and infinite, professedly gives us the *science* of universal existence and its laws. I slander no one when I affirm that such thinkers, with the entire school to which they belong, deserve no higher regard from the race than philosophical jugglers, with this difference, that the common juggler informs his audience of the deceptions he perpetrates upon them, while these authors deceptively impose upon the public their mere opinions, conjectures, and assumptions as deductions of science.

The Character of the two Systems directly considered.—A direct consideration of the intrinsic character of these two systems will still more clearly evince their distinct and opposite relations to science. Both systems, in all their forms, agree absolutely in this, that there is *some one ultimate reason* why the facts of the universe are as they are, and not otherwise. When we inquire after the nature of this ultimate reason, or first cause, all agree, also, that it must be either an eternally inhering law of nature itself, or a cause out of and above nature—a cause acting upon, organizing, and controlling nature, in accordance with the law of intelligent foresight and design. In other words, all thinkers of all schools agree that there are but two conceivable hypotheses of ultimate causation—that of natural law or that of theism; and that one, to the exclusion of the other of these, must be true. Let us, for a few moments, turn our thoughts to a consideration of each of these distinct and opposite hypotheses.

The Hypothesis of Natural Law.—Upon the hypothesis of natural law we have three very concise, but fundamentally important, remarks to make:

1. This dogma has no claims whatever to our regard as an *intuitive* truth. If true, its truth is, undeniably, not self-evident. Nor do its advocates set up any such claims in its behalf.

2. Nor can any form or degree of valid proof, positive evidence, or antecedent probability, be adduced in its favor. The reason is obvious and undeniable: no fact can, by any possibility, be adduced in favor of this hypothesis, which is not equally explicable on the opposite hypothesis. Whatever is compatible with the action of an inhering law of nature as its ultimate cause, is undeniably equally compatible with the action of a cause out of and above nature. Hence, the deduction becomes demonstrably evident, that there can be adduced from the universe of matter or spirit no fact from which the remotest

degree of valid proof, positive evidence, or antecedent probability, can be drawn in favor of the doctrine of natural law, as opposed to the hypothesis of theism.

3. No individual can hold the dogma of natural law as a positive truth without thereby violating the immutable demands of science on the one hand, and involving himself in the just charge of the grossest credulity on the other. Science absolutely prohibits the holding of positive opinions not based upon valid evidence. The individual who holds the dogma under consideration as true, holds an opinion in favor of which no real evidence or antecedent probability of any kind can be adduced. No greater violation of the immutable demands of science is, therefore, possible. To hold such an opinion is, also, credulity in its grossest form. To attempt to impose such an opinion upon the public as a truth of science, is moral criminality of the most flagrant character.

Theistic Hypothesis.—On the theistic hypothesis we have, also, three concise and fundamentally important considerations to present—considerations to which very special attention is invited:

1. This hypothesis can, by no possibility, be disproved; nor can the least degree of positive evidence or antecedent probability be adduced against it. For the same reason that the opposite hypothesis can not be proved true, this can not be disproved. For the same reason that no positive evidence or antecedent probability can be adduced in favor of the former, none can be adduced against the latter.

2. The validity of this hypothesis accords with the intuitive convictions of the race. Not a single tribe

or branch of the human race exists, who are void of the idea of creation and a creator, and who do not regard that creator as a self-conscious, personal God. We have here a form of positive evidence which will command the belief and life of every honest disciple of true science. When two hypotheses are before us, one of which must be true and the other false, and when no form or degree of evidence does or can exist in favor of one, any degree of real evidence in favor of the other binds the conscience. The issue before us is one of this kind. No evidence, in any form, renders the doctrine of natural law even probably true. The facts of the universe, as apprehended by the universal intelligence, induces, in that intelligence, the absolute intuitive conviction of the validity of the doctrine of theism. Here is real evidence which can not be doubtful, and which every honest student of science will heed.

3. On definitely assignable conditions, this hypothesis may be rendered a demonstrated truth of science, and the opposite one a demonstrated error. If there can be adduced, for example, from the wide domain of universal nature, a single real fact which can not be accounted for by a reference to natural law, that fact renders demonstrably evident the absolute validity of the theistic hypothesis. Whatever can not be accounted for by reference to any inhering law of nature, must be referred to a cause out of and above nature. This is undeniably self-evident.

Theistic Facts and Deductions.—Now, there are a multitude of facts in the universe of matter and spirit—facts of this identical character. We will make a bare reference to two of them. If we will heed the intuitive convictions of the race, or the maturest and most absolute deductions of science, we shall admit and affirm the fact of creation *as an event of time.* So absolute are the teachings of science, geological and astronomical, for example, upon this subject, that no respectable anti-theist questions the fact that the order of events in nature had a beginning. The fixed law of progress, in nature, from the less perfect in the direction of the absolutely perfect, evinces, undeniably, the same great fact. Progression in this or any other direction, by natural law, must have been from eternity, in which case the perfect would have been reached untold ages since. The perfect, however, has not yet been reached. We are, on the other hand, much nearer the beginning than the end.

Progression in nature, then, had a beginnng in time, and is not by natural law. There is no escaping this conclusion. When we admit, as we must do, the fact of creation as an event of time, we are absolutely necessitated to adopt the immutable deduction of a creator out of, and above, nature. A law of order inhering in nature, and acting potentially as the ultimate cause of the order therein existing, must, from the nature of the case, have existed and acted from eternity, or not at all. Facts of order thence resulting, must have been from eternity, and not events of time. No deduction has, or can have, more absolute validity than this. But the facts of order in nature are not from eternity, but are, undeniably, events of time. The ultimate cause of that order, therefore, is the agency of a free, self-conscious, personal God.*

If we adopt, as our next stand-point, the state of the earth, as it must have been at the subsidence of the glacial flood, we shall be conducted, by logical necessity, to the same absolute conclusion. During the continuance of that flood, such a degree of universal coldness was induced, as of necessity, in the language of Professor Agassiz, "to put an end to all living beings upon the surface of the globe." The earth could have been re-peopled, as it now is, but from one of two causes—origination by natural law, in accordance with the principles of the development theory, or by the direct and immediate creative agency of a personal God. The former hypothesis can, by no possibility, be true in this case, there having been, undeniably, no time for such originations. This theory, as the same learned professor has well observed, "is cut by the root by this winter." But one hypothesis remains for us, and that doctrine must be true—the doctrine of the all-creative agency of a personal God.

Relations of these two Hypotheses to Science.—The relations of these two hypotheses to science now

*In the annual meeting of the great Scientific Association, of Germany, held about one year since, this statement was made by one of the most distinguished scientists of Europe, no one contradicting him, to wit: That all the valid deductions of science culminate in the one great central truth *of the organization of the universe as an event of time.* "In other words," he remarked, "we have a real creation, and therefore a creator." He then added, that when science shall have reached its full maturity, it will be introductory to the Christian religion. Even Mr. Huxley affirms, as an undeniable deduction of science, that the order of events in nature had a beginning in time. Yet, with strange fatuity, he would have us believe, not in a creator, but in creation by natural law, than which no absurdity can be greater.

become perfectly obvious. At the basis of the doctrine of natural law, and consequently of anti-theism in all its forms, there lies, as we have seen, not a solitary principle (intuitive or deductive truth) known to science. In its favor not a solitary fact can be adduced, a fact rendering that dogma even probably true. Anti-theism, therefore, in none of its forms or professed deductions, can have the remotest claims to a place within the sphere of true science; and all positive claims set up in its behalf are positively condemned by science. At the basis of theism, on the other hand, we have necessary intuitive principles of science, and adamantine facts which science does and must recognize as real; while the deductions of this hypothesis are recognized by the same authority as the necessary logical consequences of those principles and facts. Here, then, we have science; or true science has no being within the domain of human thought.

The Boastful Pretensions of Anti-theists.—We are also prepared to form a just estimate of the claim, so boastfully set up by anti-theists of all ages, that they only occupy the high sphere of true science; while the dwelling-place, as they affirm, of all who believe in an infinite and perfect personal God, is the dark region of superstition and credulity. Does it not appear—permit us to ask here—does it not appear quite modest in such thinkers as Emerson, Mill, Youmans, Lyell, Spencer, and Comte, to deify themselves as great central suns in the firmament of science, and to present such minds as Thales, Socrates, Plato, Aristotle, Cicero, the Bacons, Newton, Locke, and La

Place—all uncompromising theists—as mere rush-lights in that firmament, blind thinkers, who passively received their conceptions of God from their priests? We read of a Spaniard who never pronounced his own name without reverentially taking off his hat, as expressive of the deep veneration he entertained for such an illustrious personage as himself. It would seem that these anti-theists must have taken lessons in the school of self-adulation of some such thinker as that. But what is the real ground of this self-boasting? They *deny* the being and perfections of God, a truth of real science, a truth evinced as such by proof the most absolute. They hold as a truth of science the dogma of natural law; a dogma in favor of which no form or degree of real proof, valid evidence, or antecedent probability can be adduced. This, undeniably, is all the science to which these thinkers can lay any just claim. If absolute disbelief in the presence of absolute proof is presumption, and absolute belief in the total absence of all evidence is credulity, the presumption and credulity of these thinkers must be infinite.

Let us suppose that an individual, first of all, affirms an absolute and hopeless ignorance of the matter, the productions and inhabitants (if any exist), of the planet Jupiter, and should then claim that, by a process of pure scientific deduction, he has fully revealed the geology and zoölogy of that unknown and unknowable world. Would not mankind affirm, with truth and propriety, that here is science run mad? Yet this is precisely what has been done by anti-theists of all ages, and especially by one of its most illustrious and generally accepted modern expounders, in respect to the whole universe of matter and spirit. Mr. Herbert Spencer, as we have seen, announces this as the common doctrine of all anti-theistic thinkers, from Pythagoras to Kant, and as embodying the fundamental principle of all true science; that all our knowledge of every kind is wholly "phenomenal," mere appearance, in which no reality, as it is, is manifested, and that "the reality existing behind all appearances is, and must ever be, unknown." Here, then, as we have said before, the validity of this principle being admitted, the mission of science undeniably ends. How can we have a science of that of which our ignorance is hopelessly absolute? Do anti-theistic thinkers stop here? By no means. This infinite ignorance they assume as the certain condition and ground of a scientific insight into the unknown and unknowable secrets of universal existence and its laws. The individual above named, for example, after professedly demonstrating the fact that neither the earth, the sun, nor the stars; that neither mind, matter, time, space, nor God; that nothing finite or infinite—is, or can be, in itself, the reality which we apprehend it as being; and that it is impossible for us to know what any of them is,—this same individual, after assuring us, as a deduction of science, that a personal God has, and can have, no agency in nature, goes on to tell us, on the authority of deductions purely scientific, as he affirms, just how all the events of nature, from the eternity past to the eternity to come, have resulted, do result, and will result, from three great central causes — causes of which he affirms an absolute ignorance, to wit: *matter, motion, and force*—and his expositions are accepted by anti-theists as the only true science of nature and its laws. Unless this individual has an absolute knowledge of all the facts of nature—past, present, and to come—and a knowledge equally absolute of the entire character and relations of these three causes—and he affirms an absolute ignorance of them all—he does not, and can not, know, that, through these causes, he can account for all these events; nor, indeed, for any one of them. Unless he has an absolute omniscience of all realities that have being in infinite space—and he avows utter ignorance of every one of them—he does not, and can not, know, that the words, "matter, motion, and force," represent at all every cause, or, indeed, the chief cause, that operates in nature. In affirming, as he does, an absolute and hopeless ignorance of all realities of every kind, what reason has he for affirming or denying the agency of a personal God in nature? In the name of science, then, we ask, have we not here philosophy run mad? Mr. Spencer, however, in his infinite and affirmed ignorance of all realities, not only professedly discloses to us the secrets of universal nature and its laws, but professedly reveals a still higher secret—that of life itself. Life, he tells us, is "the definite combination of definite heterogeneous changes, both simultaneous and successive, in correspondence with external co-existence and sequences." That definition, surely, is as luminous as mud, about as clear and illuminating as his definition of progression. This, he assures us, consists in "advancing from the definite homogeneous to the definite heterogeneous." The correctness of this definition is a matter of dispute among some of his learned disciples. His philosophy, and that of anti-theists of all schools, when truly and properly defined, is "only this, and nothing more"—conscious and avowed ignorance of all realities, giving professedly to the world the science of the unknowable and unknown.

The Development Theory.—With singular fatuity, anti-theists of all schools have adopted the development theory as a last stronghold of the doctrine of natural law. Their supreme aim is to exclude wholly the idea of the agency of Infinity and Perfection in the organization and government of the universe. This theory carries the origin of things back to an incalculable distance in the past. To think of the world as having existed thus long, is equivalent with anti-theists to the idea that it was never created at all; that is, to an utter exclusion of divine agency from the universe. They forget that whatever took form in time, as all things did, according to this theory, is a creation, and absolutely implies a creator, distance of time making no difference. Then, as all organizations, animal and vegetable, are, according to this theory, developed according to natural law, it seems, at first view, as if God had no agency in nature. But let us go back to the first principle, from which all things, according to this theory, have been developed. This principle could not have existed in nature by natural law. In that case it would undeniably have acted from eternity; whereas, it as undeniably commenced action in time. Nor could it have been introduced into nature by natural law; for, if natural law had failed to introduce such a principle into nature from eternity up to any given period, it could not have done it then. Nature does not and can not thus change her own laws. The principle, undeniably, must have been introduced by a power from without and above nature; which can have been nothing but the agency of infinity and perfection, the agency which these scientists would wholly exclude from nature. But what must have been the character of this principle, from which all other vital organizations have been developed? It must have contained in itself the *germs* of all that was afterward developed from it; that is, of all organizations, animal and vegetable. Now, this would have been the most wondrous form of creation to which Infinity and Perfection could have given birth, and would, if true, involve the most absolute demonstration of the agency of God in nature. Thus, to escape the idea of divine agency in nature, anti-theists have leaped into a theory which involves them in the most palpable contradiction and absurdity.

Let us now turn our thoughts for a moment to this theory itself. Mr. Darwin, its great modern expounder, is constrained to admit that, throughout the wide range of geological science, he has not found a single abnormal form of living beings indicating, in the remotest degree, the transmutation of one species into another. Turning in despair from the revelations of this science, he has made a very wide induction of facts in respect to the influence of domestication and other causes in inducing a diversity of classes in the same species. But here, as before, his argument utterly fails. While he has done much to show that domestication and other causes may induce many wide diversities in the same species, he has not adduced a solitary fact indicating in the least degree that any one species ever has been, or ever can be, developed from another by any natural cause,—the only question at issue. The argument, as really presented by the advocates of this theory, may be thus stated: An endless diversity of the grape, for example, has been developed, by domestication and other causes, from some one original form. Therefore, the grape may be developed into the apple-tree. From this, the final conclusion is deduced, as a truth of science, that *all* vital organizations were, in fact, originated in accordance with the principles of this theory. This argument, fairly stated, presents one of the widest leaps in logic ever made or attempted by any power but a crazy philosophy.

Conflicts between Science and Religion.—We have now, we remark, in the last place, attained to a standpoint from which we can most clearly determine the character of all conflicts, real or apparent, which may arise between religion and science. In the department of natural theology, it has now become perfectly apparent that no such conflict is possible. Either theism or the doctrine of natural law, as we have seen, must be true. In favor of the latter, as we have also seen, science absolutely denies all possible proof, positive evidence, and antecedent probability. Here, then, a conflict between science and religion is manifestly impossible. Religion, on the other hand, accepts of no form or degree of evidence in its favor which science does not affirm to be absolutely valid. Here, also, as before, all forms and degrees of conflict between science and religion are absolute impossibilities. While science, also, adduces, and can adduce, no form or degree of evidence against theism, it does present, as we have seen, absolute proof of the being and perfections of a personal God. When anti-theism impeaches the validity of the intelligence, as the ground of denying the claims of religion—and it can deny these claims on no other condition—the conflict is not then between religion and science, but between the intelligence and "science falsely so called."

The only conflict which can, even in appearance, arise, is not between science and theism, but between the former and *revealed* religion. Here the only peril to be apprehended is hasty deductions in the sphere of natural science on the one hand, and Biblical interpretation on the other. When geology shall have attained to the full consummation of a fixed science, and the stand-point from which the first revelator had a vision of the progress of creation, shall have been as fully and finally determined, then we shall know absolutely whether the Spirit of inspiration—the Spirit which brought order out of chaos—has, indeed, dropped an inadvertent thought

> "In that dearest of books, that excels every other,
> The old family Bible, that lies on the stand."

Most of the issues which have hitherto been raised have already been settled, and, as real science progresses onward, what remain are rapidly becoming "beautifully less." The light of a rectified philosophy and of a pure religion are piercing through the fogbanks which the reekings of false science have sent up from the death-swamps of unbelief. The era is not distant when the last cloud of darkness will have passed away, and religion and science will become visible to all the world, as having a common source and a common end and aim, the light of each proceeding from the same central sun of universal illumination, the face of Infinity unveiled.

Lecture V.

MIRACLES.

BY THE

REV. BISHOP EDWARD THOMSON, D. D., LL. D.,

Delaware, Ohio.

LECTURE V.

MIRACLES.

AS Christianity is established in the mind of Christendom, the burden of proof is with its opposers. Still, it may be well, in a skeptical age, occasionally to revert to the foundations of our faith. Infidelity has invaded the Church, often putting on the badges of ecclesiastical authority, eating the bread of the Lord's table, and teaching his children; and though in the garb of an angel of light, and speaking in the sacred names of God, Reason, and Freedom, it has all the venom of an angel of darkness. Usually, it accepts the Bible as a grand product of antiquity, and system of morality, and fountain of devotion; the Church, as a support of the State, a means of civilization, and a source of refinement; the Savior, as a teacher, of charming rhetoric, pure character, and wholesome doctrine, to which he sacrificed his life—but it would eliminate from them all the miraculous element.

This tendency of modern thought is not surprising, considering the almost exclusive cultivation of the natural sciences, and employment of human genius in material enterprises. Against it we assert that

Jesus Christ authenticated a divine mission by miraculous acts. We prove this proposition by a few sucessive steps; namely: miracles are possible, probable, provable, proved.

I. Miracles are possible. This would not be asserted if it had not been denied. Strauss says that the chain of finite causes being inviolable, a miracle is not possible. But this is assuming what ought to be proved, what can not be proved, and what can be disproved.

a. If nature is bound in an eternal, inviolable chain of finite causes and effects, religion and even Providence are impossibilities, human responsibility is a delusion, and prayer a folly. But what say the universal reason and universal heart to such conclusions? Indeed, to deny the possibility of miracles is stark atheism. God is a supernatural being. A supernatural being must have supernatural powers; he who has supernatural powers must be capable of supernatural acts.

b. To deny that God ever modifies the order of natural sequences, is to make him inferior to man, who is at all times operating on the line of causes and effects, and modifying results at his will.

c. That God has modified the order of nature, the globe itself shows; for it was not created at once, but by successive acts, as geology proves. The destruction of one set of species and the creation of a different set, and the alteration of the conditions of the globe to adapt it to the new creations, being not the results of established laws, but of the overrulings of them, are so many different miracles. The successive strata of the world's crust record more miracles than the successive leaves of the Bible; nor are the miracles spoken from the mouths of prophets more wonderful than those recorded in the lasting rocks. But regard the world as it now is. Say, if you please, that all animal forms have been developed by force of inherent laws from a single animated germ. How came that germ? It could not have been derived from the vegetable world. There is a gulf between the two which must be bridged by a miracle. Suppose we overlook that miracle and ascend through the various forms of vegetable life to a primal vegetable cell, from which all living nature has evolved itself. How came that vital cell? Here is another gulf which nothing but a miracle can bridge. Let us ignore this, and suppose that, somehow, it sprung from inorganic matter; that life leaped out of death. How came the world, on which it is planted, organized, garnished, illuminated, warmed? What gave character and weight to atoms, and order to the families of material cohesion? Between the universe and chaos is another chasm which must be bridged by a miracle. The Divine, then, must somewhere break through the chain of causes and effects. If so, who shall blasphemously seek to exclude him from the circle or say, "*Hitherto* shalt thou come, and no further?" As God has modified the established order of things in the past, there is reason to suppose he is doing so in the present. Direct your eye outward, beyond the solar system, and the nebulæ which belong to it, to those remoter nebulæ that float like separate universes in the outer depths; buried so deep in space that light, traveling twelve millions of miles a minute, would not reach our earth from thence in fifty thousand years; some of them manifesting no signs of resolvability under the most favorble circumstances and most rigorous tests of science. Have we not reason to suppose that new planets are there evolving from their centers? Suppose they issue from their furnaces and enter on their paths, by force of ordinary law; must not some creative energy be put forth to clothe their valleys with green and render them vocal with song? How are the eighteen elements which enter into the plant or animal to be selected, gathered, brought together in the exact proportions necessary and then molded into organs and systems, and animated with life? Surely we need more than the laws of the *inorganic* world.

II. Miracles are probable.

a. There is a natural necessity for them. As we have reason to believe that God has modified established order in the past and present, so have we reason to suppose that he will in the future. According to laws as well settled as that by which a stone thrown into the air will come down, the moon is drawing nearer to the earth and must soon meet it, breaking up the crust of the globe by the shock, generating intense heat by the destruction of its motion and fusing both in to one molten mass. By the same process, the earth and attendant planets are winding inward to fall into the furnace of the sun, and the suns themselves with their planetary systems are coming together into a common globe, which, though intensely hot at first, will gradually cool. When the temperature of nine hundred and ninety-seven degrees in the downward progress is reached, all physical energy will cease, light, heat and electricity will be equally diffused, all change become impossible, darkness and death will be universal, and chaos be restored. What then? Shall the universe stagnate forever? Surely he can not think so, who believes in God. No; the Creator will then come forth; at his voice there will be a resurrection, a reconstruction, a restoration of the order of things. But why not break the order to *arrest* the progress to destruction, rather than after it has taken place? What do you gain for physical science by putting off the omnific mandate to the close? And if you allow interference with material law, to save a material universe, why not to save a moral one? How much superior one man to all stellar worlds! As Pascal has justly said: "Man is but a reed, the weakest in nature; but he is a thinking reed. It is not necessary that the entire universe arm itself to crush him. A breath of air, a drop of water, suffices to kill him. But were the universe to crush him, man would still be more noble than that which kills him, because he knows that he dies, and the universe knows nothing of the advantage it has over him."

> "Behold this midnight glory: worlds on worlds!
> Amazing pomp! Redouble this amaze;
> Ten thousand add; add twice ten thousand more;
> Then weigh the whole,—one soul outweighs them all,
> And calls th' astonishing magnificence
> Of unintelligent creation poor."*

* "Young's Night Thoughts," vii, 994.

b. There is a moral necessity for them. Miracles, in the theological sense, are more than Strauss assumes; and yet, in this superior sense, they are probable. A revelation from God implies them. Faith requires evidence, and the kind of evidence is to be determined by the matter to be proved; for a proposition and its proof must be homogeneous. As moral truth requires moral evidence, algebraic truth an algebraic process, mathematical truth a mathematical demonstration, so supernatural truth requires supernatural attestation. When Jesus said, "If I had not done among them the works which no other man did, they had not had sin;"* that is, they would have been excused for rejecting him; and when Nicodemus said, "We know that thou art a teacher come from God; for no man can do these miracles that thou doest, except God be with him,"†—they expressed the general conviction of mankind, that miracles are the proper and indispensable proofs of revelation. Since, therefore, a revelation can be proved in no other way than by miracles, there is a probability in their favor measurable by the evidence that man needs further moral and religious light than nature affords.

c. There is a fitness in them. God has made the human mind with a tendency to believe in things supernatural. All ages and nations have so believed. Hence the saying of Plutarch, "As well build a city in the air, as without belief in the gods." This belief is not confined to the lower orders. Socrates, greatest among the ancients; Bacon, greatest among

* John xv, 24. † John iii, 2.

the moderns; Herbert, first among philosophical skeptics; Wesley, first among emotional preachers,—had it in equal degree. The theory that, as mankind advances in knowledge, it diminishes until, finally, it ceases, is untenable. The present age is by no means emancipated from it, even in the most enlightened states. Though we have disenchanted portents and wonders, and earthquakes and meteors and simoons; and banished witchcraft and magic, and sorcery and necromancy and ghosts; we have not even weakened the popular faith in the supernatural, or in its influence upon the natural. Even they who shake off their religious faith usually adopt another no less supernatural. Spiritualism follows in the wake of skepticism. He who was once high-priest of materialism in America, is now high-priest of spiritualism in America. Can you arrest this tendency with the laboratory? As well attempt to destroy the atmosphere with an air-pump. As we might argue the existence of light from the structure of the eye, so may we argue the probability of miracles from the universal belief in miraculous manifestations. The mind is as substantial a part of human nature as the body, and as sound a basis of reasoning.

d. There is an analogy for miracles. Every-where we see subordination of one law to a higher. The animal pumps up blood in defiance of gravitation; it appropriates elements and molds them into combinations unknown in inorganic spheres; the mind subordinates the vital laws. Thus we see successive layers of laws, as wheels within wheels in the prophet's vision; the lower subjected to the higher; the vital subordinating the physical; the mental, both. Why not a higher force subjecting all, if need be, for higher ends? Surely, this is not incredible to men who see, in the ascending series of being, the uprising of a Supreme Power, and feel coming down from all the depths, and through all the openings, and over all the walls, of the universe, the influence of a heart that speaks to our own.

e. The objections to miracles are easily answered. Say not that the world, being established under God's laws, needs no interference. So far as God is concerned, this may be; but man, created in God's image, rational and free, has, by sin, broken in upon the moral order established by infinite wisdom, and thus given occasion for miracle; even demanded it. The whole creation groaneth in pain together until now, for the miracle of redemption. When a surgeon brings together the fragments of a broken limb, does he interfere with established law?

Nor are we to suppose that miracles are incredible because incomprehensible. A clergyman asked one who would not believe what he could not comprehend, why the horns of one cow turn in and those of another turn out. The skeptic was confounded. The clergyman might have taken his antagonist upward from the horns of the cow to those of the moon, thence to the most distant star in the milky way, or downward, from the horns of the cow to those of the snail, and from the horns of the snail to the smallest insect that hums in the morning air, without finding any thing comprehensible to human mind. "It is incomprehensible that God is, and incomprehensible that he is not; that the soul is in the body, that we have no soul; that the world is created, that it is not created." And shall man, "this mean between nothing and all," to whom the end of things and their principle are inevitably and impenetrably concealed, "equally incapable of seeing the nothingness whence he is derived and the infinity in which he is swallowed up,"—shall man dare to say, as he trembles between eternities and infinities: "There is matter, attraction, impulse; beyond that, nothing. There are plants, animals, man; beyond him, nothing. There is mind, thought, law; beyond, nothing,—because I can not comprehend it?" O, folly! O, presumption!

III. Miracles are provable. Hume has said, and his argument is often repeated, that a miracle being contrary to experience, is not provable by testimony; since it is more reasonable to suppose that testimony is false than that a miracle is true. The sophism is full of ambiguities. It is sufficient to notice one. It is in the word *testimony*, which may mean either testimony in the abstract, or a particular testimony. If the word be used in the former sense, the premise is true, but the argument is void; for it is not by testimony in the abstract, but by a particular kind of testimony that miracles are established. To put the fallacy in syllogistic form: Testimony—according to experience—may be fallacious. The Gospel is testimony; therefore, the Gospel—according to experience—may be fallacious. The first premise is an indefinite proposition; put *all*, the universal sign, before it, and you have valid reasoning, but a false premise; for it is not true that *all* testimony is fallacious; though testimony in general is, there is a species of it which at once excludes the idea of fraud on the one hand and delusion on the other—the very kind we have for the Christian miracles. Change the universal sign to the particular, and the premises are true, but the reasoning becomes invalid; for, in scientific language, you have an undistributed middle. To illustrate: Suppose you go into court with proof of your title to a particular estate, what would it avail for opposing counsel to say: This is testimony; therefore, this is fallacious? You would reply: Grant that testimony in general is fallacious; it is incumbent on you, if you would defeat my claim to this estate, to show that the particular evidence on which it rests is fallacious.

IV. The miracles of Christ are proved. The evidence is found in the Gospels. We assume their authenticity not only because it is proved in works accessible to all readers, but because it is admitted by both Rénan and Colenso, the representatives of the great skeptical schools of the age. This is enough; but as some are troubled because the canon was not settled until the Council of Carthage,* be it observed that this body did not create, it merely announced, the long-settled judgment of the Church. Since some are perplexed about the apocryphal books, mark that they were not contradictory, but complementary, of the canonical; and, as many are disquieted because the works quoting the Scriptures of the New Testament are none earlier than the second century, it may be well to note

*A. D. 397.

that, in the latter part of the second century, Irenæus quotes the four Gospels by name. He could not have been imposed on by any publication which Polycarp, Bishop of Smyrna, disowned. But Polycarp, born in the year of our Lord 80, was the contemporary and companion of both St. John and Irenæus, and must have known what works were received by John as the writings of the apostles. The four Gospels, then, must have been received by the Church of the first century—the apostolic age.

The testimony of the Gospels is corroborated by an independent author—St. Paul, in his uncontested epistles. He asserts that Jesus appeared, after his resurrection, on six different occasions—to Cephas, to the twelve, to more than five hundred brethren at once, to James, to all the apostles, and to himself.* He gives the appearance of Christ to himself as a proof of his apostolic mission, and of his parity with the other apostles; and of course it must have been by sight, and not by conception or imagination, or the argument would have had no force. The whole life of the apostle, the grandest in history next to Christ's, rests upon this fact.

Is the testimony to the Savior's miracles credible? The objections to it are two—its age and its inadequacy. First. It is said to be subject to abatement from the lapse of time since it was given. But on what does the credibility of testimony depend? On the period of time when it was given, or on the ability, diligence, and honesty of the witnesses? If on the latter, then, as long as these characteristics can be

* 1 Cor. xv, 5-7.

evinced, so long will the testimony be credible. I believe that Senorita Aldama was shot in the theater of Havana, but I believe more firmly that Cæsar was stabbed in the senate house at Rome, although the former occurred only a few days since, and the latter nearly two thousand years ago. I believe that Grant took Richmond, and, with as firm a conviction, that Bonaparte crossed the Alps, Hannibal retreated from Italy, and Xerxes from Greece. Had Bonaparte not crossed the Alps, the current of history for the last ninety years would have been different. Had Hannibal invaded Italy with a different result than history records, Italian civilization would have been Punic. Had the Persians triumphed at Marathon and Salamis, the civilization of Greece might have been Asiatic. I read the Constitution of the United States to-day with as much faith as did the citizen of Philadelphia, when the ink was scarcely dry upon the parchment. I know that without this Constitution, the history and condition of the country can not be accounted for. The division, organization, and relations of the States; the General Government, Congress, the President, the Supreme Court, all grow out of the Constitution. Suppose the Government to continue a thousand years, would the Constitution be quoted with any less faith than it is to-day? The New Testament is the Constitution of the Church. Without this, how can you account for its origin, institutions, history, or for the history of Europe and the world? for it has shaped the course of science, and turned the hinges of empires. Where Gibbon has failed, we had better not try. Instead of truth's being absorbed as it descends the ages, it wears its channel deeper with the lapse of time.

But, second, the evidence is said to be insufficient. It will not do to reject it because of our prepossessions. To refuse to believe evidence because it conflicts with our theory of natural laws, is inconsistent with that (Baconian) philosophy which infidels laud; which lies at the basis of modern science; and whose primary principle is, that whatever is proved must be believed, any pre-conceived opinion to the contrary notwithstanding. Perceiving this inconsistency, the ablest skeptics of the day are compelled to admit that there is a kind of proof which would convince them of miracles.

Let a man give out that, at a certain time and place, he will perform a miracle. Suppose that he will cause a body to rise contrary to the law of gravitation. Let a committee of distinguished philosophers be appointed to witness it. Let them take all needful precautions, and exercise all needful scrutiny in its examination. If they certify that the miracle has been performed, it must be believed; though, to remove any lingering doubt, it should be repeated, somewhat varied.* Infidels may believe in such a miracle, not we. We believe in the uniformity of nature's laws, though they are under the control of infinite wisdom, and may sometimes be violated for the sake of the natural or moral world. But, in the case described, there is no great end accomplished; no new light thrown either upon science or morals; no new encouragement given to the human heart; no

* "Rénan's Life of Jesus:" Introduction, p. 44.

new strength imparted to human virtue; no opening made into the spiritual world; no communication of truth lying beyond the range of reason; no new era introduced,—a nine days' wonder, and that is all.

Now, we think either of the following suppositions—namely, that a deception has been practiced upon the senses of the committee, or that some new law has been discovered, the secret of which is with the performer—is more credible than that a law of nature has, at the bidding of a mere man, been suspended. Such a miracle is no more like our Savior's, than a school-boy's top is like the planet Jupiter. Indeed, it is not a miracle in the theological sense. In this sense, a miracle is a suspension, control, or reversal of a known law, by the act, assistance, or permission of God, performed by a lofty character, and preceded by a notification that it is wrought to attest the authority of a divine messenger, or to authenticate a divine message, of great moral and permanent benefit to mankind. In the case supposed, five things are wanting to constitute the miracle: 1. An ample notice; 2. An adequate power; 3. A sufficient motive; 4. A grand agent; 5. Important and permanent consequences. All these belong to the miracles of Christ. Mark first the pre-notification. It has sounded through the world and through the ages. This notification is in a series of prophecies by Adam, Abraham, Jacob, Moses, David, Isaiah, etc., in which Christ is presented as the Shilch, the Great Prophet, the Prince, the Deliverer, the Messiah; also, in a series of types, as the scape-goat, passover, morning and evening sacrifice, in which he is exhibited as the

Lamb of God ; and, finally, in a series of typical characters, as Joshua, Joseph, David, in which he is foreshown as he who is to save the world, and lead his people into eternity. He is predicted so minutely, that almost every incident of his life, from the manger to the tomb, is described ; so clearly, that, by an alteration of tenses, prophecy may, in many cases, be turned into biography; and so peculiarly, that in Christ only, of all the race, can the lines of Messianic promise meet. He is to come during the fourth pagan monarchy, before the scepter departed from Judah, while the second temple was still standing, and in the seventieth year of Daniel. These prophecies are held by the Jews, the enemies of Christianity. They were interpreted of the Messiah by them until his coming, and were confirmed by their rejection of him when he came. They are harmonious in doctrine, precept, promise, and both complementary and illustrative of each other. They were translated into Greek, and read by the Gentiles, before the Christian era. Many of their predictions have been clearly proved by Volney and other infidels, while none can be shown to have been falsified. They have been examined as no other book; yet after enduring eighteen hundred years of intensest criticism, they shine out more than ever. They have been hindered as no others, yet are they going forth in more lands than before, soon to be read in all the languages of the polyglossal world. They have been opposed as no other; for they oppose, as no other, the passions of man's nature, and describe, as no other, the depth of his depravity ; yet are they received by more men and nations now than ever before, and are prized by them as a general rule, in proportion to their intelligence and virtue.

You point your telescope into space, and see a set of planets arranged in order, and wheeling in harmony, at different distances around the sun. God alone, who pervades all space, can build such a system. Point, now, your telescope through past time, and you see a series of prophetic lights sphered around one great central orb, the truth that "Jesus Christ came into the world to save sinners;" they are at different distances, from the year 410 B. C. to the birth of man. First, the sixteen prophets, of different ages, nations, occupations, and locations; then the Mosaic dispensation, with its apparatus of types and ceremonies, like Jupiter and his moons; then the patriarchal history, with significant characters, altars, and sacrifices, like Saturn and its rings; then Genesis, with its first promise in the garden, like the far-distant Neptune. Who but God, that pervades all time, can construct such a moral planetary system. To herald what being save Jesus Christ, was such a system ever constructed? Such, then, is the pre-notification of his coming.

Second. The cause of Christ's miracles is adequate. It is not the power of man, or angel, but of the Almighty. They are ascribed to this agency, and are of such a character as to evince it. They occur in a series which baffle all attempts to confound them with false miracles; or to account for them on Paulus's theory of natural explanations; or on Strauss's theory of myth; or on Bauer's, of fundamental ideas; or on Rénan's, of delusion and imposture. Though the science of the sea has deprived Neptune of his scepter, and that of the earth has stripped Ceres of her authority, and chased nymphs and dryads from woods and streams, and the philosophy of the universe has disenchanted eclipses and comets; no science or philosophy has discovered a method by which the blind may be made to see with a touch, or the dead be raised by the voice of the living. These miracles must be taken in connection. A chain that might moor a man-of-war could not, if its links were separated, hold a fishing-smack to her anchor. If you could find a mode of explaining each miracle separately, ascribing one to legerdemain, another to collusion, etc., it would by no means follow that you could account for the whole series, without the supposition of supernatural power. Even if you could explain Christ's natural miracles, his clear vision, which detected thoughts in the depths of the soul, and the stater in the mouth of the fish in the depths of the sea, and his prediction of the destruction of Jerusalem and of the future triumphs of his spiritual and universal kingdom, would remain to attest his divinity. These, you perceive, are entirely different from a shrewd guess, or the prevision of human conscience, anticipating events by the grooves of Divine law in which they must needs run, or the foresight of political wisdom, which sometimes works wonderful solutions from given data; for here there are no premises to go upon, no providential chord struck, whose vibrations could be caught by the distant ear.

Third. The miracles of Christ are called forth by a sufficient motive. They are wrought to verify important truth lying beyond the range of the human reason; namely, the existence and relations of the spiritual and eternal world.

That such truth is important to mankind must be evident at once. It is truth after which the wisest of all ages have sought, as after hid treasures. Without it, our civilization, which rests upon our religion, would fall through, and we should reach a depth of barbarism worse than that of pagan states; without it, our aspirations after goodness and truth and immortality would not be adequately sustained; without it, what would support us in the sorrows of life, sustain us in the struggles of virtue, animate us with brotherly love, gird us for sublime heroism, lead us forth in the enterprises of universal philanthropy, and cheer us as we pass through the valley of death? We grant that more or less of this truth has been enjoyed by heathen states; but it has been imperfect and derived.

That such truth lies beyond the range of the reason, is equally clear. The laws of physical nature may be discovered. Matter is before us, visible, tangible; it can be experimented upon. We are under strong motives to study its laws. Their investigation is a salutary discipline of mind. But the spiritual world lies beyond our ken. No reasoning, no experimenting, no mental introversion, can give us any knowledge of it. Reason, by her wisest son, Socrates, has confessed the necessity of a Divine messenger to give it. Without asserting that it is not, either in whole or in part, discoverable by reason, we know that, as a matter of fact, the world by wisdom does not discover it. God's natural attributes may indeed be traced in his works, and glimpses of his moral attributes may be obtained from his providences; but what man, unaided by revelation, has ever reasoned himself up to the unity, spirituality, and holiness of God, or found out by nature the scheme of redemption?

Modern philosophers—of whom Carlyle is an example—sometimes tell us that they have a revelation within themselves, that their God-created souls are Mt. Sinai's, and that thunder all round the heavens could not make God's law more Godlike to them. But why are not the God-created souls of the savages Mt. Sinai's also? The difference between the philosopher's God-created soul and the cannibal's equally God-created one is not by internal, but by external, revelation. Moreover, if the inner light were enough for human guidance, whence the confusion concerning moral truth, the general depravity of man, and the universal craving for a revelation, which the oracles and altars of all ages attest?

We honor natural reason within her legitimate domain. With all due respect to natural ethics and religion, we say that they are unsatisfactory without the aid of faith to complement and confirm their conclusions. Instinct is perfect; reason is progressive. But where reason has not drawn from faith, what progress has it made in morals since the creation of man? It is a mistake to suppose that a sacred nation, in an obscure corner of the world, guarded in seclusion the deposit of the truth. Both before and after Messiah, the Divine light was diffused. Why is it that beyond the circle of the Church's influence, infanticide, polygamy, slavery, prevail, without private remorse or public condemnation? Although the codes which have presided over the public and private life of modern civilized states have not been formed in synods, yet the principles on which they rest, though they do not exceed reason, are derived from revelation.

The history of Europe for three centuries has not been the mere progress of the secular spirit, but its advance under revelation as its pillar of cloud and fire.

Let not him, who can not obtain the knowledge necessary to guide him through this world without a teacher sent from *man*, be ashamed to find his way to the next by a teacher sent from *God.*

Fourth. The miracles of Christ are performed by a miraculous agent. He comes forth at a remarkable period of preparation and watching for a deliverer. The Greek language had been diffused, and the Roman arms carried in triumph through the world. The dying Jew said, "Bury me with my shoes on and my staff in hand, that I may be ready to meet Messiah when he cometh." The living one tuned his harp to sing of his approach; the sweetest lyre of the pagan world echoed Isaiah's strains.*

His character is peculiar; a mingled lion and lamb, and both transcendent. His words of wisdom and works of charity; his spirit of blended meekness and majesty; his life of perfect purity and matchless energy; of pillowless poverty and unsearchable

*Virgil: Eclogue iv.

riches; of patient suffering and godlike action; of weeping with man and standing with God; of moving in the lowest social state, and rising infinitely above the highest; of swaying the scepter of mercy, and wielding the sword of justice; of opening at once the gates of heaven and the mouth of hell; of subordinating even superhuman wisdom and power to the ends of love, and eclipsing them both by its transcendent luster; of renouncing the world, yet founding for himself a spiritual kingdom, embracing all the nations and the ages—is unlike all else ever known on earth, conceived by philosophy, or celebrated in art or song.

His revelation is unique. What is its primal, central, final, comprehensive truth, which flashes from all prophecies, blazes from all altars, and beams from all miracles? "God so loved the world that he gave his only begotten Son, that whosoever believeth in him should not perish, but have everlasting life." Look downward over this green earth, the footstool of God; look inward upon your own soul, the image of God; look upward into this blue sky, the throne of God; listen to its utterances, as they come down through spaces unmeasured and ages unnumbered, and say whether this message is not worthy of thine almighty Father! But sound all history, and you find nothing like it.

His method is divine. His words have the charm of antiquity with the freshness of yesterday; the simplicity of a child with the wisdom of God; the softness of kisses from the lip of love, and the force of the lightning rending the tower. His parables are like groups of matchless statuary; his prayers like an organ-peal floating round the world and down the ages, echoed by the mountain-peaks and plains into rich and varied melody, in which all devout hearts find their noblest feelings at once expressed, sustained, refined. His truths are self-evidencing. They fall into the soul as seed into the ground, to rest and germinate. He speaks, and all nature and life become vocal with theology. The mustard-seed and the mountain, the prodigal and the parent, the sparrow on the wing and the lily of the field, are still his unconscious ministers.

His errand is divine. We are not what we ought to be. Sin interposes between us and God. Evil tendencies and painful apprehensions, against which we struggle in vain, seize us; so that, to the awakened soul, life is a burden and death a terror. Christ comes, the only being in all history that even assumes to be an adequate and universal deliverer. Opposed by the carnal heart, he is yet the desire of all nations. Covered with contempt and scorn, he nevertheless finds his way to kings' palaces. Though sneered at by philosophy, he yet leads the princes of science as little children. All other great men are valued for their lives; he, above all, for his death, around which mercy and truth, righteousness and peace, God and man, are reconciled; for the Cross is the magnet which sends the electric current through the telegraph between earth and heaven, and makes both Testaments thrill, through the ages of the past and future, with living, harmonious, and saving truth. Other men may be buried, and stay buried. Mankind can give their noblest dead only a place in the cathedral's crypt, a page in history, and silence and forgetfulness more and more profound as time rolls on. Napoleon, dying, said to Bertrand: "I shall soon be in my grave. Such is the fate of the Alexanders and Cæsars. I shall be forgotten; and the Marengo conqueror and emperor will be a college theme. I die before my time; and my dead body must return to the earth, and be food for worms. Behold the destiny, near at hand, of him who has always been called the great Napoleon! What an abyss between my great misery and the eternal reign of Christ, who is proclaimed, loved, adored, and whose kingdom is extending over all the earth." Well might the great conqueror say so. But the world can not bury Christ. The earth is not deep enough for his tomb, the clouds are not wide enough for his winding-sheet; he ascends into the heavens, but the heavens can not contain him. He still lives—in the Church which burns unconsumed with his love; in the truth which reflects his image; in the hearts which burn as he talks with them by the way. There are suns so distant that, if they were blotted out to-day, the world would be thirty thousand years in ascertaining the fact. Practically, so far as the world is concerned, they would still exist. So with Christ, Sun of righteousness: he still shines; so that if we were not certified of his death, we might suppose, from the calls upon his name, the anthems in his praise, and the fruits of his Spirit with which the Church is blessed, that he is still on earth. And so he is. He is here to-day. Wherever the soldier bows in his tent, or the sailor on his deck; wherever the saint seeks grace, or the philanthropist help; wherever the orphan lifts up his cry, or the widow raises her despairing eyes, or the father weeps over his dying child, or the heart breaks under the weight of its sins, and calls on Jesus, he is there; there with the sympathies of man and the attributes of God; there to forgive sin, to fold the lamb, to purify the soul, and to lead the departing spirit in his own image to the skies; and every revolving day widens the sphere of mind over which his scepter sways and his blessing falls.

Vain to call this character a myth. It were easier for a rude peasant, without genius or geometry, or knowledge of artists or works of art, to produce the grandest historical painting, than for the fishermen of Galilee to draw the picture of our Lord. As Rousseau has shown, the myth would be as great a miracle as the reality. The line of cause and effect must be broken to produce the picture; why not to produce the reality, and to group around the reality miraculous acts?

Fifth. The miracles of Christ have produced wonderful and permanent results. The Church, in its origin, spread, present prosperity, and prospective triumphs, is miraculous. By preaching Jesus and the resurrection, it changed the religion of the world. It had no social or physical force; no civil or intellectual authority; no other element but the moral and miraculous. It has not lost its power. It still opens blind eyes, unstops deaf ears, cleanses lepers, makes the Ethiopian white, changes the lion to a lamb, and raises the dead; not, indeed, physically, but morally.

It constitutes the coast and cascade ranges of the moral world, condensing upon their summits the clouds of spiritual blessing, and inclosing the only valley of earth through which crystal streams meander among green pastures to the city of God. Beyond, on one side, are the arid sands of idolatry; on the other, the stormy ocean of unbelief. We may find objections to it, as we may to nature when we look into the recesses of the rocks for the snake, or the depths of the forest for the bear; but when we stand upon Mt. Zion, as when we stand upon Mt. Hood, to survey the whole landscape, we see on all its outlines the hand of the Almighty.

Now, to sum up and show how these five facts bear upon the argument, let me suppose a case. Were you to tell me that a carpenter in Brooklyn had risen from the grave the third day after his interment, I should give no heed to your tale, but let it pass as the idle wind. Bring before me twelve men, of unimpeachable character and good sense, who make oath to the fact, I should think them deceived. Prove that they could not be mistaken; that they knew the carpenter well; were with him when he died, heard his last words, and saw his breath depart; that after his death they stood by while the surgeons opened his breast and examined his heart and lungs; that after his resurrection, they had talked with him, eaten with him, and put their hands into his open side. I might suppose they had taken a strong conception for an object of sight. Show that, instead of expecting such a vision, they were disheartened after his death; that he had subsequently appeared to different parties, at different times, and, on one occasion, to five hundred and more at once—I might think there was an anomalous mental epidemic prevailing. Prove that, although the proclamation of this truth was upsetting the civil government and the religion of the world, and charging a damning crime upon the Supreme Court, the body of the carpenter, which, if brought from the tomb where his enemies had sealed it, would have vindicated the Court, saved the nation, and forever silenced the witnesses, was never produced,—I might then suppose that the witnesses had themselves concealed the body, and were dishonest. Prove that for their testimony they had suffered the loss of goods, reputation, office, and that they were engaged in proclaiming this miracle in pain, privation, and persecution. Lead them out before a platoon of soldiers, and read them an order from government that if they persisted in their testimony they should every one be shot. If, while the bullets were speeding to their mark, they should joyfully renew the statement, I should be in a quandary. Mind has its laws as well as matter. It is contrary to physical law that a dead man should come to life and burst from the grave; it is equally inconsistent with mental laws that human mind should burst from motive influence, and reverse its mode of action. Here, then, I should have, on the one hand, a physical miracle, on the other, a moral one. Which I should choose, I wot not; perhaps the latter. Add another circumstance—namely, that the resurrection was announced beforehand as a work of God, in attestation of an indispensable revelation to mankind—and the balance would incline in favor of the natural miracle. At this point, prove that the carpenter was more than a carpenter; a great, a popular, a blameless, an effective reformer; a miraculous being; the antitype of a long line of types, and the subject of prophetic song in all past ages, my doubts would be dissipated, and I should cry:

> "All hail, the power of Jesus' name!
> Let angels prostrate fall;
> Bring forth the royal diadem,
> And crown him Lord of all."

We believe more firmly than the skeptic in the uniformity of natural law, and reject more promptly those reports of isolated miracles performed at tombs, or at the bidding of mendicants or mountebanks, and which excite only the wonder of gaping multitudes, or the curiosity of prying historians. But we believe in a moral as well as a physical world, and in a supernatural series of events running athwart the natural laws, to verify a revelation for the instruction and salvation of the world—not so much contrary to natural laws, as according to higher laws in a loftier plane and for a nobler purpose. The miracles of Christ are but parts of a conglomerate miracle, of which the Jewish dispensation and the Christian, the Bible and the Church, the character of the Messiah, and the doctrines, precepts, power, and results of the faith, are all elements,—elements which we see and handle; which enter into practical life and human experience; which run through history, and modify nature, whose laws, physiological, mental, and moral, are dovetailed to them.

But it may be said, "You have only proved the miracles of Christ, leaving those of the Old Testament untouched." That phase of infidelity which accepts Christ and rejects Moses is the most absurd; for it accepts the major and rejects the minor included in it. Christ quotes the books of the Old Testament as of Divine authority. Grant that he is divine, and you must let us regard them so too. It is Christ that says, "If ye believe not Moses and the prophets, neither would ye believe though one rose from the dead."

The language with which a French philosopher, Pascal, closes one of his expostulations, I trust I may adopt in closing this.

Whether this argument pleases you, and appears strong or not, "know that it proceeds from one who, both before and after it, fell on his knees before that Infinite and Invisible Being to whom he has subjected his whole soul, to pray that he would also subject you, for your good and his glory; and that thus Omnipotence might give efficacy to his feebleness."

LECTURE VI.

THE

BIBLE A REVELATION FROM GOD.

BY THE

REV. BISHOP DAVIS W. CLARK, D. D.,

CINCINNATI, OHIO.

LECTURE VI.

THE BIBLE A REVELATION FROM GOD.

"*In the beginning, God.*" GEN. I, I.

I AM challenged to-day to perform two impossibilities. The first is, to bring forth a popular lecture upon one of the profoundest subjects that ever occupied the intelligence of man. The other is, to comprehend, in the discussion of one brief hour, a compass and breadth of thought that labored volumes could scarcely reach. I can do neither the one nor the other. All that can be hoped for is, that I shall skirt along the coast, taking soundings here and there, that, in the end, we may discover where the true harbor is.

As I am to speak of the Bible in its relation to God, no text more appropriate than its very first utterance can be found: "In the beginning, God." The alpha and the omega of the Bible is God. It commences with his being; it closes with his benediction. And, like a golden thread interweaving the whole texture and binding the genesis to the benediction, is God. It is, therefore, not a far-fetched proposition which asserts that the Bible is a revelation from God.

There are three generic problems in philosophy,

around which the deepest interest has gathered—the origin and collocations of matter in the realm of nature; the origin of man in the realm of mind; and the origin of the Bible in the realm of thought. The last of these problems is, however, the key to both the others. Solve this, and both the others become clear.

This is the problem that now claims our attention. Let us state the issue, and confine our inquiry to the narrowest limits that issue will admit. The Bible exists. It is printed in almost all languages, and spread abroad into all lands. Its wonderful history, and its still more wonderful literature, and its influence in forming the character of men and shaping the destinies of the world, are facts claimed by Christians, conceded by infidels, and known to all. They form, then, no part of the issue before us.

So much vantage-ground has the believer in this conflict. It makes the issue plain, simple, and single. The infidel, who would exclude God from the authorship of the Bible, can not deny its existence. He must, therefore, account for its origin in some other way. For him to assert that he does not know who its author was, does not meet the case; because this is a mere confession of ignorance, and accounts for nothing. If he does not know how the Bible originated, or who its author was, how does he know but that God was its author, and that it originated just as it claims? The whole history of skepticism shows how earnestly, and yet how vainly, it has sought to account for the origin of the Bible so as to exclude God.

It is a question vital to religion. If the Bible is a divinely attested message from God, then we find in it a solvent of the mysteries of human life and history, a harmonizer of the contradictions of philosophy, and an infallible teacher and guide. If it is not from God, then it only adds another element of mystery to that boundless and endless maze of darkness and doubt from which humanity may not hope to emerge without help from some higher source. This is the problem of the hour.

I. *We have presumptive proof that the Bible is a revelation from God, in that a written revelation is a necessary complement of natural religion.*

Nature speaks of God. But who will claim that she is a sufficient teacher of God? What significant teaching is there in the expression, "The unsearchable God"—handed down through all ages, felt in all human hearts!

While Job is enumerating the tokens by which God is seen in nature, the current of his thought is suddenly arrested, and he exclaims, "Lo, these are parts of his ways"—the extremities, the outer edge of his works—" but how little a portion is heard of him?" or, to give the passage a more true as well as forceful rendering, "What a whisper of a word is heard of him; but the thunder of his power who can understand?"* There are intimations of God in nature. She proclaims the great fact of his being; and, with unerring finger, evermore points to him as her author. But these disclosures are dimly seen. They are only glimpses of the Eternal. The mysterious dwelling of God in the universe; the workings of his mind

* Job xxvi, 14.

upon created things; the mighty sweep of his government through the ages; the spirituality and eternity of his character,—have wrung from the profoundest explorers, after all their research and their grandest discoveries, the confession, "Lo, these are parts of his ways!"

We stand only upon "the borders of his works"—on the outer edge of the creation of God. The grand center is full of God. Myriads of intelligences dwell there. Grander emblems of his power and glory brighten in their heavens, and speak to them from all his works. But, alas! there comes to us only "the whisper of a word." Go to him who has most profoundly explored the works of creation—the sage, philosopher, student of the handy-workmanship of God. Hear him speak of his discoveries and achievements. He has analyzed the hidden elements of nature; fathomed the depths of all oceans; measured the distances of all stars; solved the mysteries of all science; the winds and the waves obey him; the lightnings bear his messages across all continents and through all oceans; his thought spans all the broad spaces of astronomy. But put to him that question of profounder moment than all: "Canst thou, by searching, find out God? canst thou find out the Almighty to perfection?"* Mark the humility of his answer: "Lo, these are parts of his ways; we have trodden only upon the borders of his works; and only the whisper of a word have we heard of him."

Newton, who surveyed the amplitude of creation, and brought to light her all-pervading, all-controlling

* Job xi, 7.

laws, could say no more; Sir Humphrey Davy, who, with before unknown processes of science, analyzed the wondrous compositions of inorganic bodies, tracing the plans and purposes of the Creator in each, could say no more; and Hugh Miller, the Christian geologist, who, with science angelic, studied God in the earth's formation, could only rejoice in the discovery of the "foot-prints of the Creator" upon the everlasting rock.

Was man never designed to know more of God than this? Was it never intended that he should know how to approach his God and Creator? Never know how he might become like God? Never have more than a faint conception of his perfections? Was it intended that he should labor forever under the most painful uncertainty about his own destiny, and never for once feel the inspiration of the knowledge of his own grand immortality? Nature teaches us much. She has some grand lessons her children may learn from her. But there are higher, sublimer truths essential for man to know, which she can not teach. Turning away from, or rather, looking beyond, all the teachings of nature, the human heart instinctively yearns for higher and holier utterances. In its perplexity, doubt and darkness, it cries out, "O, that God would speak unto me!"

II. *Can God speak? Is utterance from him possible?*

Nature shows the workings of the mind of God. He embodies his thought in material creations, and through them speaks to man. Why, then, may he not embody his thought in the utterances of speech, and thus make known his will and truth to man? "He that planted the ear, shall he not hear? He that formed the eye, shall he not see?" and, pushing the inquiry of the Psalmist a step further, "He that gave the power of speech to the human tongue, can not he speak?" To deny that the Infinite, whose utterances are made to the human heart and understanding through all the avenues of material nature, can embody his thought or convey intelligence of himself in the utterances of language, is equally inconsistent and absurd. It is, in fact, to rob the Infinite of his infinitude.

III. *A revelation, written, recorded in permanent form, is the only one that can meet this demand concerning God.*

"It is written," "written in the law," "written with the finger of God," "written in earth," "written in heaven," and all "written for our learning, that we might have hope!" Glorious words are these! Had the Almighty only spoken, and left his words unwritten, no matter how august the scene when his voice was uttered, though with ten-fold more grandeur than when he uttered it amid the smoke and black darkness and pealing thunder of Sinai, the impression could not be transferred to others—could not be handed down to succeeding generations; and the unwritten tradition would, in the lapse of ages, become mixed with fable, till the grandest truths uttered by God would be perverted and lost. To such a peril God has not suffered the race to be exposed. To such an uncertain and perishable ark he has not committed the destinies of his own eternal truth.

The written revelation is the test of the unwritten tradition. The one is ever changing, the other ever abiding. "It is written," is the standard and the test of all truth, and in its sacred investiture it shall bear the truth onward through all ages and to all people.

IV. *If a revelation from God be a necessary complement of natural religion, in what written document shall we look for such revelation?*

Does it exist? Where shall it be found? In what book or literature shall we seek it? Shall we go to the Shasters of the Hindoos; to the Veda of Brahma; to the works of Confucius; to the Zenda-vesta of the Parsees; to the Koran; to the Book of Mormon? Shall we find it in the "Age of Reason;" in the rationalist's "System of Nature;" in the boasted "intuitions of the human mind," or the "internal consciousness," so strongly asserted by modern skepticism? Or, shall we find it in the Bible? Who can doubt for one moment where, among all these, is to be found the true revelation from God? The Bible stands out in its character, claims, and influence, infinitely above all the others. It distances every competitor. It is the only one that can stand the test. If God has given us a revelation, that this is it must be the conviction of every intelligent mind and every uncorrupted heart.

The whole question, then, is narrowed down to

this: If God has made a written revelation of himself to the race, this Bible must be that revelation. And if it is, then may we expect to find not only direct testimony of the fact, but, in the Bible itself, and in its character, history, and relations, we shall be sure to find circumstantial and corroborating evidence that it is from God.

V. *The early origin of the Bible, taken in connection with its wonderful character, affords strong evidence that it is a revelation from God.*

To say that the Bible is the oldest book extant of which we have any knowledge, is to make only a trite assertion; but it is an assertion pregnant with suggestive thought. The writings of Moses carry us up to the very origin of our race, and form the only connected line of human history from the creation. The Psalms of David, which contain some of the sweetest and sublimest poetry ever uttered by human tongue or recorded by human pen, were composed three thousand years ago. Many of the prophetic records were made a thousand years before the coming of Christ. The earlier portions of the Bible were undoubtedly written in the first language spoken by man. It is not improbable that the very first use made of letters was to record the revelations of God to the human race. The very fact that a book so wonderful in its character—the admiration of cultured mind in all ages, the crowning gem of all literature—antedates all science, all literature, and almost all intelligence, is demonstration that its origin is higher than human.

VI. *The survivance of the Bible as one of the living forces of the world is demonstration that it is from God.*

The works of men crumble and perish away. The mightiest productions of human intellect, however profound the impression made, or controlling their influence, at the beginning, will, after the lapse of ages, if not of years, pass gradually out of the current literature of the world. They will lose their hold upon the public mind, will cease to be read, and their influence be no longer discernible among the living forces that mold the characters of men and shape the destiny of the world. But the Bible, this earliest embodiment of thought, this earliest record of literature, has somehow escaped the operation of this universal law. It has come down to us, not as the dry, dead, blackened mummies of Egypt, but as a living force. The Bible lives. Never before did it enter so largely into the hopes of humanity or exert so wide an influence over nations and men as in this very age. Never before did it enter so largely, not only into the daily reading of unnumbered millions of the race, but also as a living force into the languages and literature of the world. A tree of life for the healing of the nations, the lapse of ages has brought no decay to its roots, left no rust upon its branches, no blight upon its fruit. Whence does it derive its living energy? Whence has it those vital powers that forbid it to die? Whence has it those irrepressible energies that have kept it, like the bush in the mount of God, unconsumed amid the flames?

Inspiration itself answers, "The Word of God liveth and abideth forever."*

VII. *The Bible has also overcome the opposition of its enemies, and survived their assaults in such a manner as to prove it incontestibly Divine.*

No other book has ever been so foully and so persistently assailed as the Bible. In this respect, the Bible has had a wonderful history. No form of attack has been spared. The arm of power has gathered the fagots, and applied the torch; but it has not been consumed. It has been cast into the crucible of criticism, and tortured in every conceivable form; yet it would not die. Infidelity has exhausted the arsenals of unsanctified wit, and croaking hypocrisy and damnable heresy have spread around it the pestiferous mildew of their breath; but it has come forth from its thousand conflicts triumphing alike over the open assaults of implacable foes and the machinations of pretended friends. Popery has not been able to chain it; the devil has not been able to destroy it.

Infidelity and false science have traveled the world over to explore the archives of history, to find some traces back of the Mosaic chronology, which might show the Bible history to be a fiction. Heathen traditions have been consulted; the chronological myths of the East, purporting to extend thousands of years anterior to the creation, have been brought forward; ancient astronomical calculations, whose dates were fixed long before sun or moon or stars began their courses in the heavens, have been sought out;

* 1 Peter i, 23.

obscure hieroglyphics, inscribed on enduring obelisks, have been tortured to draw from them something inimical to the Bible records; the most abstruse mathematical calculations have been made to falsify, if possible, the Mosaic history; the bowels of the earth have been penetrated, and nature forced to yield up the secrets of her birth, in the vain hope of discovering something which might give the lie to her Author.

All these objections to the Bible have been brought forward again and again. They have been reiterated with an audacious boldness and insisted upon with a pertinacity almost transcending human belief. This has been no ordinary ordeal through which the Bible has passed. Had it not been founded in truth and had God for its protector, it could not have survived the conflict. But the very weapons of its enemies have been turned against themselves. Even heathen traditions, when traced back along the converging lines toward their origin, present a thousand coincident features arresting the attention of archæologists, and tending to confirm the Word of God. The boasted chronological and astronomical records of antiquity, when founded in fact, and when truly interpreted, have been found coincident with the Bible, instead of being in antagonism to it.

Along the frontiers of every science, infidelity has planted its standard and raised its bulwarks against the Bible. But as scientific knowledge has advanced, it has been obliged to surrender one stronghold after another, till no place is left on which it can rest, except in the regions of conjecture and speculation.

The Bible, assailed by wicked men through all ages, has fought its way down along the line of opposing forces, and to-day it comes forth from its last conflict as it did from its first—bearing no scar or wound, with no singe of fire upon its garments, and no perturbations upon its brow. Like Milton's Angel, it is immortal in every part.

Take the last bold venture of modern rationalism, which claims that all higher forms of life are derived from the lower forms by a series of developments requiring unnumbered ages for their completion, and thus on down to the very lowest form of life, scarcely distinguishable from the inanimate lump of earth out of which it springs. Marvelous philosophy! But who made the clod that produced the polypus, that begot the monkey, that made the man? Who put the lump of earth there? Force, do you say? But what is this mysterious, intangible force? When, where, how, did it originate? What the fulcrum on which it plants its lever? How can it account for the work of creation, when it is not accounted for itself? How can it solve the mysteries of nature when, if it has any thing real in it, it is the most mysterious of all things in nature? What unmitigated effrontery is it that propounds such a scheme as this, unsustained by a single fact in all history, or by a single discovery in all science! A generation has hardly passed since this new "instauration of philosophy" undertook to solve the mysteries of creation, yet it is fast becoming a by-word; while, on the other hand, the very inquiries into the Bible account of creation, provoked by these attacks, gather around that account, from history, from science, and from philosophy, the sublimest attestations of its truth.

What intellect was that which enthroned the Bible, in the very morning of time, in advance of and above all science and all philosophy, so that the ages bow down to it with reverence? What inherent power is it that has given the Bible its double triumph over the unholy passions and the depraved intellects of men? The first utterance of revelation, "In the beginning, God," has stood the test of ages. It is the beginning of all history, the seed-thought of all philosophy. You must uproot this before you can invalidate the authority of the Bible.

VIII. *The entire freedom of the Bible from false science and fictitious history is no small evidence that it is a revelation from God.*

The Bible was not intended to be a summary of human history, but of the plans and dealings of God with humanity. It was not designed to teach science or philosophy, but religion. Its mission was to the race. Its communications, therefore, must be conveyed not in the precise, technical terms of science, but in the language current among men.

Science, through thirty centuries, has been searching out her facts, and molding and remolding her theories in every department of human knowledge. But though human interpreters have had oft occasion to modify their commentaries on the sacred text, yet the old record stands to-day unimpeached. The knowledge of the earth's form and its topography has been wholly reconstructed and boundlessly enlarged;

the facts of history have been more fully investigated; but no rashness of utterance on the part of the Bible in regard to things unknown, can be found to weaken its authority or expose it to contradiction. Even when the Ptolemaic system of astronomy gave way to the Copernican, and Galileo stamped his foot upon the earth, exclaiming, "Nevertheless, it moves!" he was not warring against the Bible itself, but against the glosses of mistaken commentators, who had failed to understand it. Now mark this fact: The Bible was written long before science had given rise to any theory, or formed a nomenclature, or been enriched by any of the great facts of her later discovery. But it contains no statement, no allusion even, that is contradicted by them. It does not employ any form of phrase that could be even improved by any of the discoveries of modern science. The most that can be said of it, or against it, is that it employs the "language of the common people."

The Veda and the Shasters of the Hindoos have not escaped this danger. The authors of these sacred books were ignorant of the form and geography of the earth; ignorant of many facts in the history of the race. They were without a knowledge of the true solar system. Hence, they hazarded statements about the form of the earth, the system of the universe, the ages of empire, and the lives of men, that harmonized with the traditions and mythologies of their age, but have been found, by later discoveries in science and a more accurate knowledge of human history, to be utterly unfounded in fact. Put a common school geography, or the simplest treatise upon astronomy, or any well-composed work on ancient history, into the hands of an intelligent Hindoo, and in just so far as he comes to the knowledge of their facts, he is compelled to give up his faith in his Shasters. It is for this very reason that these sacred books are losing all their authority among the intelligent and inquiring of the people.

Compare, also, the Koran with the Bible. What the Bible once uttered was uttered for all races and all time. The emergencies of the moment never affect its principles. The crises of an empire never turn it back upon itself; never even divert it from its main design.

On the other hand, the author of the Koran conformed his instructions to his followers; not to any deep and broad underlying principle, but to the pressing necessities of the moment. Hence, he was compelled frequently to recall what he had once promulgated, and to suppress what he had once proclaimed. Thus, the Koran is not only filled with false philosophy and historical untruths, but it is in itself "one complicated mass of irreconcilable contradictions." Skeptics have pronounced it the great religious rival of the Bible. It is the cripple entering the lists against an athlete, only to suffer defeat in every possible encounter.

Look at the Bible. It spreads over a wider range of history, looking into the future as well as recording the past. It is more definite in its account of creation, more specific in its wondrous scheme of salvation. How happens it that it has escaped the rock on which the systems of false religions have split? There is but one answer that can be given, and that is, its Author held in his hand the key of all knowledge. Not only is there an absence of false science and history in the Bible, but there are the most wonderful confirmations of even its most remarkable facts, brought to light in the investigations of philosophy. The mistakes of the Hindoo astronomy, which would have given the lie to the Bible, have been exposed and rendered harmless. Explorations in the crust of the earth's surface confirm the Bible history of the origin of man, by showing that it dates among the later geological periods. They also demonstrate that the order in which the elements were organized in the earth's formation, and in which vegetable and animal life were developed, was precisely that recorded in the Bible. The traditions of all nations confirm the fact of the Mosaic deluge. The Egyptian hieroglyphics confirm the exodus of Israel. Pagan oracles have been demonstrated to be only perversions, or rather imitations, of the utterances of God to the patriarchs, prophets, and kings of his chosen people. Nineveh rises from the grave to confirm the prophecies of Nahum and Zephaniah; Babylon rises to confirm Isaiah and Daniel. The scientific generalization of the races of the human family brings us back to the Bible account of Shem, Ham, and Japhet. There are more than two hundred different languages, and dialects almost innumerable, yet scientific analysis traces all forms of language back to one common type, thus illustrating the confusion of tongues, and making the tower of Babel a historical reality.

Science not only brings to light confirmations of the Bible in the ages past, but points forward to possible confirmations in the ages yet to come. Her theories of human progress are a prediction and a proof of the coming millennium. The "lost pleiad" from the heavens is also a foreshadowing of the destruction of our own world by fire.

Nor is this all. In this age of skepticism and infidelity, when the strongholds of the Christian's hope have been so ruthlessly assailed, God seems to have especially come forth for the vindication of his Word. A voice has been given to the very desolations of the earth. The buried and long-lost cities that perished beneath the curse of God, and whose desolation was so entire, and their very sites so long lost, that infidelity had come to question whether they ever existed, have been exhumed from the grave of ages. They have come up from their dusty beds, with the cerements of the charnel-house wrapped around them, and, before all men, utter their irresistible testimony to the truth of God. Infidelity and skepticism stand aghast at the spectacle, while the believer joins in the mighty acclaim, "Great and mighty art thou, O Lord God, and fearful are the judgments thou hast executed upon the face of the earth!"

IX. *The harmony of the various parts of the Bible, blending together so as to make it not merely homogeneous, but an absolute unit, is demonstration that one ruling mind gave it conception, and one master genius molded its form, however numerous the instruments employed in its development.*

The Bible is made up of sixty-six different books, written in different ages, and by forty-five different authors. And what is peculiar in the whole, each one of all those authors, separately, voluntarily, and for himself, surrenders the right, the honor, and the prerogative of authorship, and only professes to write as he is "moved by the Holy Ghost." There is incontestable evidence that there was only one Great Designer, who contrived the whole plot, from the beginning to the end, and who directed the execution of all the parts.

From the time that the record—"In the beginning, God"—was made, nearly sixteen hundred years elapsed before the "Amen" of the Apocalypse was uttered. During that time, what changes marked the world's history! Fifty generations lived and died; dynasties and kingdoms rose and fell; cities, walled and mighty, perished utterly, and were forgotten; new languages and new literatures received the impress of new forms of thought, and, in turn, gave new forms to the thought and culture of the age; the very face of nature was changed, and regions once populous became barren and desolate. But none of all this change reached up to the source whence the Bible sprung.

It starts out with, "In the beginning, God;" and every note struck thenceforward down through the ages, was in perfect harmony with the key-note struck in the beginning. Its instruments were many; their gifts and culture and external surroundings were endlessly varied. But, behold! What a wonder! The spirit, scope, and teachings are the same in all ages!

Though this sublime temple of revelation was so many ages in going up, and employed so many and various workmen, and its parts were wrought out in divers places—one in Mesopotamia, another in Egyyt, most of them by the mountains and lakes of Palestine, and the last on the isle of Patmos—yet all these parts, when brought together, harmonize into one, demonstrating that it had only one Architect from beginning to end. Creation does not more clearly indicate one Creator than the Bible one Author, whose thought and purpose and plan run through it all. One spirit only pervades the sacred Volume, and that spirit is divine. The volume of nature and the volume of revelation point to a common authorship. You may as well claim that man is the author of the one as of the other.

This thought is all the more striking when we come to compare the Old Testament and the New. Unlike, and yet alike, they fulfill their peculiar functions in perfect harmony. The one is the counterpart of the other. The one is the preliminary, the other the completion. All through the New Testament there are vast ranges of preliminaries assumed. In the Old Testament all these preliminaries are found recorded, each one pointing forward to something yet to come. In this harmony of the Old and the New Testaments, the whole structure of revelation stands complete.

You have seen buildings, partially completed, so arranged that, while present emergencies are met, future enlargement and a more perfect structure are indicated. This, you perceive, entered into the design of the architect at the beginning. The building as it now stands lacks symmetry, lacks completeness;

something is to be added. There are projecting stones and sunken mortises along the angles and at one end. The thought flashes upon you that the building is to be enlarged in this direction. The new is to be matched upon the old. These projecting stones are to be mortised into the new structure, and similar projections in the new building are to reach back and fill these mortises in the old. By this means the old and the new are to be dovetailed together, and made to constitute one great building.

Such were the Old and the New Testaments. The Old Testament, with prophetic jetties reaching forward into the future, finds its counterpart in the New; and the two together complete the symmetry, strength, and unity of the whole building. Whoever was the author of the former, most evidently anticipated the latter, even in its most delicate minutia. Not one of the projecting stones in the partial structure of the Old Testament but enters into its appropriate mortise in the New. The inspired writers of the New Testament constantly recognize this fact. Hence the oft-repeated expressions: "That it might be fulfilled which was spoken by the prophet;" "As it was written in the prophets;" "As the Holy Ghost spake by the mouth of the prophet;" "The Scripture can not be broken;" and so forth. There is a striking significance in that declaration of our Lord, that "one jot," the least letter in the Hebrew alphabet, or "one tittle," the minutest point in Hebrew writing, "shall in no wise pass from the law," the old dispensation, "till all be fulfilled." Every projecting stone enters into its appropriate mortise, and the building stands complete.

Whence this sublime harmony that pervades the Bible in all ages; its history, so accredited and true; its prophecies, so far reaching and yet so complete in their fulfillment; its religious truths, so lifted up above the range of human intellect, and yet so accordant with man's deepest and holiest intuitions; its great doctrines of Providence and grace, so unlike any thing that ever fell from the lip of sage or philosopher, and yet so in harmony with God's world and man's necessities; its great decalogue, born of God before literature was formed or history was written, an embodiment of moral precepts that has commanded the homage of the learned and the good in all ages, and which no subsequent age, however cultured and refined, has ever been able to equal, much less to surpass? What is there in all this that can be regarded as man's work? Could the unaided intellect conceive so wondrous a scheme? Or, if its conception were possible, how could frail, dying man inaugurate and carry forward a scheme so stupendous, requiring ages for its development, employing and controlling agencies so innumerable and so diverse, and working out, among all people and in all ages, results so grand and far-reaching? Impossible! simply impossible! It would be scarcely less absurd to say that the vast machinery of material nature was guided by human brain and impelled by human muscle.

Listen to the music of the spheres, as they roll along in their boundless orbits through the regions of space. How harmonious their concerts; how sweet the blending of all their notes!

> "Forever singing as they shine,
> The hand that made us is divine!"

We listen; we wonder; we adore. That wondrous harmony proclaims that the God of nature is one. Turn to revelation: from every book and chapter and verse; from every revelation, stretching through a period of four thousand years,—there comes up in responsive harmony the proclamation, "All Scripture is given by inspiration of God." "In the beginning, God," is no less the formula of revelation than of creation.

X. *There are certain analogies between nature and revelation, which indicate a common author.*

Whatever comes from God bears the impress of his character. His thought pervades alike his word and his work. There is comprehensiveness of plan, perfectness of adaptation, unity of design, together with a mysterious mastery of means, which are ever more reaching forward and working to bring about predetermined ends. This point can be made more palpable by a direct comparison of some common traits of nature and of the Bible, showing how both bear the finger-marks of God.

1. *In both there is the most surprising and wonderful adaptations.*

Nature is so perfectly adapted to man, that no one can fail to discover the fitness between the two. For man the day and the night succeed each other, bringing seasons of labor and of rest. For him the earth brings forth its flowers and its fruits. Had there been perpetual darkness, where would have been the use for the eye? Had the earth's crust been covered with one unbroken sheet of ice, like an immense glacier, it would have been totally unadapted to man. But we see every-where innumerable adaptations, great and small—adaptations wonderful beyond our thought; and the further we advance in the study of nature, and the more minute our examination, the more real and wonderful will these adaptations appear. They are infinite in number and infinite in variety.

Turn to revelation. You there find this same wonderful adaptation. To our intellectual nature, how complete the adaptation of the Bible; power to quicken the thought, to hallow the emotions, to kindle the imagination, to enlarge the conceptions, and to develop and perfect his power of utterance. To man as an individual, conscious that a few years ago he was not, and in a few years more he will not be, yearning to know for what purpose he is here, and what is to become of him in the future, the Bible comes with its lessons of immortality; for the victim of sin, the child of sorrow, here is deliverance from sin, and joy of heart. It comprehends all necessities, is adapted to all conditions, from the cradle to the grave!

We think it wonderful that the solid earth is adapted to one class of animals, the air to another, and the sea to a third; but how much more wonderful are the endlessly varied and perpetually continued adaptations of the Bible! John Williams, the early and eminent missionary of the South Sea Islands, gives, in his biography, a striking incident in point. The British ship-of-war *Seringapatam* was cruising in those waters, and the officers desired to see what effect religion had wrought upon the natives, and especially to hear them express their views of the doctrines of the Bible in their own way. Among the questions asked was this: "Why do you believe the Bible is the Word of God, and that Christianity came from him?" Several answers were given. After a while the question was repeated to an old and shrewd pagan priest, who had been converted and become an ardent student of the Bible. Instead of replying to it at once, he held up his hands, and rapidly moved the joints of his wrists and fingers; he then opened and shut his mouth, and closed these singular actions by raising his leg and moving it in various directions. Having done this, he said: "See, I have hinges all over me. If the thought grows in my heart that I wish to handle any thing, the hinges in my hands enable me to do so; if I want to utter any thing, the hinges of my jaws enable me to say it; and if I desire to go anywhere, here are hinges in my legs to enable me to walk. My body is just adapted to the wants of my mind. When I look into the Bible, I see there are proofs of adaptation which correspond exactly with those which appear in my body; I therefore conclude that the Maker of my body is also the Author of that Book." What more conclusive argument could be drawn, to prove that the Author of nature and of the Bible *is one?*

2. *In both nature and the Bible there are anticipations of and preparations for coming events, which could spring only from the infinite knowledge of God.*

The broad prairies that lie untilled and waste are a prophecy of the hand that shall cultivate them in the ages to come. The vast mineral resources hid away in the bowels of the earth, and the riches of the great sea, were so many prophecies of coming generations of men, who should delve in the mine and traverse the ocean. The immense beds of coal stored away in the earth, what were they but a prophecy of generations of men that should live far off in the future, and a preparation for them when the primeval forests have been cleared away? While the rich soil was designed to produce bread for the eater, the coal deposit was designed to provide fuel for the dwelling; and each is an anticipation of the future. Thus, in all the creation of God, "one thing is set over against another."

The same thread of anticipation and preparation runs through the whole Bible. As in nature there are events beyond the reach of unaided intellect, never dreamed of before in science or philosophy, so in the Bible there are events which no human experience could suggest, and no earlier facts of history lead us to expect. The ark was built while yet no cloud, visible to the human eye, shaded the heavens; but its grand mission was to bear the elements of a better civilization to a new world this side of the flood. The gauze-like threads floating in the mottled contents of the egg-shell are prophetic of a strong wing, that shall erelong come forth to cleave the clouds and scale the heavens. So all along, in Jewish altar and sacrifice and most holy place, we behold the gauze-like threads, the mystic prophecy of the strong wing, that was to bear our humanity heavenward in the Gospel day.

Amid all the sublime symbols of the temple and the altar, who, among all the earlier generations of men, had any adequate conception of the wondrous work of redemption upon the cross of Calvary? Yet the whole plan runs like a thread along the whole line of revelation, from the beginning to the end. Its key-note was struck amid the anguish and darkness of the fall; its final harmony is blended with the song of the angels of God. Such anticipations of the great and mysterious events of the future, whether in nature or in revelation, have foundation evidently in God's great, underlying law: One God, one universe, one humanity! Such far-reaching insight, such unerring anticipation of events hidden far away in the bosom of the future, belongs not to the philosophy of the earth; it is a revelation from the skies.

3. *The same great law of gradual development or growth that characterizes nature, is also manifest in revelation.*

"All created nature is in the process of development. From the solid and sterile rock up to the ethereal seraph, you see movement, transition, elevation, progress." God might have created an oak complete, instead of having it grow up from the acorn; he might have created the man instead of the infant; but he leaves the one to become the outgrowth of the other. So it is with the kingdom of heaven. It is the mustard-seed sown in the earth. He sheds upon it the light and warmth of his Spirit; the dews of heavenly grace fall upon it and quicken it into life; the vigor of his truth gives it strength. Thus it *grows* up.

The mineral, the vegetable, the animal, the intellectual, the spiritual, are only so many successive grades of ascent in the wonderful creative energy of God. The acorn grows into a mighty oak. The full-blown rose is but the unfolded petals bursting into a higher life. The eaglet's wing, whose microscopic fibers are scarcely discernible floating in the shapeless fluids of the egg-shell, shall yet soar majestically through the air, bidding defiance to cloud and storm. The feeble and helpless child infolds manhood in all its strength and glory.

What is here suggested in the natural world is revealed and confirmed in the Bible. The processes of development in the natural world have their counterpart in the spiritual. The resemblance is so precise, the two schemes interlacing at so many points, fitting as exactly as the bone is fitted into its socket, that no one can doubt that both had a common origin, and that the one was made for the other. *One God, one universe, one Bible!*

4. *Again, there is a oneness in the mode in which nature and the Bible impart knowledge, which clearly indicates that they are parts of one great plan, having a common Author.*

They both simply indicate practical facts, without assigning a reason, or attempting to explain the inner being, cause, or mode of any of them. Nature gives us water to drink and be refreshed, but does not stop to explain how or why. She gives us light, and allows us to open our eyes and behold her glories; but the philosophy of the solar ray she leaves us to study. Ages pass by before we have advanced so far in that philosophy as to know that seven distinct colors are blended into one to make the solar ray. Nor, when we have made the discovery, have we made any practical addition to the value of light. So Christianity gives us facts. The Bible announces God; but the mysteriousness of his being and eternity, it does not attempt to explain. It teaches the facts of the fall—sin, redemption, regeneration, adoption, resurrection, heaven; but it takes no pains to disclose the philosophic element that underlies and pervades all these truths. It does not even take pains to explain the harmony that exists among them all. The Bible and nature stand side by side. Each one says, Here are my facts, use them; then study them. Wonderful is this harmony! What shall we say of these two, but that they are twin ministers, receiving their commissions from one common Source?

5. *Inexhaustibleness is also characteristic alike of nature and of revelation, as it is of nothing else.*

We can soon reach the bottom of the works and thoughts of man, and comprehend all they contain. The author is finite, and a finite mind may comprehend his work. But when we come to the works of the Infinite One, we are struck with their inexhaustibleness. All our discoveries in the natural world are so suggestive of undiscovered wonders which lie beyond, so suggestive of new and more wonderful problems yet to be solved, that we deem ourselves only to have made an advance, but never to have reached the bottom. The broader our survey of the material universe, the more absolutely limitless and beyond finite comprehension it seems. Even a single drop of water embodies forms of life wonderful and innumerable, suggesting how inexhaustible nature is.

And so it is, also, with the Bible. Its profound depths have never yet been fathomed by finite mind, while portions and passages open up to the reader new beauties and sublimer truths, even at the thousandth perusal. The art of Christopher Wren and the philosophy of Bacon we may exhaust and go beyond; but go far as we may in the study of nature or of revelation, we find that the lines of thought in each stretch out in perfect harmony, like parts of one great whole, limitlessly beyond our farthest advance. What other conclusion can we reach, but that both are the productions of one Infinite Mind?

XI. *The Bible only has given us the true idea of God, and this is a presumption of its being a revelation from himself.*

The intuitions of the human mind suggest God; reason demonstrates him. But who, unaided by revelation, can comprehend him? The King of Syracuse proposed this question to Simonides, "What is God?" The sage desired a day to consider the question. On the morrow he asked for two days more. When they were ended, he asked for four days, then eight days, and so on, doubling the number each time. The King became impatient, and demanded the reason for this delay. The sage answered, "It is because the more I consider the question, the more obscure and difficult it appears." Greece had a wonderful history. She had Aristotle and Plato; she had Thucydides and Pheidias; she had Demosthenes and Homer; philosophy, profound and far-reaching; history, that has furnished the world with models; art, admired and copied in all ages; eloquence, entrancing, vehement, omnipotent; poetry, the vibrations of whose melodies will cease only as the earth's pulses stand still; a language and literature, sparkling with classic beauty, and rich with classic lore. She had her conquering Alexander. But she had no God! Saturn, her oldest deity, devoured his own children. Jupiter dethroned his father, and became sovereign of gods; but his life was a history of corruption and debauchery. Juno, his wife, was a vixen and a shrew, and yet a goddess. Venus, his daughter, was the patroness of all licentiousness; Bacchus, the patron of wine and drunkenness; Mercury, expert as a thief, and a god of all thieves; Mars and Bellona, patrons of war and blood. These be thy gods, O, Reason! O, Philosophy!

But behold, away back in the dim antiquity of the race—ages before Grecian art or culture had being—here is an outcast child, drifting in a frail ark down the Nile! He is saved from the waters and the crocodiles only to become first a foundling, then a slave. Then, when grown to manhood, kindling at the wrong inflicted upon one of his race, he smites the oppressor, and goes forth a fugitive into the desert, branded as a murderer. Tell me, how did this poor wanderer among the wastes of Arabia gather that knowledge of God, to which Grecian culture and art and philosophy utterly failed even to make the faintest approach? Nay, how was it that he should have grasped conceptions of God upon which no subsequent age has been able to improve, and which all subsequent revelations have only confirmed? Where, in what literature, ancient or modern, can you find a substitute for that grand conception of God, as the one Lord and Father, spiritual, holy, almighty, eternal? Mark how he appears to Moses, as he is sheltered in the cleft of the rock from the overwhelming glory of the Divine presence: "And the Lord descended in the cloud, and stood with him there, and proclaimed the name of the Lord. And the Lord passed by before him, and proclaimed, The Lord, the Lord God, merciful and gracious, long-suffering and abundant in goodness and truth; keeping mercy for thousands, forgiving iniquity and transgression and sin, and that will by no means clear the guilty; visiting the iniquities of the fathers upon the children, and upon the children's children, unto the third and fourth generation."* Can any thing be more sublime, more true? In what age of the world, and among what people or race, did poet or philosopher ever originate conceptions of God so grand or so true as this poor fugitive was made the vehicle of communicating to the race? From this old Bible, then, lifting up its voice in the gray dawn of the world, we

* Exodus xxxiv, 5–7.

have the grandest utterance of God that has ever fallen upon human ear. How can this be, unless God himself spoke?

XII. *The Bible has done more to keep alive the idea of God, and make that idea felt and active, than all other causes combined.*

It utterly ignores the theories of philosophy; pays little respect to the arguments of the naturalist; but, by a sort of magnetism peculiar to itself, it touches the intuitions of the heart, and the soul recognizes that it is God who speaks. The Bible does not demonstrate God, but it is full of God. You need no other proof that the sun is shining than to look at it. You can not commune with the Bible without the felt presence of God. Among Oriental fables, we read of a mirror with such wonderful properties that to one looking into it distance and time were annihilated; things past, present, and future could be seen with equal distinctness; and objects invisible to human sight, and too grand for human comprehension, were brought to view. What was fiction with the pagan has become fact with the Christian. Such a mirror he has in the Bible. It sweeps the whole range of creation, and reveals God every-where. Under the reflections of this wonderful mirror, "the heavens declare the glory of God, and the firmament showeth his handiwork." He is seen walking among the constellations; giving brightness to every sunbeam; giving the landscape its verdure, the rose its beauty; whispering in the gentle breezes of evening; feeding the young ravens when they cry; providing pasture for the cattle upon a thousand hills; uttering his voice in the thunder; going forth upon the dark bosom of the tempest, and making the winds and the waves his messengers. Creation becomes instinct with a new life; God appears not merely in its majestic worlds, moving through the cycles of uncounted ages; but in the flitting of a wing, as well as in the fall of a world; for even the sparrow has the notice and care of God. It reveals God, present, living, active—threading all the mazes of human history and shaping the destinies of all events, from the beginning of creation to the end of time. The grandest creations of the human imagination are unequal to such a result as this. None of them have ever been, none of them can ever be, so impregnated with God. The great lessons and the grand pictures of the Bible abide from age to age. They speak to all generations and all ages. They never become obsolete, never become old; they are like God, living and eternal. Theism can not die while the Bible lives. Atheism with the Bible becomes impossible. The theories of philosophy and the arguments of the schools, however conclusive, may fail in their power to convince; they have no key with which to reach the heart; but human conscience must respond to the Bible revelation of God. Pantheism may resolve God into an airy abstraction, deny his personality, banish him from creation or confound him with it; but the moment the Bible appears, God stands forth, personal, active, mighty. The Bible formula—"In the beginning, God"—places him at once in immediate contact with human beings as their great Creator and Lord. "It appeals to the eye, the ear, the imagination, the intellect, the heart, and enshrines God in the most vivid conceptions and the deepest sentiments of the human soul." It enters into all the interests of humanity, fires the heart with the loftiest aspirations, lays before it the grandest work, and appeals to it with the noblest motives. This is not the sphere of philosophy. Human philosophy has never yet risen so high. It is not human teaching, but Divine.

XIII. *The truths revealed in the Bible are above the range of the human intellect, and such as human reason could never have discovered.*

Many of these truths are of profound and abiding moment. They permeate all philosophy and endure through all time; and though they are essential to man's nature, yet his unaided reason never discovered them. Take a single grand truth, the priceless revelation of the Bible, that God is one, and that the universe is not the offspring of chance, nor a resulting condition of an endless development of previous states, but the work of His hands, and so the object of His almighty, fatherly, ceaseless care. Take a single commandment, the first commandment of all, and the second, which grows out of it, "Thou shalt love thy neighbor as thyself,"—in these two primary and capital truths is the foundation of all religious duty, sentiment and action. They confront us every-where, surround us evermore, permeate all doctrines and all duties, and at once bind the whole race together in one common brotherhood, and point them all to the love and care of one common Father. "In the revelation of them is an evidence of the Divine, which may be seen and read of all men. And until it can be explained how these grand truths, which neither the East nor the West discovered, which escaped the earnest searchings of Zoroaster, with his profound Magian philosophy, which dawned not upon the soaring intellect of Plato, and which was, in fact, hidden to all philosophy; until it is explained how these truths, so solemn and yet so salutary, defying the utmost scrutiny of the mere intellect of man, and yet, when sent down from heaven, harmonizing with all his clearest conceptions, and loftiest aspirations; until it is explained how these great truths, thus lying beyond the reach of the noblest minds of the race, were, or could be elaborated out of the thoughts of Moses himself,—until then, I shall not think it unreasonable to recognize in these truths and these facts a light from heaven, an instance of Divine interposition, a proof of the Divine origin, and an illustration of the high worth of the religion of the Bible."*

XIV. *The doctrines of religion which originated in the Bible, and are taught by the Bible, are evidently above human invention.*

The human mind never originated them—never could have originated them. Human philosophy never taught them. They are above and beyond the scope of both. For the most part, indeed, human philosophy has stood apart from the Bible and its

* "The Divine in Christianity," pp. 59, 60.

teachings, and ofttimes been in antagonism to both. It did not, therefore, originate either, even if it had power to do so.

But these doctrines are interwoven with the facts of history. The same is true of the miracles of the Bible. The doctrines, the miracles and the history, were all recorded by the same hand. They are all blended into the same system, and have become conjointed parts of one great building. Now, if we accept the history, as we must, then almost inevitably the miracles are conjoined with it; and these together become the "two witnesses" who attest that the doctrines are of God.

Then, too, these doctrines of grace, holiness, heaven, bear the impress of God. Nowhere in them is there to be found such limitation as always characterizes the finite mind, or such defects as inevitably inhere in imperfect natures. They admit no exception, but extend to all. They are applicable to all races and peoples, and sweep down through the ages, a boon and a blessing for every generation and every individual. The wonder—"God manifest in the flesh"—was as surely born in heaven as it was heralded by angels to earth.

Thus we are made to *feel*, as the first converts of Christianity said, "Satan never devised those doctrines, man never wrought those miracles." And thus are we driven back to God. His is the word, his the work! One is the document, the other the seal. If the seal shows the finger of God, it demonstrates that the document is from God. If the document comports with the seal, as the doctrines of the Bible do comport and harmonize with its miracles and its history, then the two mutually strengthen and confirm each other, and the demonstration that both are from God is complete.

XV. *Finally, I know that the Bible must be from God, because it is the great intellectual regenerator of the race, as no other work is or can be.*

Most works of human authorship have but a limited influence and an early death. A few in their own specific departments have attained to distinguished honor and brought forth grand results. But even these were limited in their sphere, and not one of them could survive the slow wasting of the ages. What human genius has not attempted, and what it must have failed to accomplish, if it had attempted, the Bible has actually done. In its practical lessons, it discovers to us how intimately our personal interests are associated with those great truths and agencies by which God is leading our humanity onward to its final destiny.

The Bible, setting aside all questions of its Divine authenticity, of its inspiration, and even of its theology, stands before us in the light of fact as the intellectual regenerator of the race. This pre-eminence is assured by the purity and truth of its philosophy, and by that inspiration of its genius through which the minds of men are quickened with intellectual vigor. And to these must be added the sublime earthly, as well as heavenly, destiny it reveals to man.

It embodies history the most wonderful, spanning the entire cycle of the race, from the birth of creation to its apocalypse; ethnography, the most minute and accurate, challenging the profoundest deference of the archæologist and antiquarian; biography, the most thrilling and instructive, giving portraitures of characters, with a distinctness, fullness, and beauty, no human skill can equal; civil polity, laws, and jurisprudence, which not only transcend the wisest legislation of the time, but furnish the germ and the model of all that is humane and just and noble in the enlightened legislation of the most enlightened nations and periods of the world; delineations of the domestic affections and virtues, such as ennoble humanity, and enchant, by their simplicity, truthfulness, and purity; patriotism, love of country and people, such as led the world's first great statesman and legislator to choose to suffer affliction with the people of God rather than to dwell in the tents of wickedness, such as girded with might the sword of David, and inspired his songs with undying melody, such as hallowed the tears of Jeremiah, and kindled the eloquence of Isaiah; proverbs for instruction, maxims for the regulation of human conduct, and oracles to clear away the darkness of human reason, which, for pertinence, for adaptation, force, and universal applicability, are unequaled in the uninspired literature of the world; eloquence, the most impassioned and sublime; poetry, soaring on seraphic wing into sublime altitudes unreached by Milton or Young; moral virtues and æsthetic beauties, such as human philosophy, confessing its own impotence, can only wonder at and admire, without attempting to rival; science, comprehending mysteries of the earth and the heavens, before which, even after the lapse of six thousand years, all mere human philosophies pale into insignificance ; theologies, teachings of God, bringing within the range of human cognizance, Him that filleth all things with his fullness and glory !

It is thus that Divine revelation sweeps across every field of human thought, and underlies every interest of human life. The Bible is not a mere lesson-book of duty, nor yet a mere manual of theology. Had it been such, and no more, a hundredth part of the present volume would have been all that was required. Such a book would not have been diversified by varied and thrilling history, nor by sublime imagery and wonderful announcements of prophetic inspiration, such as have proved in all ages a bulwark against the rude assaults of infidelity, and are a standing demonstration of the truth of revelation, growing stronger and more convincing as the ages roll on, and at the same time making the Bible a book of unceasing study and criticism, to sound its depths and unravel its meaning. Nor would it have contained those sacred songs that so move the hearts of men, nor those fascinating stories, beautiful narrations, striking fables, proverbs, and parables so attractive to the fancy of the young, and so rich in practical wisdom for the common people. Thanks be to God that he has given us, not the lesson-book, but the Bible ! The former would have fallen still-born and powerless ; it would have been forgotten ages ago. But the Bible is the life-thought of the world. It is replete with all that can excite the fancy or give wings to the imagination ; all that can refine the taste, ennoble the affections, and enlarge the intellect ; all, in fine, that can call forth the sublimest thoughts, present the grandest motives of action, and enkindle the loftiest expectation in the illimitable future. It enters into all thought and all feeling, and is allied to all interests, earthly and heavenly. It is just such a book as must be read, will be read. It will travel through all lands, dwell among all people, find a home in all languages, permeate all thought. However skeptical and unbelieving men may be, they can not ignore the Bible. It confronts them. They must read it, if it be only to learn how to combat its doctrines and claims; they must study it, if it be only to join in the vain effort for its overthrow. The very study and effort to destroy it will only cause it to penetrate still more deeply into the world's thought, and imbed it still more firmly in the literature of all ages. Thus the very efforts of infidelity to destroy the Bible only cause it to strike its roots still deeper into the earthly soil, where it shall live and grow forever.

St. Paul rejoiced that Christ was preached, even though it was done by some "of envy and strife." So say I of the Bible. Let skeptics and the false and deceiving philosophers of the day read and study the Bible, though it be only for envy and strife, though it be only to cavil at its truths and claims; yet "I therein do rejoice, yea, and will rejoice;" for I know that by it all, the Bible will be only the more firmly intrenched in the thought and life of the world.

There is no department of taste or thought, or culture or art, that has not felt the invigorating power of the Bible. It has furnished some of the grandest themes for the sculptor, the painter and the musical composer, in all ages; it has given to the great masters their inspiration, and they, in turn, have laid their grandest trophies at the foot of the cross.

The Bible contains some of the sublimest poetry, which the most gifted of our race have ever found unapproachable in beauty and grandeur. But this is not all. It has actually furnished the material, the subjects, and even the thought, for the sublimest poems in the literature of the world. The sacred songs that enliven the worship of Christian temples in all lands, find their source and fountain-head in the songs of David, written three thousand years ago. Who does not recognize this every-where in the sacred hymns of Watts and Wesley, of Montgomery and Cowper, of Heber and White? Even Byron's gifted but wayward muse kindled with unwonted fervor and grace, as he sung anew the "Hebrew Melodies." Strike out from the sacred song of the ages all that had its origin in this old fountain, and there would be little left to touch the heart or inspire the faith. The voice of melody would become silent in the temples of God and in the dwellings of the saints.

Then, too, see how largely all poets have drawn upon the Bible for their subjects, their materials, and their inspiration. "Paradise Lost," the great epic of the world, had never enthroned its author as the master of song, but for the inspiration drawn from the Bible. Pollok's "Course of Time;" the "Messiah," of Klopstock; the "Night Thoughts," of Young; Tasso's "Jerusalem Delivered;" Dante's "Inferno;" Burns's "Cotter's Saturday Night;" Scott's

"Hebrew Maid;" and Moore's "Song of Miriam,"—are only a few of the examples that might be cited. Thus, in the poetry of all ages and all languages, we find every-where, mingling in the song, notes borrowed from the sacred poets of Israel.

Shakspeare has been claimed to be the most original of the poets. And so he was. But in almost every scene and act of Shakspeare there are gems gathered from the Bible, to deck the bright conceptions of his own genius. Do you question this? Let me cite a few of the many examples. The blood of Abel crying from the ground for justice; the three-score years and ten as the measure of human life; the sleeping of the righteous dead in Abraham's bosom; the fearful thing of being blotted from the Book of Life; the camel threading the eye of the needle; the serpent as the tempter; the ministering angel from heaven; the "All hail" of Judas; the dropping of manna from the skies; the mote and the beam in the eye; the wail of the Jewish mothers over the slaughtering of the infants; Pilate washing his hands to remove the foul stain of murder; the grand remedy of redemption for souls forfeited; the peacemaker's blessing; the voice of wisdom crying in the streets,—are so many of the samples of the imagery and language borrowed by Shakspeare from the Bible. Thus, the great dramatist of the world was scarcely less indebted to the Bible than was the author of the grand epic of the Fall of Man. And who will not say that both these grand authors were immensely enriched by that indebtedness?

The Bible, it is true, does not undertake to teach

science, just as it does not undertake to teach painting or poetry. One has said, "The Bible has no mission to teach philosophy how to cast her measuring-lines into the sea, or sink her shafts into the heart of the earth, or stretch her telescopes through the untrodden fields of space." But, after all, it does have to do with science as well as with art. It is the moving spirit, the upheaving energy, that has stimulated the discoveries of science, and shed its benign radiance upon the brilliant pathway of her explorations, even in the material universe. Why is it that in no age has science, or the arts of industry, or the economies of life, or the humanities of society or of legislation, made any essential progress without the Bible? Why is it that, in all ages, this reviled, scorned, hated book has stood at the head of the science and the literature of the world?

Have we, indeed, come up here to the fountain-head, the great inspirer of all thought, and the source of all human progress? Do we here find the great orb of light in the intellectual heavens, whose beams shine from pole to pole? Who but God himself could set it in the heavens, and sustain it there, undimmed in its glory, from age to age?

And now, young gentlemen, having presented these few initial points, which, to every unprejudiced mind, must be decisive of the great question before us; having seen that God is at once in the Bible and the Author of the Bible, just as he is in creation and the Author of it; and that the Bible, by the comprehensiveness of its plans, the marvelous variety of its adaptations, the wonderful resources of its power, and the sweep of its influence down along the line of human history, is worthy of its author and equal to the grandeur of its mission,—we can not better close these remarks than in the exultant language of Kepler, when, with rapt soul, he contemplated one of the sublime laws of astronomy, just then disclosed to human intelligence: "The wisdom of the Lord is infinite, as are also his glory and his power. Ye heavens, sing his praises; sun, moon, and planets, glorify him in your ineffable language! Praise him, celestial harmonies, and all ye who can comprehend them! And thou, my soul, praise thy Creator! It is by him and in him that all exist. What we know not, is contained in him, as well as our vain science. To him be praise, honor, and glory, forever and ever!"

This, young gentlemen, is language not copied from any sentimental or doctrinal work of the Church. It is not the exultant triumph of Christian joy; but it is the outgushing homage of science itself, and expressed by one whose laws circle the earth and comprehend the heavens. If in your college curricculum it shall be your ennobling privilege to try to follow the pathway of the immortal Kepler among the globes of light, tread that sacred ground with the same reverent recognition of God. Return from it rejoicing in the great central truth of all science, as well as of all revelation, "that it is by him and in him that all exists."

Lecture VII.

SCRIPTURE INSPIRATION.

BY THE

REV. WILLIAM F. WARREN, D. D.,

President of the School of Theology of Boston University,

Boston, Massachusetts.

LECTURE VII.

SCRIPTURE INSPIRATION.

THE theme assigned for to-day's lecture is the Inspiration of the Bible. It is a high theme. It is one of vital interest to every Christian, yet difficult of treatment apart from the technicalities of the schools. Our time is short. Omitting all introductory formalities, allow me to limit and define the discussion by first stating a few points, respecting which I shall assume a perfect agreement at the outset.

And, first of all, I assume that a man is not a beast. I shall take it for granted that you claim for yourselves and for your kind a spiritual nature. You do not believe with Moleschott, that "thought is a movement of matter," nor with Karl Vogt, that "the thoughts stand in the same relation to the brain as gall to the liver or urine to the bladder." If any man chooses to hold such language as this, we have many other questions to settle with him before coming to that of Scripture inspiration. Perhaps I should rather say that, if any creature in human shape shall be pleased to profess himself nothing different from a brute, it will be eminently fitting to postpone all argument with him until he shall become a man. Lunatics, we are told, should never be contradicted.

I assume, secondly, that there is a personal God, who has created man and given him his spiritual nature. And I assume that, in making man, this Divine Being did not forever exhaust himself, and sink into an eternal swoon. I shall take it for granted, without argument, that he is still God enough to act upon the creature of his hand, and to influence him as one spirit may influence another. If any of my hearers is disposed to say he knows nothing of any such Being, I shall reply by recommending him to make his acquaintance.

Thirdly, I assume that this Divine Creator and natural companion of man is not locked up in the sky-parlor of the universe, unable or unwilling to do more than indolently to watch, through the crystal floor of his prison, the swing of his spheres and the tumultuations of human history. I shall take it for granted that you all reject this deistic notion of a cock-loft divinity, far removed from all human affairs, a cold and idle spectator of the world of men. I assume that, as the air inspheres all trees, so God all souls. In him is our living, our movement, our being. He touches us on every side. The Divine and human spirits not only can, but do, communicate to and with each other. God can take knowledge of my thought; I of his. God can breathe peaceful benedictions into my spirit; I can cause grief to his. God can woo my love by his goodness; I his, in prayers and grateful service. If any man hesitates to concede me this, let him take lessons of Theodore Parker; even of him he may learn thus much.

Finally, I assume that the Christian Church is

not the fabric of a dream, nor a paper plan found only in books, but a great historic institution. I shall not try to prove that Jesus Christ was neither a knave nor a fool; neither myth-made nor a myth-maker. I shall assume it as tolerably well settled that Abraham was the father of the Israelitish nation; that there was a servitude in Egypt; a law-giving at Sinai; a theocracy in Palestine; a crucifixion in Jerusalem. The kingdom of God among men has stood long enough to be recognized in every history. It spreads widely enough to be seen on the smallest map. Its foundation-stones are under the world; its pinnacles are lost in the heavens.

These, then, are our preliminary assumptions: a spiritual psychology, speculative theism, and a personal relationship between God and men, historically mediated by Jesus Christ. I make them the more unhesitatingly, from the fact that each of them has been already vindicated by the lecturers who have preceded me in the course. They give us, as you see, first, an inspirable Soul; second, a Being capable of inspiring it; and, third, the fit historic occasion.

These preliminaries being thus settled, we are prepared to state the exact question proposed to us for discussion. Much confusion has characterized some of our treatises on this subject, from the failure of their authors clearly to apprehend, and persistently adhere to, the precise point in debate.

Observe, then, first of all, that the question before us is not the question whether or not the ancient prophets and apostles received immediate communications from God. This is assumed. It is the question, not of Scripture inspiration, but of Christian revelation.

Again, our question is not whether or not these organs or mediums of Divine revelation were in an inspired condition at the time of their receiving the immediate Divine communications vouchsafed to them. This may be taken for granted, if they received Divine communications at all. It is, however, a question relating not to the recorders, but to the recipients of God's revelations.

Finally, the point at issue is not whether or not the holy prophets and apostles were under an especial Divine influence, when engaged in orally declaring and carrying out their Divine commissions. That is a point to be settled on its own evidence; but it is not the question of Scripture inspiration.

The real question of Scripture inspiration is simply and solely this: Is there satisfactory evidence that, in the labor of composing our Holy Scriptures, the sacred writers were aided in an extraordinary and peculiar manner by the Holy Ghost? and, if so, what was the nature, and what the effect, of that aid? Remember, then, that we do not here inquire respecting the fact of a Divine revelation, or the psychical state of its recipients at the time of its reception, or the normality of their state of mind in orally delivering it to others; our one and only business is with the sacred writers, *as writers*, and *as writing*. The general inquiry ramifies, as we have just seen, into three special ones; the first relating to the fact, the second to the nature, and the third to the effects, of Scripture inspiration. Let us take up each in order.

I. THE FACT. That the sacred writers were directly and extraordinarily aided by the Holy Spirit in writing down what they did, is not so easily proved as some, who have attempted the task, would seem to imagine. The sacred writers themselves nowhere make the assertion. In one place they tell us that "holy men *spake* as they were moved by the Holy Ghost;"* but nowhere, that they thus *wrote*. Often, along with the Divine message, vision, or prophecy, they record the Divine command which bade them write it; *but that, at the time of making the record*, they were under an extraordinary Divine influence, they nowhere tell us. We can not claim, therefore, that they were under such Divine influence, on the ground of any direct assertion of the writers themselves.

To some before me, very possibly, this may seem a very grave and unnecessary concession. To such I can only say, that no concession to truth is to be feared. Nothing is so perilous to the ascendancy of Christian ideas and beliefs, in a community like ours, as an over-anxious, disingenuous, special-pleading spirit in the professed expounders and defenders of the faith. Nothing ever came so near swamping my own faith in the Divine origin of Christianity as the discovery of this pitiful pettifoggery on the part of some of the accredited apologists of the system. There are defenses of Christianity which are more dangerous than the attacks which called them forth. There are vindica-cations of the inspiration of the Holy Scriptures, of which we may emphatically affirm, it had been better

*2 Peter i, 21.

for the cause had they never been born. Take any fifty ordinary treatises or discussions of this subject, and you will find at least forty of them commencing their argument for the fact of Scripture inspiration with the assertion, "The sacred writers claim it." When I recall the emotions with which I first perused and sifted the course of argument employed in proof of this initial proposition, I can not reply indignantly enough, "They claim no such thing." Call not my position a perilous concession. It is the old position which is perilous. The logical jugglery required to cover up its falsity has fatally disgusted many an ingenuous mind. Nothing is so safe as truth, nothing so persuasive as honesty.

There is another argument, almost invariably employed by those who have elaborated the proof of Scripture inspiration, of which I can say nothing better than of the last. I refer to the argument *a priori*, from the necessity of such a Divine influence in order to make the Bible authoritative. It runs as follows: The Bible must have been written under a Divine inspiration, since, without such an inspiration, it would have no power to command man's faith, would have no authority. This, as you observe, is arguing a matter of fact from an alleged *a priori* necessity—a logical procedure always suspicious, and most frequently fallacious. I must leave such an argument to others. It does not carry conviction to my mind. It seems to me that the Gospel would have been worthy of all acceptation, even if it had never been committed to writing at all. Methinks the Israelites were bound to believe Moses or Isaiah, when they declared what Jehovah had said to them, even if these prophets gave no proof that God was, at the moment, dictating, or in any wise extraordinarily affecting, their narration of his message. Methinks that, if the writings of the holy prophets and apostles contained no hint that God assisted in a peculiar manner in their composition, I should still be under obligation to believe the great facts of sacred history; to accept the cardinal doctrines and practice the pure precepts of Christianity. Even these same theologians grant, and indeed strenuously maintain, that uninspired testimony may make a belief in miracles morally obligatory. If it can do that, what is there, in the whole compass of the Bible, which the ordinary testimony of the holy prophets and apostles, and the witnessing Church, could not cover? Let us remember, too, that, if uninspired testimony has no power to command men's faith, the Bible has no power to command faith in its own genuineness; for the only testimonies we have that our sacred books were really written by the holy men to whom they are ascribed, are confessedly uninspired.

Again, the argument either excludes all Scripture proofs for the fact of inspiration, or involves the fallacy of reasoning in a circle. If, as we are told, we can never be absolutely sure that a Scripture statement is true, until it has been shown that every word and syllable was infallibly inspired of God, then, evidently, no Scripture statements, were they never so numerous and never so explicit, could establish the doctrine of inspiration itself, for the simple reason, we have as yet no proof that those Scripture statements affirming it are themselves reliable. If we employ them, we necessarily reason in a circle. We say, in effect: All Scripture must be Divinely inspired, for such and such Divinely inspired passages say so.

Without wasting further words upon the traditional mode of arguing our question, I will here say, that, while I most heartily and unwaveringly believe in the inspiration of the sacred writers as writers, I am of the opinion that my faith, and the universal faith of the Church, on this point, is *purely inferential.* The Scriptures teach it only as they teach the doctrine of the Holy Trinity, or the hypostatic union of the two natures in Christ. Nor is its evidence, on this account, in my opinion, any the less. I should rather call it all the greater. Mere professions are cheap in all religions, and in our day even authority goes for little. The very best evidences which a system can have are those which are imbedded in its very structure, ingrained in its very fiber. These must be as enduring as the system itself. Just such, as I view them, are the evidences of Scripture inspiration.

The reasons in view of which we accept the doctrine are chiefly, I think, the following:

1. The grand analogies of Christian experience.

The true Christian has a very vivid realization of his own utter impotence and worthlessness apart from Divine grace. He has learned from experience that no man can even call Jesus Lord, but by the Holy Ghost. He has learned that the new life is a living in the Spirit, and a walking in the Spirit; that they only who are led by the Spirit are the sons of God. The

Comforter is nearer to him than his own flesh and blood. He helps his infirmities, bears witness to his sonship, indites his petitions, makes intercession for him, prompts to good, restrains from evil, sanctifies the heart, and hallows the life. Such a man views himself as a temple of the Holy Ghost, a worker together with God. When called upon to witness to the truth before the ungodly, he asks for Divine assistance, and is conscious of receiving it. In interceding for others, he asks to be taught how to pray, and believes that he is thus taught. If a preacher of the Word, he never prepares or preaches a sermon without asking, and, as he firmly believes, receiving, Divine aid. With such views and convictions and experiences, he instinctively assumes that the sacred writers, walking more closely with God, called to higher responsibilities, and intrusted with higher work, must have enjoyed in an exceptional degree these aids and influences of the Spirit. It is an argument *a fortiori*. If put into logical form by the understanding, it would run thus: If I daily receive such Divine strength and aid and direction in the discharge of my comparatively insignificant duties, how much more must the holy prophets and apostles have had the higher aid they needed in every thing pertaining to the revelation of God's will, and the government of his Church! The force of this presumption is immense. Its practical influence, in maintaining the faith of the Church in the extraordinary inspiration of the sacred writers, is, in my opinion, immeasurably greater than that of all the argumentative treatises ever written upon the point, from the beginning until now. It is true it is only a presumptive argument; but the presumption is so vitally grounded in the facts and experiences of the Christian life itself, that nothing can neutralize its influence over the genuine Christian mind. And the higher sense such a mind has of the responsibility and importance of the work of committing the Divine Oracles to writing, and thus furnishing to the Church of all ages an authoritative norm of doctrine and practice, the more vivid and firm will be its faith that, in the execution of that work, unusual aids of the Spirit were granted.

2. I think the faith of the Church in the fact of Scripture inspiration reposes, further, upon the representations given us, in the Scriptures, of the authority and inspiration of the prophets and apostles in their *oral* teachings.

I need not detain you with any extended proof that a peculiar and exceptional Divine aid was afforded to God's ancient prophets and to the apostles of Christ, when acting in their proper capacity, as divinely commissioned teachers and authorities in the Church. Such extraordinary aid was absolutely essential to the right discharge of the extraordinary duties of their office. They were constituted the authorized heralds and interpreters of the whole counsel of God with respect to human salvation. To the apostles were committed the keys of the kingdom of heaven, with the solemn assurance that whatsoever they should bind on earth should be bound in heaven, and whatsoever they should loose on earth should be loosed in heaven. Christ made them so completely his representatives and mouthpieces as to assume the full responsibility of their words and acts. To those who should refuse to receive them and to hear their words, he threatens judgments more intolerable than those which overtook Sodom and Gomorrah. He declares to them, "He that heareth you heareth me, and he that despiseth you despiseth me." And when, at the close of his earthly career, he tarries yet a little to issue his last solemn commands to his almost bewildered disciples, he deliberately suspends upon the teachings of these men the eternal destinies of all the nations and unborn generations to whom their words shall ever come. "Go ye and teach all nations; . . . teaching them to observe all things whatsoever I have commanded you. . . . He that believeth and is baptized shall be saved; but he that believeth not shall be damned."* In the old dispensation, like power and authority was committed. God demanded of the people and of their rulers, and even of the priests and high-priests, that they should hear and obey his special prophetic messengers. He declared that if any man should refuse, he would require it of him. If such was the office of these organs of revelation in God's kingdom, surely an extraordinary Divine aid was essential to its right discharge.

This antecedent expectation we find fully met in the representations given us in the Bible. We are told that such a special official charisma was promised and conferred. Christ pledged it to his dis-

* Matthew xxviii, 19, 20; Mark xvi, 16.

ciples the first time he sent them forth to preach.* He renews it in his prophecy of the destruction of Jerusalem and the persecutions which awaited them. He tells them, "Settle it, therefore, in your hearts, not to meditate before what ye shall answer; for I will give you a mouth and wisdom, which all your adversaries shall not be able to gainsay nor resist."† In his farewell discourse, just previous to his death, he repeated and enlarged the promise;‡ and after his resurrection, one of his last injunctions to his disciples was to tarry at Jerusalem until they should be endued with power from on high.|| Similar promises were often vouchsafed to the ancient prophets.§

All these promises were duly fulfilled. The apostles were endued with the promised power; and, as if to intimate the Divine significance of the baptism, as designed to qualify them for the publication of the Gospel, the charisma was bestowed under the visible type of cloven "tongues," like as of fire resting upon each of them. Thenceforth their preaching was with the Holy Ghost sent down from heaven.¶ They represented their teachings and ordinances as of Divine authority.** They demanded for the spirit within them the respect due to the Divine.†† They asserted that their preaching was not with words of man's wisdom, but in the demonstration of the spirit and of power; that it was revealed unto them by God's Spirit, the same Divine Agent who searcheth all

* Matthew x, 19, 20; Luke xii, 11, 12. † Luke xxi, 14, 15.
‡ John xiv, 16–18. || Luke xxiv, 49; Acts i, 8.
§ Jeremiah i, 8, 18, 19; xv, 19–21; Ezra iii, 8, 9, etc. ¶ 1 Peter i, 12.
** Acts xv, 28; 1 Corinthians vii. 40; xiv, 37; Ephesians iii, 5.
†† Acts v, 3, 4; 1 Thessalonians iv, 8.

things, even the depths of God; that by this Spirit they knew the mind of the Lord; and, finally, that what they thus knew, they spoke, "not in words, which men's wisdom teacheth, but which the Holy Ghost teacheth."* Of the prophets they affirm that they spake as they were moved by the Holy Ghost. At the same time they claim for themselves perfect equality with, and even pre-eminence above, said prophets.† No one, who believes the Bible true, can doubt that the prophets and apostles were truly and extraordinarily inspired in the work of *oral* teaching. Inspiration in oral teaching, however, being granted, inspiration in the work of written instruction, and especially in the preparation of a perpetual norm of faith for the Church, is a simple, natural, almost inevitable, inference. Contrasting the character and foreseen historic influences of their spoken, and of their written, words, we should say that such Divine aid was even more needful for the writer than for the speaker. Hence, the pious mind of the Church has, in all ages, consciously, or unconsciously, reasoned as follows: If the Holy Spirit secured an absolute and continual authority to the chosen *media* of revelation, then must they have been as truly under Divine guidance when laboring with the pen, as when laboring with the tongue. Indeed, as what they wrote was designed of God to be preserved through all generations, and to serve the Church as a permanent and authentic record of sacred history, doctrine, and ordinance, there was greater

* 1 Corinthians ii.

† 2 Peter iii, 2; Romans xvi, 25, 26; 1 Corinthians xii, 28; Ephesians ii, 20; iv, 11.

reason for affording them extraordinary aid when writing, than when delivering oral discourses, which could reach but a few hundred of their own generation. To suppose that the promised and received Spirit of truth was withdrawn from the apostles, when they betook themselves to the task of writing the Scriptures of the New Dispensation, would be to suppose that they were deserted just when Divine help was more needed than at any other time; would be to assume that especial assistance was afforded in the easier portion of their work, but withheld in the more difficult. The argument loses none of its force when applied to the ancient prophets, since in almost every case the critical and decisive test of the truth of their prophecies was to be the historic fulfillment, or non-fulfillment, not of remembered words which had been spoken, but of exact declarations, written down ofttimes centuries before, in black and white. Evidently, if the prophet needed to be supernaturally preserved from error at all, it was not so much in his spoken, as in his written, declarations.

Such, I imagine, to be the second ground of the Christian faith in the inspiration of the prophets and apostles as writers.

3. The third basis of the same belief is found in the peculiar deference every-where and always paid to the Old Testament Scriptures by Christ and his apostles.

Here, as on other points, I think the defenders of the Bible have often overstrained the argument, and so broken its force. Many of them have represented the language of Christ and of the apostles, as directly and unequivocally asserting that the authors of the Old Testament books wrote under an extraordinary Divine afflatus. I can find no such assertion in the New Testament. Even the classical passage—2 Timothy iii, 16—whether rendered, "All Scripture is theopneustic and profitable," or, "All theopneustic Scripture is profitable," does not assert it. It contains no reference to the sacred writers. It does not even indicate whether the affirmed or assumed theopneustia relates to the matter, or to the form, of ancient Scripture. It does not even define the unfamiliar term which it applies to ancient Scripture, a term found nowhere else in the Bible. It does not *compel* us to predicate of the Old Testament any thing more than that theopneumatic quality which is predicable, for example, of a good man's prayers. But if this passage does not sustain the affirmation in question, surely there is none which does. Here, as in the former cases, the argument is first made clear and forcible, when we make our conclusion an inference from the facts before us.

What are these facts? I can not state them in detail; but, in general, they are these. Christ everywhere appealed to the Scriptures of the Old Testament, as to an authoritative arbiter in all controversy. He declared that it can not be falsified;* that the whole law, even to its iotas and tittles, must be fulfilled;† that every thing in his own life and death must conform to what was written of him, "in Moses, and in the prophets, and in the Psalms."‡ The same is true of the apostles. Their constant appeal is to

* John vii, 23; x, 35. † Matt. v, 18. ‡ Luke xxiv, 44.

the Scriptures. They call them the Word of God, God's Oracles. They quote them with such introductory expressions as these: "The Holy Ghost saith;" "God saith;" "The Lord by the mouth of his servant David hath said," etc. They style them, in distinction from all other compositions, "*The Scriptures,*" "*The Scriptures of Truth,*" "*The Holy Scriptures.*" They affirm that they are theopneustic,* that they are able to make us wise unto salvation. And while most, if not all, of these and similar declarations are employed with reference to the Old Testament Scriptures, it is not to be overlooked that they claim for their own apostolic writings a full equality with the more ancient Scriptures of the Church.† Now, in all these and equivalent expressions, there is no direct assertion that either the prophets or apostles wrote under extraordinary influences of the Spirit; but there is such a patent assumption of the fact, both by Christ and his apostles, that no candid and right-minded believer in their authority can resist the clear inference. Taken in connection with the considerations already presented, its force far surpasses that of any mere declarations of authority, however numerous or explicit. It is perceived to be a necessary implication of the faith.

Such I believe to be the chief grounds on which the Church's belief in Scripture inspiration rests. Others no doubt contribute to its confirmation, but these are the chief. I believe them abundantly sufficient. Granting the facts from which our inference is drawn, and for all of which we have highest direct

*2 Tim. iii, 16. †2 Peter iii, 16.

evidence, the legitimacy of the inference can never be questioned. So long, therefore, as the Church shall retain her Christian life, her faith in the official charismata of the prophets and apostles, and, finally, her histories of the manner in which Christ and the apostles deferred to Old Testament Scripture, just so long will she believe in the fact of Scripture inspiration.

II. The Nature of Scripture Inspiration.

Enough with respect to the Fact; let us pass to consider the Nature of this extraordinary Divine influence.

On this point, as you all know, a great variety of views have been entertained. There is, for instance, on the one hand, the dictational theory, or the theory of an exact and universal verbal inspiration. According to this conception of the matter, God literally dictated to the sacred writers, as to so many amanuenses, every word of the Bible, verbatim, from Genesis to Revelation. One Calvinistic Confession insists that even the Hebrew vowel-points were given by the inspiration of God;* though they are well known to have been added centuries after the original composition of some of the books. On this theory the sacred writer was only a penman, a transcriber; his part was simply and solely the reproduction upon parchment of the precise words revealed to his inner sense by the dictating Spirit. Whether he penned history, prophecy, psalm, or doctrine, Divine

* "Tum quoad consonas, tum quoad vocalia, *sive puncta ipsa, sive punctorum saltem potestatem*, et tum quoad res, tum quoad verba θεόπνευστος." (Formula Consensus Helvetici, A. D. 1675.)

thoughts or human feelings, things already known, or now for the first time revealed, the operation of the Spirit was the same. The writer was merely the passive organ of the Divine Spirit, as much so as the hand with which you write is an organ of your mind. Gerhard calls them, in so many words, "Manus Christi"—the hands of Christ. Here the Divine agency is at its maximum, human agency reduced to its minimum.

The natural reaction from this mechanical and most unsatisfactory view carries many to the opposite extreme of a mere Divine supervision or superintendence of the sacred writers, by which they were simply restrained from material error. Their language is their own; their style is their own; their statements, arguments, and reflections, with perhaps the exception of those introduced directly with a "Thus saith the Lord," are all their own. The only Divine agency attending the composition was the somewhat negative one of excluding from the mind of the writer all statements and inculcations inconsistent with the great object of Divine revelation. Here we have the maximum of human, with the minimum of Divine, agency.

But these two antipodal theories are by no means all. Between these, as extremes, we find almost every conceivable modification of the two related agencies. To increase the confusion, old Rabbinical distinctions between different kinds of inspiration are rehabilitated; and we are told of "the inspiration of superintendence," "the inspiration of elevation," and "the inspiration of suggestion." Then come distinctions with respect to the writers; one class being historic, another didactic, and a third prophetic. Finally, to render the discrepancies as nearly infinite as possible, all these classes of writers are combined with all these kinds of inspiration, through almost the whole scale of possible mathematic permutations. How, now, in such a Babel of conflicting opinions, are we to ascertain the true one? How can we expect to arrive at a view satisfactory even to ourselves?

It would detain us quite too long were I to attempt even the hastiest review of the arguments by which any one of these theories has been defended or assailed. The controversy, particularly between the verbalists and the non-verbalists, has been long and earnest. The arguments, pro and contra, fill volumes. Nor do I think that such a review, even were it practicable, would bring us to any satisfactory conclusion. No business is more utterly profitless than that of weighing the relative advantages or defects of theories all equally false. This I understand to be the exact difficulty with all these theories of the nature of Scripture inspiration. And I suppose the great reason why no one of them has ever been able to secure general acquiescence, is to be found precisely in their common, and perhaps equal, untruth.

I style them all false, and equally so, because they all equally proceed upon the false and Deistical dogma that Divine agency and human agency are mutually exclusive. Some things man, unaided, or left to himself, can do; those he is left to do. Only when the requirement surpasses man's ability are we to bring in the supposition of Divine efficiency. Whatever, therefore, is required in the Bible over and above what its human authors were able to furnish, that is God's; all else is theirs. This principle underlies all these theories alike. They all conceive of God's agency and man's agency as similar, in their relationship, to two antagonistic mechanical forces. Increase the one, and the effect of the other is correspondingly reduced; diminish the one, and the other proportionately preponderates. The moment God's agency in a prophet becomes extraordinarily great, his own becomes extraordinarily small. In like manner, the less the Divine influence, through withdrawal of the Spirit, the greater the human. It is a see-saw relationship, in which the higher the Divine element rises, the lower the human falls; and, *vice versa*, the higher the human rises, the lower the Divine falls.

Now a more radically anti-Christian notion never found entrance into the Christian Church. The principle is borrowed from the Deistic world-view. It is not only not true, but even the exact reverse of truth. Christianity teaches us that such is the relation of God and man, that, in all their mutual bearings over against each other, *the greater the Divine agency the greater the human, and the less the Divine the less the human.* I need not prove this by any formal argument; its mere statement carries conviction to every truly Christian mind. Christianity is radically and eternally at war with that whole conception of the world and of man, according to which each, under normal conditions, exists and acts independently of Divine agency. It tells us that all things are constantly upheld by the word of his power. Man lives and moves and has his being in God. His dower of freedom gives him, indeed, sufficient personal independence to enable him personally to antagonize or personally to choose God; but even in the exercise of this freedom he is not independent of God. Indeed, he can not become fully and truly human without that supernatural Divine light, which lighteth every man that cometh into the world. He can never become a proper moral agent without that insphering atmosphere of God's Spirit, in whose light he discerns moral distinctions, and in whose promptings and reproofs he finds impulses to action. Especially in the phenomena of specifically religious life do we note the great law I have enunciated. The greater the awakening and convicting agency of the Spirit, the intenser the contrition and agony of the sinner; the livelier the testimony of the Spirit to adoption, the keener the joy of the pardoned; the more perfect the indwelling of the Spirit, the higher-toned and more active the Christian's life. Even the heightened joys and activities of the ultimately glorified, are represented by Christianity as conditioned upon the fuller and higher Divine manifestations, which await them in the future state. I repeat it, then, that the conception of the relationship subsisting between God and man, which underlies the dictational theory, the supervisional theory, and all compromises between the two, is Deistic, anti-Christian, not merely untrue, but the exact reverse of truth. Inspiration, like every other fact, conditioned upon the co-efficiency of God and man, is a product, not of *contra*, but of *con*-spiring forces.

Such being the Christian view of the relationship between Divine agency and human agency, it necessarily follows that the most thoroughly inspired man is the most thoroughly self-active. This is as we should antecedently expect, when we remember that man was originally created in God's image, and was designed to share in his life. It corresponds, too, with the uniform Scripture representation of the natural man as dead, and of the Spirit as life-giving. If God is the fountain of our life and archetype of our nature, how can we expect to acquire more and more of self-life, except by appropriating more and more of his vivific inflowings? Apart from God's power, we could not exist at all; apart from his Spirit, our life can only be earthy, psychic, animal. True normal activities of spirit can wake to life only when we become partakers of the Divine nature.

You see at a glance how instantaneously and completely this thought revolutionizes the traditional conceptions of Bible inspiration. According to all those theories, from highest verbalistic to lowest supervisional, the trance-mediumship of the prophet was regarded as the highest form of inspiration. Here the human activity was least; *ergo*, so it was assumed, the Divine must be at its highest pitch. Instead of being the highest form of inspiration, it is in reality the lowest. Only distinguish correctly between *inspiration*, as that Divine operation upon the soul by which it is prepared to apprehend a Divine communication, and *revelation*, which is the Divine act of presenting such communication to a soul so prepared, and you see at once that the mere production of a prophetic trance or ecstasy is the lowest operation of the Holy Spirit, to which we should in any wise feel authorized to apply the word *inspiration*. Indeed, it can not be proved that it *necessarily* involves any thing more than an influence upon the nervous organism. We see essentially the same thing in the phenomena of animal magnetism. The hypnotized subject is in the same relation to the operator, as the entranced seer to God. The magnetizer can even make revelations to him; can cause him to see, hear, taste, think, desire what he will. He can cause him to relate, under this influence, what he sees, hears, tastes, thinks, desires. It is mysterious, indeed; but it shows us that the mere entrancing of a man is the lowest, most natural, most mechanical of all forms of theopneustic inspiration. It was for this very reason, doubtless, that it was the first employed by God, after visible theophanies gave place to spiritual manifestations in the history of redemption. Very analogous effects of Divine power have often been witnessed under the preaching of the Word, in the history of every living branch of the Church.

But whatever may be thought of the relative rank and dignity of the trance, as distinguished from other forms of the inspired state, one thing is certain, and that is, that we have no proof whatever that one syllable of our Holy Scriptures was ever *written* in that psychical condition. However frequent an experience it may or may not have been, in connection with the reception of Divine communications, there is not a particle of evidence that ever a prophet or apostle, while yet in his trance, wrote down such Divine communications. Every natural probability lies against the supposition. All questions, therefore, with respect to the nature and rank of so-called prophetic inspiration are ruled out of this discussion; they have no connection with our question of *Scripture* inspiration, as defined at the outset.

How, then, are we to conceive of the extraordinary Divine influence under which the sacred writers wrote? In my own opinion, it was identical with that Divine influence under which the same Divine messengers orally taught and personally governed the Church. It was the distinctive charisma of their office, as authorized expounders and plenipotentiary executors of God's will. That it was one thing when they taught with the pen, and another thing when they taught by the voice, is nowhere hinted, even in the remotest manner. Peter's pentecostal sermon must have been just as theopneustic, when it fell upon the ears of the congregated multitudes, as after Luke had written it down on a piece of parchment. If Paul's discourse on Mars' Hill is to-day inspired truth, it must have been inspired truth when first it rang out above the classic landscape in which it was pronounced. The apostles every-where place their written and spoken instructions on a perfect equality, claiming for the one as truly as for the other, full Divine authority.*

The precise psychological characteristics of this inspired state, in which the "holy men" spoke and

*2 Thessalonians ii, 15; 1 Corinthians xi, 2; Galatians i, 8, 9; 2 Thessalonians ii, 2, etc.

wrote, we can never expect, in the utter absence of the like experience, to discover. It seems, however, clearly inferable, from intimations in their writings, that the apostles, in all their official teachings by tongue or pen, retained and exercised their full rational consciousness and freedom. Thus Paul declares, "In the church I had rather speak five words with my understanding, that by my voice I might teach others also, than ten thousand words in an unknown tongue."* Again, he affirms that "the spirits of the prophets are subject to the prophets."† When charged by Festus with being a crazy ranter, he replied, "I am not mad, most noble Festus, but speak forth the words of truth and soberness."‡ In the case of the prophets it might be thought that Peter's declaration, that they spake, "borne ‖ by the Holy Ghost," would exclude a normal consciousness and freedom on their part; but this evidently can not be maintained. All sons of God are said to be *led* by the Spirit; but does this exclude consciousness and freedom on the part of the led? Does it necessitate the supposition that they are led like so many somnambulators or drunken persons? This would be falling back into the wretched mechanical conception, which constitutes the substructure of the false theories already rejected. We are rather to conceive of even the prophets, when they stood before the people and delivered to them God's messages, or when in their chambers they penned them for future generations, as more truly, widely, conscious and free,

* 1 Corinthians xiv, 19.
† 1 Corinthians xiv, 32.
‡ Acts xxvi, 25.
‖ Φερόμενοι, 2 Peter i, 21.

than those to whom they spoke. They were conscious, not only of their own inner and personal experiences, but also of God's presence, and of the impending judgments just ready to fall upon their guilty countrymen. The range of their lifted powers was broader, freer, than without Divine inspiration it could have been. The necessary effect of the Divine inworking upon intellect, sensibilities, and will, was not to stupefy, but to quicken; not to repress, but to energize; not to smother, but to ignite. All theopneustic inspiration is generically one; the peculiarities of the official prophetic and apostolic inspiration grew out of their special offices, as Divinely authorized intermediaries between Jehovah and man. In its nature it was such a Divine influence, as lifted the soul to where it could work in perfect unison of power and purpose with God. It had its varying limits and conditions, both in the nature and spiritual attainments of the subject, and in the extent and character of the revelations enjoyed; but for its specific purpose—to wit, to secure authoritative forms of Divine teaching and requirement in his Church—it was, in all cases, and under all dispensations, perfect. This brings us to consider, in the last place,

III. The Effects of Scripture Inspiration.

The question is, What did this extraordinary Divine influence upon the sacred writers, while writing, secure? I reply:

1. It did not secure to the Church, so far as we know, any new truth.

The disclosure of new truths is one operation;

inspiration another. The work of revealing is usually ascribed in Scripture to the second person in the Adorable Trinity, the work of inspiring to the third. Revelations were often given without inspiration; inspiration, often, without revelations. Doubtless, every degree of inspiration was, by reason of its natural effect upon the soul, a degree of preparation for the receiving of Divine communications; but it does not appear that any great distinctive doctrine of revealed religion was first revealed to one of the sacred writers while engaged in writing. We say, therefore, that the inspiration vouchsafed to the sacred writers, while writing, did not secure to the Church, so far as we know, any new truth.

2. It did not secure to us, if I rightly apprehend the matter, an exclusively Divine expression of sacred history and revealed doctrine and duty, as claimed by the advocates of the dictational theory. It is absurd, in speaking of the language of Scripture, to speak of it as Divine, or as human. It is neither purely the one, nor purely the other. It is rather Divine and human in inseparable unity, theanthropic in the strictest sense.

Look at yonder inexperienced exhorter; last week a rude and reckless sinner, to-day pleading with mighty and effectual eloquence before the touched and awe-struck throng. How the swift periods of burning statement, and entreaty, and argument, and expostulation, roll from his lips! Do you ask me whose are those words? Foolish question. You surely can not say they are literally and strictly the words of the Holy Ghost. Neither are they strictly and properly his own. A week ago he could not have uttered them, to save his soul. Even now, lift from his heart the mighty burden of gracious prophecy which the Spirit is laying upon him, and in three sentences he will flounder to an inglorious end. Every such attempt to draw the dividing line between the Divine and the human, in religious phenomena, is as hopeless and absurd as to ask the apple-blossom whether it is a child of the soil or of the sun. Every Christian's prayers and praises and right relations of religious experience, while human, are yet, in a most real and true sense, theopneustic. They are not, on the one hand, the words of God, independent of man; nor are they, on the other, the words of a man, independent of God. They are the utterances of a soul lifted above the low level of sinful and natural experiences; enlightened, vitalized, created anew in Christ Jesus. They are not necessarily unerring utterances, since God has not constituted them prophets and apostles; but neither are they human, as excluding the Divine. The words of Holy Writ differ from such words in authority, but not in this peculiarity of authorship. They are neither Divine nor human, in the disjunctive sense; but, conjunctively, both, at one and the same time. They constitute neither a Divine expression, nor a human expression of the truth; but an expression at once perfectly Divine and perfectly human.

3. Precisely what the inspiration of the sacred writers did secure the Church was, a rule of faith and practice exactly equal in authority to the oral teachings and commands of these God-sent messengers.

This we must suppose to have been the grand leading purpose of God in causing the Holy Scriptures to be written. Nothing more than such a rule was needed; nothing less would well answer. He *could* have preserved the purity of the Church's faith by continuing the succession of individual prophets down to the end of time; he *could* have done it by constituting the Roman popes and their clergy a body of infallible Rabbins; but having chosen to pour out his Spirit upon *all flesh,* and slowly build up a kingdom of heaven under the imperfect forms and processes of historic evolution, it was needful that there should exist somewhere in the Church a standard by which all teachings and practices could be tested. So long as the apostles lived, such a standard existed in their oral instructions; since their departure, it exists in the writings in which God caused them to sum up those instructions. These are to us all that prophets or apostles could be without additional revelations. They are as authoritative for us as would be the vocal accents of Christ. They are God's word to us; and evermore throughout the Church resounds the requisition, "If any man speak, let him speak as these oracles of God."

The lapse of time forbids my taking up any of the doubter's threadbare arguments against the fact of Scripture inspiration, or anticipating, in any wise, objections which may be raised against the view above presented of its nature and effects. I think the view I have imperfectly suggested would aid in giving new and solid answers to some at least of the traditional arguments against the fact; but already I have detained you much too long. Accept, in place of further argument, one word of wisdom. An honest, truth-loving mind, willing to seek the truth on this or almost any other point, to seek it by the light of Christian experience and revelation, and especially by the aids of God's Spirit, will seldom fail of satisfaction. Even if darkness shroud here and there a point, such a mind has learned enough to know that, with increasing light, all darkness must disappear. He therefore seeks the light, the true light; walks in it; and his path grows brighter and brighter unto perfect day.

Young men, if you will take this one thought to heart, I shall feel that I have not come a thousand miles to speak to you in vain. The way to find the truth is to love the truth. The way to escape from our natural darkness is to enter into the light of God.

While we have been reasoning together here, the millions of Christian Europe have been celebrating the martyr-death of Mark. Eighteen hundred and one years ago yesterday, they tell us, on the feast-day of Serapis, tutelar deity of Alexandria, the holy evangelist, then laboring in that city, fell into the hands of the maddened heathen. They tied his feet to a chariot, and dragged him through the streets and down to the sea-shore, dragged him the livelong day over hot sands and stony banks, every-where marking their track with shreds of flesh and a lengthening trail of blood. Exhausted at last, and marveling that their victim died not, they cast him into a dungeon for the night. Eighteen hundred and one years ago this morning,* they found him where they had placed him the night preceding, but wondrously refreshed and quickened by two visions of glory, which had been vouchsafed him during the darkness. Again they bind him to the chariot, and drag his mangled form till God, in mercy, grants him in death a happy deliverance.

History tells us that, a little more than three centuries from that day, the colossal image of Serapis was dragged, mutilated and dishonored, through those same streets of Alexandria, and Mark proclaimed the patron saint of the city. The proud temple of the idol—one of the grandest in the whole world—was demolished, while fanes sacred to Mark began to rise throughout the earth. May we not discover in the fortunes of this perhaps latest of all the sacred writers save John, a significant type of the fortunes of that inspired Word on which we have been dwelling? Ofttimes has it been dragged over the sharp rocks of hostile criticism, ofttimes across the hot sands of scorching sarcasm, ofttimes through the mire of filthy jesting: but God has been with it. It refuses to die. Even when its enemies have fancied it finally and forever dispatched, it has erelong reasserted its indestructible vitality, overtoppling earth-born fanes of superstition, and replacing them with temples not made with hands. Even the works of nature are frail, caducous, and transitory, when compared with this inspired Book. The grass withereth, the flower fadeth, but the Word of our God abideth forever.

* April 25, 1869: Feast of St. Mark.

Lecture VIII.

THE ALLEGED

DISCREPANCIES OF SCRIPTURE.

BY THE

REV. FALES H. NEWHALL, D. D.,

Professor in Wesleyan University,

Middletown, Conn.

LECTURE VIII.

THE ALLEGED DISCREPANCIES OF SCRIPTURE.

Δεῖ πᾶν τὸ ἀληθὲς αὐτὸ ἑαυτῷ ὁμολογούμενον εἶναι πάντῃ. Τῷ μὲν γὰρ ἀληθεῖ πάντα συνᾴδει.

ARISTOTLE.

IT is very obvious that the question of the essential truthfulness of Scripture is not to remain open until all its manifold facts are seen to be woven into a harmonious and symmetrical whole. Every candid objector must concede that there may be evidence sufficient to produce the conviction of essential truthfulness, although many details and minutiæ may appear exceptional. Not until we know all things, can we see all truth to be perfectly harmonious with itself. In our study of nature and of history, after being perfectly convinced of certain truths, we always find ourselves carrying along packages of exceptional facts, which we can not at the time adjust to others, but which we are sure that we can, as we grow wiser, drop into their proper places. "Nature," says Tyndall, "is full of anomalies, which no foresight can predict, and which experiment alone can reveal. From the deportment of a vast number of bodies, we should be led to conclude that heat always produces expansion, and that cold always produces contraction. But water steps in, and bismuth steps in, to qualify this conclusion." Yet the anomalies of which Tyndall speaks, when followed out, lead to the discovery of higher harmonies in nature. By a bold sweep of inductive reasoning, Newton grasped the truth of universal gravitation. He came into that close sympathy with nature that led him to judge, by unmistakable intuition, that he felt the throb of her heart. There were certain facts that could not then be reconciled with this induction ; yet so overwhelming was the evidence in its favor, that he felt sure that deeper study and broader observation would bring them into harmony. The history of physical science has justified this faith.

Apparent irregularities in celestial phenomena have led to some of the grandest discoveries of astronomy. Mysterious variations in the position of certain fixed stars, carefully observed and studied for more than twenty years, led Bradley to the discovery of the great and fruitful facts of aberration and nutation ; the first furnishing final proof of the progressive motion of light, and the second showing that the pole of the earth, instead of describing a smooth and uniform circle in its revolution, traces a wave-like curve among the stars. These two facts have given to modern astronomy its precision and accuracy. Planetary perturbations have been the harvest-field of recent astronomical discoverers. Certain irregularities in the path of Uranus led some who feebly held the clew of nature, to speculate whether the law of gravity at that immense distance operated in all its rigor; but the true astronomer saw mirrored in these perturbations another world, pacing its solitary round as the outmost sentinel of the solar system. Nature's laws are thus often found by the philosopher to be knotted in discrepancies, which, when patiently disentangled, have furnished him threads to guide him through new labyrinths of fact and law. Scripture discrepancies are thus the clews to higher harmonies. The true philosopher does not demand a demonstrated theory of these irregularities in nature. The logical understanding is not troubled by them, if a plausible hypothesis of reconciliation can be invented. A reasonable mind, which has satisfied itself on independent evidence, as to the essential truth, is content if imagination can suggest any adjustment of exceptional facts. In this respect we should go to Scripture, as the true philosopher goes to nature.

It may be, in the first place, remarked, that modern criticism, with all its acuteness, has not discovered new discrepancies of any importance. Colenso and Strauss repeat objections that were urged against the first Christian apologists. The "Wolfenbüttel Fragments" urge the same difficulties in the Gospel genealogies, and the same differences between the Jesus of John and the Jesus of the synoptics, that were fully discussed by the early Christian fathers. Mr. Parker thus stated the discrepancy between the law and the Gospel: "Here are two forms of religion, which differ widely, set forth and enforced by miracles; the one ritual and formal, the other actual and spiritual; the one the religion of fear, the other of love; one finite, and resting entirely on the special revelation made to Moses, the other absolute, and based on the universal revelation of God, who enlightens all that come into the world; one offers only earthly recompense, the other makes immortality a motive to Divine life; one compels men, the other invites them. One-half the Bible repeals the other half; the Gospel annihilates the law."*

But we find the apostles themselves profoundly pondering this problem of the antithesis between the law and the Gospel, and the first generation of Christians bewildered and confused about its solution. Paul's acutest logic and profoundest spiritual apprehension were taxed, to state clearly and fairly solve this problem. It rent the first Church at Jerusalem; it brought upon Paul his heaviest labors and fiercest persecutions; it gave rise to the Epistles to the Romans, the Galatians, and the Hebrews; the echoes of this controversy ring through every Pauline speech and letter; it was one of the causes, or occasions, of the formidable and wide-consuming heresy of Gnosticism. Mr. Parker declared this discrepancy irreconcilable and fatal. So did the heretics and persecutors of the first two centuries; and they stated the discrepancy as sharply and urged it more vehemently than Mr. Parker. Yet, in spite of it, Christianity has become what she is. In her very cradle she throttled this dragon; and will she tremble before the dragon's seed to-day? If she proved the old and the new covenants to be identical in essence, when it was only by faith that she saw the Christian

* "Discourses," page 324.

flower and fruit in the Judaic husk, much more will she triumph, when the fragrance of those flowers comes wafted to us through historic centuries, when those ripened fruits are dropping on all lands.

Another preliminary thought of special importance is this: the perfect simplicity, the guileless confidence, with which the Scripture writers spread apparently conflicting statements before us, is most suggestive and instructive. While the earliest commentators, Jewish and Christian, often manifest the greatest anxiety to reconcile and harmonize these discrepancies, the Scripture writers calmly go on their way without giving them the least attention. No editorial explanation is offered to adjust the two narratives of creation; they are simply set side by side, with all their divergencies and contrasts. There is no editorial weighing of conflicting statements in the Gospels, no word of comment to harmonize the different accounts of Christ's birth and resurrection. Thus is spread over all the Scripture the artlessness of conscious truth. To the candid mind this impression is irresistible. Every-where assuming in the most solemn manner its own Divine truthfulness, yet nowhere anxious to vindicate its consistency with itself, it reveals a sublime consciousness of integrity, most impressive and convincing to a healthy soul. So, when Moses wove into his history the patriarchal narratives of creation, he left each to tell its own story. So he wrote down the Decalogue of Exodus and the Decalogue of Deuteronomy, without minute reference to the stony tablets; not careful to use the identical words in both, as a forger would be sure to do where a copy is professedly given. So Ezra gives us the first and second records of the kings of Judah and of Israel, without editorial alterations and corrections to bring them into harmony.

The value of these discrepancies is thus very high in enabling us to understand the real nature of the documents in which they occur. They show that we have in the Scripture narratives the original documents, the genealogical records, statutes, speeches, songs, having all the flavor of contemporary authorship, such as would be called, in our day, the raw material for history, rather than history itself. These materials have never been digested and assimilated into a uniform whole, in the mind of any philosphical historian: no Thucydides has woven them into an artistic treatise. So the Gospels are memoirs, memorabilia of Christ's life, sayings, and doings; set down by different authors, at different times and places. The original facts have not been filtered through the imaginations or judgments of professional authors, but are spread before us in what criticism calls rawness, incompleteness, and redundancy; not fitted to each other, or adjusted to any system or theory whatever. Thus the narratives are often abrupt, fragmentary, assuming and suggesting much that is not said; or disappointing, by leaving much unsaid. Thus Mark assumes that the reader is already well acquainted with Jesus and with John the Baptist. John adds a supplement to his Gospel, giving an account of Christ's appearance at the Lake of Tiberias. The history of the Acts breaks off abruptly in the midst of Paul's imprisonment, without hinting any thing about the result of his appeal to Cæsar. Discrepancies are inevitable in such a mass of materials; but how valuable are they, as showing the real character of the materials, proving them to be the original data on which all systematic history must be founded! We have here no secondary formations of critical conclusions or mythic imaginings to dig through, in order to reach the primitive facts. The discrepancies of the Gospels thus furnish weapons with which Strauss's whole theory may be overturned. This must be admitted by any candid mind that does not start with the dogmatic assumption that the supernatural, being unnatural, is never to be believed on any evidence whatever.

I. The first class of discrepancies that we note are those which present us with diversities in form, while yet there is identity in matter. Truth is presented us here in manifold draperies; in phenomena terrestrial and celestial; in shadows and symbols; in actions and language; in history, biography, argument, speech, and song; in exhortation, parable, and proverb. It is declared, inferred, intimated, presupposed; yet it is ever one and the same truth, speaking with all these various voices to the various moods and conditions of humanity. Historic statement may be essential to reach one phase of mind, and parable or allegory to reach another; and this drapery of truth may, by its wonderful variety, display the highest wisdom. As matter is obviously more essential than form, if there be essential identity in matter, diversity in manner and form is not only not to be deprecated, but is to be desired.

For example: In the evangelical narratives, Matthew says that at Jesus' baptism a voice from heaven was heard, which said, "This is my beloved Son, in whom I am well pleased;"* while Luke† tells us that the words were, "*Thou art* my beloved Son; in *thee* I am well pleased." Now, it is perfectly clear that *both* Matthew and Luke can not have given us the precise form of words. One uses the second person, and the other the third; in the one the voice addresses the Savior, in the other John, or the multitude; yet the matter is identical. The truth is the same, whether spoken in the second person or the third. Such discrepancies as this may make insuperable difficulties for an interpreter who regards the Scripture writers as the mere amanuenses of the revealing Spirit; but can not perplex him who intelligently distinguishes between matter and form. That the inspired writers themselves made this distinction is obvious, both from the freedom that they exercise in quoting each other, and from the varied phraseology in which the same writer describes the same events, and reports the same spoken words. For example, in Luke's narrative of Saul's conversion,‡ we read, "And he trembling and astonished said, Lord, what wilt thou have me to do? And the Lord said unto him, Arise, and go into the city, and it shall be told thee what thou must do." Paul himself relates this conversation, in his speech on the stairs of the tower of Antonia,§ in this language: "And I said,

* Matt. iii, 17. † Luke iii, 22. ‡ Acts ix, 6. § Acts xxii, 10.

What shall I do, Lord? [instead of '*What wilt thou have me to do?*']* And the Lord said unto me, Arise, and go into *Damascus* [instead of '*the city*']; and there it shall be told thee *of all things which are appointed for thee to do* [instead of '*what thou must do*']."† Again, in Paul's speech before Agrippa,‡ we have the revelation made to him after his visit to Ananias, blended with that made on the road to Damascus; for there we read that Christ says, "But rise, and stand upon thy feet: for I have appeared unto thee for this purpose, to make thee a minister and a witness both of these things which thou hast seen, and of those things in the which I shall appear unto thee." In his defense before Agrippa, the time and place of this revelation were not essential; it was the fact that he preached to the Gentiles in obedience to a heavenly vision that he would emphasize.

If there were any place where literal exactness might have been expected, it would certainly be in the copying of the Decalogue, the commands written in tables of stone; where the *verba ipsissima* would not only seem to be of the highest importance, but where they must also have been familiar. Yet, in comparing the two records of the Decalogue given in the Pentateuch,§ it is perfectly clear that both can not be literal copies from the tables. Thus, in the opening of the Fourth Commandment, "Remember the Sabbath-day," Exodus‖ gives us the verb זָכוֹר, *zachor*, and Deuteronomy¶ the verb שָׁמוֹר, *shamor*,

* Τί ποιήσω, instead of Τί με θέλεις ποιῆσαι.

† Περὶ πάντων ὧν, instead of ὅ τι; and τέτακταί σοι ποιῆσαι, instead of σε δεῖ ποιεῖν.

‡ Acts xxvi, 16.

§ Ex. xx, and Deut. v.

‖ Ex. xx, 8.

¶ Deut. v, 12.

while the Deuteronomy copy inserts the connective particle ו, *ve,* before all the Commandments, from the Sixth to the Tenth, inclusive. In fact, the reason for the observance of the Fourth Commandment, as given in the Exodus copy, "For in six days the Lord made the heaven and the earth," etc., is wholly omitted in Deuteronomy; and in its stead we find an exhortation parenthetically interjected: "And remember that thou wast a servant in the land of Egypt," etc. Colenso presses these discrepancies as demonstrating that the Pentateuch is not historically reliable; but the objection can have no weight, except with one who confounds matter and form. The Scripture writers are all too much busied with the essentials of truth to be critically punctilious about its drapery. They produce broad impressions, aiming at the average heart and conscience, instead of choosing phrases for critical ears. Spiritual freedom emancipated them from the restraints that cramped and fettered Rabbis and Fathers, as with fetters of iron. The early Christian Fathers, as Clement, Polycarp, and Justin, show much of the same freedom in quoting Scripture phraseology; but, as we approach the mediæval era, the letter stiffens into a stony hardness and coldness, that chills and crushes out the spirit.

If, then, the objector press the question, "Was the word spoken on Sinai זָכוֹר, or שָׁמוֹר? was the declaration at the baptism σὺ εἶ, or οὗτος ἐστιν?" we reply that we do not know; and it is not essential that we should know, for literal exactness is not essential to the real purpose of revelation. Had it been so, faithful phonographers could have given us better Gospels than the inspired evangelists; a Galilean Boswell would have been selected, rather than the spiritual and contemplative John. But while the Divine Spirit, bringing all things to the remembrance of the disciple, does not call up in his memory the precise language of the heavenly message, he does suggest its precise import,—in Luke, as related to the world without; in John, as related to the world within. Not to the weakness or ignorance of the human co-worker in revelation, not to caprice or accident, are we to charge these irregularities, or variations from literal exactness in the records. Not because the substance is from the Spirit, and the form from the man, do we find these diversities; for both form and substance are from the Spirit and from the man. The Word is Divine *and* human; the Divine coming through the human. By this variety in form, the Divine Spirit would teach us that truth, while ever the same, is yet ever manifold. The stiff, precise formula can set forth only one of its aspects; its whole meaning can not be cramped into an inflexible sentence. The Scripture is not addressed to the logical understanding, but to the man. It is not a collection of dry and bristling formulas, but of living truths; which, like the cherubim of the apocalyptic vision, look before and after, above and beneath, without and within. Science may gather up these truths as well as she can, and arrange them in her cabinets of philosophical theology; but she has no right to demand that the winds of the Spirit should blow, and the

Sun of Righteousness shine, by her tables and formulas.

II. In the second place, there are apparent discrepancies, not only between different Scripture authors, but between different works of the same author, arising from differences in the point of view. The same truth is viewed on different sides, or in different connections, or is differently applied, for the enlightenment and instruction of the reader. Under this head comes the subjective condition of Scripture authors. They are greatly diverse in mental character, education, and circumstances. They are scattered through a series of ages, in different lands, in different civilizations and barbarisms. This it is that gives the Scripture its infinite variety; its wonderful manifoldness in thought and expression; its inexhaustible adaptability to man, at all periods of life, and in all the varied phases of thought and feeling, and even to the whims and caprices of this manifold human nature. God speaks through kings and through herdsmen; through lawgiver and statesman, philosopher and poet; through shepherd, fisherman, and tent-maker. He calls a lonely nomad from far-off Ur of the Chaldees, who wanders all his life, pitching his tent among his flocks and herds. He talks with the lawgiver among the grandeurs of Egyptian civilization. He speaks to the prophet-orator, who pours forth warning and invective and consolation, in the gate-ways of Jerusalem. He touches the harp-string of the shepherd-poet, so that it thrills through all time. He speaks from the miry prison of Jeremiah; and from the banks of the Chebar, where Ezekiel sits amid the solemn and sublime monuments of Assyria. He speaks through Solomon, the royal sage, as on his ivory throne he receives embassadors from the ends of the earth; through Daniel, the captive; and Nehemiah, the cup-bearer, mourning the desolations of Zion. The dry Matthew, the graphic Mark, the circumstantial Luke, the mystic John, the stern James, the fiery Peter, and the logical Paul, are various channels through which one and the same spirit pours the water of life upon a thirsty world. This wonderful variety can not exist without wonderful diversities. Seer and sage, poet and logician, king and peasant, each sees his own vision of the same truth, and tells us what he sees. He who hath ears to hear can feel that the Epistle to the Romans chords with the Psalms of David, and the Lamentations of Jeremiah with the great shout of the triumphant Church in the Apocalypse. Many-sided humanity could be reached only by this many-voiced revelation. Man must be addressed by man, else he could not understand; but manifold men are requisite to touch all the sides of man. The Infinite Spirit must use a vast number and variety of finite channels, to pour itself upon the world.

Take, as a first illustration of this species of discrepancy, the two distinct narratives of the creation, as given in the first two chapters of Genesis. The second narrative is evidently distinct and independent, going back to the very beginning, and bearing a regular title: "These are the generations of the heavens and the earth"—as we afterward read as titles before the histories of the successive patriarchs—"These are the generations of Adam, Seth, Noah," etc. Whether the two narratives originally proceeded from one author or from two different authors, we do not now consider; for, whether they were originally composed, or only finally revised, by the inspired author of the Pentateuch, is comparatively unimportant. The contrast between the two records is striking, and objectors have declared the discrepancies to be inexplicable. If the book of Genesis commenced with the fourth verse of the second chapter, although we should have no distinct account of the creation of the heavenly bodies, we should still have a full narrative of the formation of the earth and all its inhabitants, and especially a full detail of the primeval history of man. The first narrative gives a record of six creative days; the second speaks of *the day* when God created the heavens and the earth. If the second narrative stood alone, we should certainly speak of the creative *day*, instead of the creative *week*. The first narrative brings man upon the scene at its close; the second at its opening. The first narrative speaks of man as created in God's image, male and female; while the second speaks of a single man formed from the dust of the earth, and of the woman formed from the man. Thus, if we had the first narrative without the second, we should think of the human race as brought into being in numbers, like the lower animals, at the close of the sixth creative day. Of the individuals Adam and Eve, we should know nothing. Had we the second narrative without the first, we should certainly think that a single man was created as the first solitary inhabitant of the earth; that after he had begun to feel his solitude, the lower orders of animals were brought into being; and that the woman was created last of all. But all these diversities vanish when we consider that we have here the same events described from two different points of view. The first gives us creation as viewed from without, as it might be described by a spectator from another planet, taking his stand upon the earth, and from thence beholding the grand panorama move for the six successive days; the second, as viewed from within, as described by the being for whom earth with its furniture and all its lower inhabitants were made. It is earth as seen by man, and as related to man. In the first narrative the successive creative steps are followed and described with serene, impassive grandeur, and man is beheld taking his throne of dominion at the close of the scene; it is creation as it might have been outlined by a seraph, adoring the creative Majesty, but having no throb of interest in us. But man is the center of the second narrative. All nature is focalized in him. As it is interesting only from its relations to him, it is described not as it was made, feature after feature, in historical succession, but simply as related to him. The first is the world as it is in itself, the second is the world as related to man. Thus are the two narratives not contradictory, but supplementary to each other; the first furnishing a broad and grand background for the fuller and warmer detail of the second. They are related to each other as a landscape sketch to the picture of a single inhabited spot, which may be but a speck or a line on the sketch, but which so enlarges in the picture as to dwarf or hide whole landscapes of background. The man of the first narrative is a far-off, solitary king, with earth as his palace, the animate creation at his feet, the sun and stars burning as his lamps in the firmamental ceiling above. We can not clearly see his face nor hear his voice. The man of the second narrative stands so near us as to hide the mountains, sun, and stars; but we can hear him talk with God and with his own heart, as it first throbs toward the being who was made bone of his bones and flesh of his flesh.

The greater part of the supposed discrepancies between the different Gospels disappear when we consider that the same facts are seen from four different points of view. Many, most, indeed, of these difficulties have been created by the presupposition that either one of the evangelists composed a strictly consecutive chronological history. Rules of composition deduced from the classic models have been vainly appealed to and applied in the interpretation of the Gospel narratives. Neither one of these writers aimed to produce a history after the model of Tacitus or of Thucydides. There is no attempt at a philosophical history of the origin of Christianity, no analysis of the character of the Savior, no skillful historic perspective, no artistic grouping of events, no chronological unfolding of the mustard-seed truth, which is destined to root itself through the entire earth and lift its head to heaven. While men who insist on judging solely by the rules of classic rhetoric, may regret that the Divine Spirit chose such forms in which to drape these momentous truths, they can not fairly criticise the work, unless they candidly compare it with what it professes to be. It is not to be judged by the standard which our science decides it ought to have reached, but simply by the standard it claims to reach. These histories are trustworthy if they really are what they profess to be. That this is what they really are, is the Christian apologist's only claim. It would seem to be a very obvious principle, too trite to need to be stated, that an author's point of sight is not to be learned from *a priori* assumptions of what it ought to have been, but from the author himself.

The discrepancies which have been most insisted on as real, and not apparent, are chronological diversities, the order of a few minute events in time, events which all describe as transpiring within the limit of three brief years. Now, while all these historians paint the same general series of great events, from our Lord's birth to his resurrection, yet none of them profess to give such minute chronological data of his public ministry, as would be necessary to cast the events of those last three years into the form of a diary. Although many eminent authors have written as if this were possible, and many critics seem to regard it as a great *desideratum*, we neither expect that it will ever be attained, nor do we think that it was ever designed by the Spirit, who is the real author of the Gospel. But while neither evangelist professes to write a journal, each not only has his own object, but makes it sufficiently plain. Matthew, who wrote in Hebrew, or rather Aramaic, for the Christian Jews of Palestine, tells us, at the opening of his work, that he is to set forth Christ as the *son of David, the son of Abraham.* Mark, the preacher to the Gentiles, calls his work the Gospel of Jesus Christ, *the Son of God.* Luke, the companion of Paul, who had stood by that mighty apostle, as, amidst the stormiest persecution, he aimed his heaven-directed blows at the partition-wall which separated Jew and Gentile, writes for the instruction and edification of those Gentile Churches which he had helped to plant in the soil prepared by the Jewish synagogues scattered through all the Mediterranean islands and peninsulas. Matthew looks backward, as indicated by his Hebrew garb, and sees the Gospel linked to prophetic Judaism; Mark's eye and heart are filled with the present; while Luke, with something of a Pauline intuition, looks far into the future and abroad over the Gentile nations. These three writers regard the Gospel in its aggressive aspect; their eye is on its foes; they give us the words and the works of Christ as directed to those without; it is Christ as seen and heard by a world lying in wickedness. But John gives us the Gospel as seen from within, the Gospel as it was poured into his heart, while he leaned on Jesus' bosom. These are the rich, deep discourses in which, when shut in with the chosen twelve, or when gathering still closer to his heart the chosen three, Jesus removed the veil from the most awful mysteries. Rénan tells us that the Christ of John is not the Christ of the first three evangelists.

This statement is true, and yet it is false. Socrates in the cell, talking of immortality in that little circle of chosen, devoted friends, is not Socrates before the tribunal, defending himself against the charge of blasphemy. The face that was turned toward the tyrant and the sophist was not the face that was turned toward Phædo and Crito. Yet without the quiet faith and calm philosophy of the cell, we could not understand the bold plea and stern rebuke at the tribunal. So, while the other evangelists trace the streams, John leads us to the fountain; the synoptics show us the beams of light that burst from little Galilee upon a darkened world; John shows us the Sun of Righteousness.

As a single illustration of minor discrepancies arising from diverse points of view, may be mentioned the diverse accounts of the time of our Savior's passion. Mark states* that he was crucified at the third hour, and that he remained on the cross until the ninth hour; that is, from nine in the morning till three in the afternoon. Matthew and Luke do not mention the precise hour of the crucifixion, but state that he hung on the cross at noon, the sixth hour, and suffered until the ninth hour, when he cried with a loud voice and gave up the ghost.† But John states that it was about the sixth hour when Pilate sat down in his judgment-seat, on the pavement before his palace, and called Jesus before him.‡ If, now, the trial commenced at noon, it is evident that the execution could not have taken

* Chap. xv, 35.

† Matthew xxvii, 45; Luke xxiii, 44.

‡ Chap. xix, 14.

place at nine in the morning. A simple consideration, however, harmonizes these accounts at once. There were at Jerusalem two different modes of estimating time, the one used by the people and the other by the Government.* The people adopted the Hebrew mode of computation, and commenced the day with daylight; while the Government, the courts, and official persons generally, all followed the old Roman mode of computation, commencing the day with midnight. In all official transactions there must, then, have been a mingling of the two modes of computation, the one being employed by the officers and the other by the people. Jews who had received a Greek education, sometimes used one and sometimes the other.† Now, granting that it would be more natural for John to use the popular reckoning, it is not at all unlikely that, in describing the arraignment of Jesus and his trial before Pilate, John should have used the official designations of time; in other words, have spoken of the hours in the language used by Pilate and his officers, by those who tried and crucified Jesus. The sixth hour of the Roman was the first hour of the Jew, and all the circumstances of the trial, such as the cock-crowing, the morning chill, which drove Peter into the high-priest's hall to warm himself among the servants, show that Jesus was led to Caiaphas very early in the day, and the trial before Pilate followed immediately. It can not be demonstrated that this view is correct, but with so easy a solution of the difficulty

*Cf. Tholuck on John, I. 39 and 19, 14.

†Cf. Josephus de bell. Jud., Lib. VI, cap. 9, 3, and Vita, cap. 54.

at hand, it would be very rash to assume that there is a real discrepancy.

III. Not only may apparent discrepancy arise from difference in the points of sight taken by the authors, but also from the same difference in the hearers or readers of Scripture. Scripture is as diverse as man, whose infinitely diversified wants it mirrors, whose myriad-chorded nature it touches; as diverse as the nature on whose bosom man is cradled. As man is one, under all shades of color, babbling all varieties of language, dwelling in all climes, having ever the same central wants, the same sadness and gladness,—so is this book most Divinely human, in its vital unity amid infinite diversity. Now, if we take up our abode in the center of Sahara, it may be easy to quarrel with nature; so if we pitch our tent amid the rites of Leviticus, the cavils and doubts of Ecclesiastes, or the strange and startling symbols of Ezekiel, we may easily quarrel with Scripture; yet there is an Arab to whom the desert is home, and there is a tropic soul for whom the jungles of Ezekiel are none too rank and warm. He who stands on John's mount of vision, does not care to follow the steps of a Pauline demonstration; and he who ever plods along logical highways, can never swoop upon truth with apocalyptic intuition.

Scripture addresses diverse faculties, as well as diverse men. The song may perfectly harmonize with the syllogism; yet it is hard for the man who is influenced mainly by reason to agree with him who is swayed mainly by feeling, and harder to see that it is the same truth, under different aspects, that they both believe. It takes a comprehensive mind to distinguish the same voice, now speaking to reason, now to understanding, and now to imagination, as the chemist sees the same water, now exhaling in vapor, now dropping in rain, now feathering in snow, and now flashing in ice. The graceful drapery of a symbol reveals to one a truth that another refuses to see unless skeletoned in a dogma. When Socrates roused himself from his last stupor to adjure Crito not to forget to sacrifice a cock to Æsculapius, he declared his faith in immortality far more clearly and beautifully than when arguing away the doubts of Simmias. He would have his friend carry a thank-offering for him to the god of health, because that, through death, he has found life at last. Yet dull men have quoted this passage of the Phædo, to prove that Socrates died in superstitious doubt. They could understand the reasoning that plodded toward truth by short, slow steps, but could not understand the Platonic symbolism that revealed truth as by a flash of lightning.*

IV. There is also an apparent discrepancy between the whole and the part, between the concise and the detailed narratives of the same events. This is closely connected with what we have just discussed; as discrepancy arising from diverse points of view, in fact, as will appear from our illustrations, is the same, under another phase. Sometimes one writer sketches what another paints, as the second chapter of Gen-

* Phædo, Ed. Stallb., 118 A.; cf. Stallbaums' Note.

esis fills out a sketch given in two verses of the first; as Mark adds graphic touches and warm colorings to the bare outline of Matthew; as Luke, in the book of Acts, draws out into minute narrative, incidents just alluded to in the Pauline epistles. Events are grouped together, in single verses or lines of the Psalms and the prophets, which, in the Old Testament narratives, are painted in full historical perspective. Under this head are to be explained most of the diversities in the genealogical tables of Scripture. As these records of lineage furnished the framework for the most cherished hopes of the Hebrew people, they are preserved with exceeding care.* The prerogatives and privileges of the priesthood, the fulfillment of the ancient prophecies and of historic promises, and especially the splendid Messianic hopes of the nation, all were guarded and guaranteed by these genealogical catalogues. Yet, where the ancestors of the same individual are several times given, comparison shows that some links in the chain are frequently dropped; it is not necessary in the mind of the author always to unroll it at full length; it is enough to mention several selected ancestors scattered along the line, and thus a man may be styled the son of an ancestor of the third or fourth generation. Ezra, the scribe, who had complete access to all these records, gives his priestly lineage up to Aaron, the founder of the priesthood, and yet omits several generations that are given in the first book of Chronicles. So when Matthew, for mnemonic purposes, as well as to set forth the three great

*Cf. Josephus, in his first Book against Apion.

epochs of Hebrew history—its patriarchal childhood, its royal maturity, and its provincial decline—groups the ancestors of the Savior in three fourteens, or double-sevens, headed respectively by Abraham, the patriarch, by David, the royal minstrel, and Jechonias, the exiled monarch, he drops out three generations. Yet that these three omitted names were perfectly familiar to him, is evident from the fact that they were well-known historic names, the names of kings of Judah, the events of whose reigns were fully recorded in the books of Kings and Chronicles. Every Jew, with the Old Testament in his hand, knew the names of Amaziah, Joash, and Ahaziah. Had these been the names of obscure or unknown individuals, the case would have been very different. But no objector at this day doubts that Matthew had before him the Old Testament history, in Hebrew and Greek, subtantially the same as we have it today. It was not, then, through ignorance that these historic names were omitted, but by design; because their insertion would not agree with the author's plan in the presentation of his subject. Objectors may criticise this plan, that it is not according to classic models; they may object to the Hebrew conception of the object and character of history, and may complain that these records are imperfect and unsatisfactory, when judged by the rules of composition that have been drawn from heathen histories,—but all this does not prove that these authors are inconsistent with themselves or with each other, and does not in the least impeach their reliability, when their real stand-point is found.

And in this respect no more is demanded for them than for any heathen authors; for no author can be understood, and seem to be consistent with himself and with truth, until we fully understand his point of view. In this respect every author is a law unto himself; and so every school of authors, and every literature, has its own laws, which are to be candidly and thoroughly studied, as facts, before any theory of the subject can properly be constructed. A man has no right to dogmatize about the Hebrew histories who is willfully blind to the principles on which those writers looked at all historical events. Every thing is viewed by them in its relation to the Divine government and purposes. Events are selected and grouped, and set in the foreground or the background, according to this plan. Thus, in the passage before us, generations are so selected, from Abraham, the father of the Jewish nation, to Joseph, the last descendant of Judah's royal line, as to set forth, in three corresponding and symmetrical pictures, the successive phases of Hebrew history, till God's purposes concerning that wonderful people ripened into fulfillment. When the long-promised seed of Abraham, the Branch from the stem of Jesse, the King of all kings, appeared in this royal line, the nation, having fulfilled its mission, sank from human history.

The same law of Hebrew composition is also seen in the apocalyptic vision of the hundred and forty-four thousand that were sealed of the twelve tribes of Israel. Dan is omitted from the list, probably because of its idolatrous apostasy, and Joseph is inserted instead of Ephraim, his son, who is regarded as joined to his idols. No one will pretend that the author of Revelation was ignorant on so familiar a subject as the names of the tribes.

This habit of compressing a genealogical series, dropping out intermediate links, thus giving a part for the whole, when it is not the author's design to spread out the whole family history of an individual, but simply to show the relation to some remote an-ancestor; as when Ezra is shown to be the son of Aaron by the mention of several intermediate generations, and as when, in like manner, Christ is set forth as the son of David, the son of Abraham,—this habit of representation should be considered, in calculating chronology from genealogical series. Much more time may have elapsed than would be inferred from supposing the series before us to be complete.

Another peculiarity of the Hebrew narratives may here be mentioned, which, although chiefly to be assigned to the difference in the point of view, combines both sources of discrepancy already discussed. The narrative follows a logical, rather than a chronological, order, tracing an event out to its consequences, paying no attention to contemporary or immediately subsequent events at the time, but afterward returning to take them up and follow them out in like order. Thus successive portions of narrative are not chronologically successive, but lap over each other in time, like a series of parallel lines in which the beginning of the second is opposite the middle of the first, the beginning of the third opposite the middle of the second, and so on. Thus, the history of a patriarch is traced through, and then that of his son is taken up from the beginning. Sometimes the narratives resemble a series of parallels of different lengths, yet all beginning on the same perpendicular line. Thus, the first and second narratives of the creation, at the beginning of Genesis, commenced at the same point; but the second runs out into a full detail of the sixth day's work, and is followed by the history of Cain and his posterity. The fifth chapter then commences back again at the creation of man, as if it had not been mentioned before, and follows the line of Seth as far as Noah. The sixth chapter begins back again amid the corruption which ensued when men first began to multiply on the face of the earth, and comes down through the generations again to Noah, entering on his family history as if it had not been alluded to before; and then follows the detail of the flood. Thus, an event which is just sketched in one narrative, may be fully painted in the parallel narrative, and the contrast may easily be magnified into a discrepancy.

V. There are two other kinds of apparent discrepancy that we will mention, arising from the limitations of the human mind considered as the recipient of revelation. The first is the discrepancy, or rather contrast, between the subjective and the objective, between things as they are and things as they seem to man. We know things only through their attributes, and have no right to assume that all attributes come within reach of our cognitions. By what we can cognize we learn enough about different natures to answer all life's practical ends; but it would be very short-sighted to suppose that thus we can learn enough to satisfy all speculative cravings, or can thus infer how things appear to more highly endowed intelligences. Human perception is not the gauge of the universe. For aught we know, the rose may show to superior beings, or even to the insects that hover over its petals, a hundred other attributes as pleasing as color and odor, for which human language has no names. Our faculties can be relied on as far as they go, yet they go but a short distance into the infinite.

God, the Infinite, can never be fully known to any finite intelligence. Here there must ever be an antithesis between the subjective conception and the objective reality. Yet the conception may be correct as far as it goes; deficient, rather than erroneous. Our conceptions may thus be used to reveal the inconceivable, while yet we are saved from error by counter-statements addressed to the reason. "His ways are not our ways, nor his thoughts our thoughts." . . . "No man hath seen God at any time;" yet, through these very thoughts and ways of ours, he reveals himself in the written word, while the Incarnate Word makes us *see* the Invisible God. This is a paradox, but it is not the paradox of revelation only, but of all instruction. The lessons of the instructor, to be of any value whatever, must be accommodated to the capacity of the pupil. The objective must be made subjectively apprehensible. Thus must there ever be an antithesis between truth absolute and truth as conceived by a finite intelligence.

If we insist on the objective reality, and proudly scorn all subjective aids, our God becomes an inaccessible, icy Absolute, the thought of whom freezes every moral impulse into death; but if we allow ourselves to be instructed by God through the same symbolism by which we instruct each other, then can we accept the statements, "They saw the God of Israel," and "No man hath seen God at any time," and feel that there is no contradiction. In manifold modes is the truth enforced and reiterated, that God is not limited by a material form. "God is a Spirit," said Christ to the Samaritan woman at Jacob's well. "Ye saw no manner of similitude in the day that Jehovah spake unto you in Horeb out of the midst of the fire," says Moses to Israel. Yet this formless God *speaks* with Moses, and that, "face to face!" Yea, the Psalm that sets forth, in language of unparalleled grandeur, the omnipresent spirituality of Jehovah, yet assigns him human hands! "If I ascend up into heaven, thou art there: if I make my bed in hell, behold, thou art there. If I take the wings of the morning, and dwell in the uttermost parts of the sea; even there shall thy hand lead me, and thy right-hand shall hold me."* With what Divine skill is the ineffable, and wholly inconceivable, objective truth made, in this wondrous Psalm, subjectively apprehensible to the soul!

VI. The last kind of discrepancy that we shall mention, is that which necessarily arises from progress in revelation. It is the contrast between the

* Psalm cxxxix, 8–10.

sketch and the picture, between the seed and the tree, between the foundations and the temple. The egg would be called dead, most confidently, by him who had never seen the eagle that is folded in the germ; the law is dead to him who has never felt, through the embryonic envelope of precept and ceremony, the quickening of the Gospel germ that waits the age-long broodings of the Spirit to bring it into perfect life. Revelation comes in successive stages adapted to advancing man. The wisdom of the Divine Teacher commends itself to us, in that it adapts its lessons to the capacity of the pupil. The patriarchal, Mosaic, prophetic, and Christian revelations are successive stages in the same great process, each intermediate step starting from those which precede and suggesting those that follow. The lofty ethics and sublime visions of the prophets, both in form and substance, presuppose the Mosaic law and ritual. The Psalms of David could never have been sung in a nation that had not been trained for centuries in the statutes of the Pentateuch; the Epistle to the Romans requires as its preface not only the Gospel according to the evangelists, but the Gospel according to Abraham, Moses, and Isaiah. Revelation is to be judged by its own claim to be the Word of God to *man*, not scattered utterances to diverse peoples in different ages. It is spoken to the race as one, in all nations, ages, and grades of progress; and this is the claim by which it is to be judged. It is not Jewish, Greek, or Roman, but human; it is cosmic in its aims and plans. Its utterances should, therefore, have a depth and breadth and weight, such as to penetrate all lands and ages. It hastes not, and yet it rests not, until its message is complete. Abraham, the God-fearing patriarch, is called to go forth from his father's house in Chaldea, and wander in a strange land, pitching his tent in the grove, the plain, and the desert, that day by day and year by year he may be trained to become the father of a missionary nation, whose message to the world shall be faith in the one only God. This nation is then educated in the school of centuries, by the Nile and by the Jordan; in the terrible Syrian Desert, and in the delightful land where the vales ran milk and the rocks dropped honey; at the feet of the bare black peaks of Sinai, and on the slopes of Ebal and Gerizim; by centuries of royal splendor, and by generations of heart-breaking captivity; by lawgiver, warrior, orator, poet, priest, and seer; by tabernacle and temple; by statute, ceremony, and sacrifice; by the loftiest commands, most terrible threats, and most inspiring promises. In a word, by a history, national literature, faith, and character, wholly unique, was the Hebrew people trained to be God's messenger to all nations. This was the John the Baptist crying in the wilderness of heathen idolatries, to prepare the way before the Desire of all nations. When he appeared, that nation's work was done; its temple fell; and the glory which had waxed from Moses to Solomon, and waned from Solomon to Herod, went out in darkness forever. . . . The great day of revelation advanced from the gray twilight of the patriarchal era to the deeper hues of the Mosaic covenant, through the morning tints of prophecy, to the splendid Gospel noon; yet was the light ever from the Sun of Righteousness. Christianity, that mighty tree,* which is fast drawing up into its branches all the juices of the earth, was wrapped up in the mustard-seed promise given to the woman on the day of the fall. Abraham saw Christ's day, and was glad; yet he knew not what he saw. Moses never saw the rich kernel that God had hidden in the ceremonial husk. The Hebrew nation toiled for weary centuries on the Mosaic scaffolding around the Christian temple; yet most of these busy workmen saw nothing but the scaffolding, and dreamed not of the Divine beauty and harmony of pillar and architrave, frieze and cornice, within. At last the top-stone was laid, the Lord of hosts came suddenly to his temple, and lo! the scaffolding fell, and the workmen, who knew not what they builded, were scattered forever. It is easy to show that the messenger does not understand the full import of the message; that the workman, whose life is spent on a single column, has no conception of the temple; that there is a contrast between the rough scaffolding and the polished marble; but let revelation be judged by its own claims, and there is no discrepancy. Prickly rites and thorny ceremonies were absolutely necessary to guard the precious flower, whose fragrance was to fill all lands and ages. The law seemed slavish; but, as Paul said,† it was the slave whose office it was to lead humanity to the feet of the great Teacher. Christ proclaimed a contrast, not a contradiction, between

*Neander's "Church History:" Introduction. †Galatians iii, 24.

law and Gospel. He brushed away Pharisaic glosses, wiping off the mold that had gathered on the tablets of Móses; as he said, "Ye have heard that it hath been said, . . . but I say unto you." Yet he pointed to the traces of the Divine finger, as he declared, "Verily, I say unto you, till heaven and earth pass, one jot or one tittle shall in no wise pass from the law till all be fulfilled." Paul, in whom the Christian Church burst complete from the Hebrew chrysalis, asked, "Do we, then, make void the law through faith?" and replied, "Nay, we establish the law." Certainly, Paul, who presided over that revolution, amid whose earthquake-throes the Church was born, better understood the nature of the struggle than those who to-day preach Christianity without Judaism. For Christianity without Judaism is an oak without roots, a cathedral without foundations.

As the man sees truths that are hidden from the child, so great doctrines concerning the nature of God and of man, and their mutual relations, of which the race in its childhood had but a shadowy apprehension, are revealed to the mature man. Thus is it with the doctrines of the Trinity, the incarnation, immortality, and resurrection. Yet these great truths are outlined in the earliest revelations. The finished picture of the Gospel but completes the sketch of the patriarchal age. Those wandering shepherds of Syria, those Egyptian slaves of the age of the Pharaohs, who believed that their ancestor, Enoch, "walked with God, and was not, because God took him," had views of immortality far more clear to the intellect and comforting to the heart than

Plato taught, a thousand years later, in the groves of the academy. Yet the splendor that Christ has shed upon immortal life makes that patriarchal faith appear as a twilight gleam. Creation, by the Divine Word, as revealed on the first page of the Scripture, corresponds mysteriously with the profound utterances on the first page of John's Gospel—"The Word was God; all things were made by him." The Jehovah-angel who hears and answers the prayers of the patriarchs, identifying himself with the one only God in whom they so firmly believed, was the morning star before the Sun of Righteousness, or rather that Sun himself, shining through the mists of the morning. In the blood-besprinkled altars of patriarch and Levite, were given the preparatory instructions for the profoundly mysterious lesson of Calvary, which concentrates, in one dazzling focus, all the manifold rays of revelation.

There is much error in our day concerning the progress of religious ideas. The most advanced culture of our day may profitably sit at the feet of those far-off Syrian shepherds. The grand fundamental truths that lie at the foundation of all theology, the truths of the Divine unity, spirituality, and supremacy, did not come to the world from the New Testament revelation, nor from Greek or Oriental philosophy; they are as clearly written on the oldest pages of the Hebrew Bible as anywhere in literature.

When will our advancing race, in its spiritual development, outgrow the Hebrew Psalms? The most advanced Christian of to-day finds these ancient songs and prayers, which burst from the hearts of

Hebrew minstrels, prophets, priests, and kings, twenty to thirty centuries ago, voicing more perfectly than any other language his profoundest meditations, his sternest struggles, his sublimest joys and aspirations. It is not mere traditional reverence that has bound the Hebrew Psalter on the heart of the Christian Church. The eternal glow of the wondrous book draws humanity of all ages to its quenchless warmth. Some of these strains drop like angels to the darkest depths of human agony; and there are others that blow the hurricanes from their trumpets, and clash the thunders from their cymbals, to pour forth the grandest joys a mortal heart can know. It is significant and instructive, that the fierce conflicts and triumphant victories of New Testament saints, find adequate utterance only in Old Testament songs. Even the Savior, at the midnight moment of his mysterious agony, gave vent to his soul in a line of an ancient Psalm. Paul, as he finishes his survey of the resurrection, the distinctive doctrine of the New Testament, which lay at the core of every apostolic sermon, could close only in the triumphant strain of Isaiah, "Death shall be swallowed up in victory." John, who had leaned on Jesus' breast, and whose very soul was steeped in the essence of the New Testament revelations; this John of Tabor, and Gethsemane, and Calvary, when he would paint the final visions of the prophetic Gospel, uses the brush and canvas and colors of Daniel and Ezekiel; nay, he leads us back to the very spot whence we started with Moses on this wondrous circuit of revelation, and leaves us at last under the branches of that same tree of life where stood Adam and Eve, to hear the first whispers of revelation. Is this a discrepancy between the New Testament and the Old? Is it not rather a profound, world-wide, and age-long harmony?

We have thus looked at the apparent discrepancies of Scripture under six different heads, as resulting, (I) from the difference in form; (II) from the difference in the author's points of view; (III) from the difference in readers or hearers; (IV) from the difference between the whole and the part; (V) from the difference between the subjective and objective; and (VI) from the difference between the seed and the tree. We are confident that, by some one or more of these formulas, all the problems of discrepancy can be solved. The more deeply we study Scripture, the more deeply do we feel its profound analogy with nature. Nature does not arrange her flowers in herbariums; her animals and minerals, and elements, in museums, cabinets, and laboratory phials. She intermingles all together in that beautiful and sublime confusion that clothes the world with an infinite charm and makes it a gymnasium for all the faculties of the soul. The chemist may dwell among his powders and gases; the botanist may love his dried leaves and seeds; but the *man* loves the multitudinous forest, the myriad-mooded sea. An uninspired theologian would have cast the Epistle to the Romans in a series of metallic syllogisms, and nailed down its theses in a sort of Nicene creed; and it would have been read by men who love logic and system, and by no others; a

Strauss, who had seen the truths that John saw, would have arranged them like shelves of fossils; a Niebuhr or a Hallam, among the disciples, would have written gospels which would have met the wants of the world as the histories of Niebuhr and Hallam do to-day; but the Scriptures are written, not for scholars or philosophers, but for men. Our scientific technicalities and classifications of natural facts satisfy for a year or a generation, and then vanish, after giving birth to new classifications and technicalities; but the facts themselves abide forever. Pythagoras vanishes before Copernicus, and Copernicus before Newton; but the stars shine on the same. So the facts of revelation, with all their startling irregularities, their abruptness, their soul-quickening contrasts, give rise to systems which oppose, supplement, and succeed each other, age after age, while the facts themselves abide forever. Athanasius, Augustine, Anselm, vanish; but the great Gospel facts are constellated in eternal beauty.

Again, the Bible is like nature, omnivorous, yet healthful. It has a Divine vitality, which enables it to absorb and assimilate elements most diverse and contradictory. Nature is ever clean, healthful, and serene. Though teeming cities may shed their filth upon her bosom, though the malaria may reek, and the earthquake throb here and there, yet she has an exhaustless, recuperative, and assimilative energy, which distills perfume from carrion, sweetness from rottenness, exudes and absorbs volcanoes like pimples upon the cuticle. So the Bible, with all its contradictory moods, and conflicting statements, is ever infinitely calm and healthful, because infinitely vital. Nature, man, and Scripture, when read with an open eye, prove themselves to be successive volumes on the same theme, and from the same Hand.

LECTURE IX.

ADAPTATION OF THE SCRIPTURES

TO

Man's Moral and Spiritual Nature.

BY THE

REV. DANIEL CURRY, D. D.,

Editor of the Christian Advocate,

NEW YORK CITY.

LECTURE IX.

ADAPTATION OF THE SCRIPTURES TO MAN'S MORAL AND SPIRITUAL NATURE.

THAT the universe of beings is not a mass of dissociated individualities, but a system of closely related parts, is an almost universally prevalent notion. The savage or rustic that might for the first time examine the half-shell of a bivalve, would see that it lacked completeness, and would be led to suspect that there must be another, corresponding to, yet unlike, the one found. Thoughtful minds, from such suggestions, verified in nature, deduce the laws of philosophical relations found pervading all things. Poetical minds contemplate it as a kind of soul of the universe, that

> "Lives through all life, extends through all extent;
> Spreads undivided, operates unspent."

Philosophers call it "the reign of law," and the superstitious speak of it as destiny—

> "A divinity that shapes our ends,
> Rough-hew them how we will."

By virtue of this universal prevalence of law—itself the outflow of the power and authority of the one great *Lawgiver*—there is unity over all the diversities of creation; there is harmony of purpose in the apparently discordant actions of individuals; and consolidation, without the confusion of the parts, of the one great whole. Nothing is independent or segregated; and the harmony of the universe is secured by the adaptation of each to all other mutually related individualities. And, as the comparative anatomist constructs a complete skeleton from a single part, by producing, in material forms, the ideals suggested by the requirements of that one member, so, by following up the all-pervading order of adaptations, the philosophical mind is brought to the truth, whether proceeding upwards or downwards in the scale of being.

Beyond all others of the denizens of our world, man's relations are multiform, and his susceptibilities delicate. He is therefore, above all others, remarkable for the multitude and the greatness of his wants. He sympathizes with all about him, because of his relations to them; and these, in turn, exercise effective influences over him. And, further, these relations, and the influences that grow out of them, determine his character, both as to its original capabilities and its ultimate attainments. The eye that could trace out all these varying relations and their intertwining influences, might also foresee all the various stages of growth and development, up to the highest completeness.

Physical natures require an order of things in their surroundings adapted to their sustentation and growth. There must be an atmosphere for the lungs, and food for the stomach, and often a covering for the body as a protection against atmospherical changes. There must be light for the eyes, and for the ears the sonorousness of bodies and the conducting power of the atmosphere; and, answering to the universal sense of touch, is provided the resistance of matter, which returns touch for touch, and thus suggests, to the reflective reason, the idea of externality and individuality, and distinguishes the *objective* and the *subjective.* There are also certain social wants of man's nature, which look beyond the individual for their supplies. Not only is it not good for a man that he should be alone, but solitude is wholly incompatible with the elevation, or even the continuance, of either the race or the individual. Accordingly, he is endowed with certain controlling social appetences, fellow-feelings, paternal tenderness, and the loves that draw together and hold individuals in the closest and most sacred relations of life. In all these things, *wants* and their required *provisions* lie over against each other, as foins and foils, answering to each other, and each implying its opposite. Every-where in nature may we detect an ever-recurring adaptation of related objects. Each is the answer to the other's necessities; so that adaptation has come to be accepted as evidence of purposed co-existence, or of the original provisions of certain things to meet the requirements of others.

It must also be observed that men's wants are not the creatures of their own purposes and voluntary fancyings. Rather, they are instinctive and spontaneous. Having their germs in the elements of our being, they are developed with our normal growth, and force themselves upon the consciousness unasked and undesired. They may, indeed, in some cases, be repressed and dwarfed in their development, but they can be extinguished only with the extinction of all that is ennobling, or productive of good in human nature; and by their proper culture and discipline the character is formed for the highest excellence.

Man's spiritual pre-eminence is indicated by the multitude and greatness of his *spiritual wants*. Irrational creatures have only physical desires and necessities. The strong lion reposes in his lair, if only his hunger is satisfied; and the fierce tiger desires nothing more, when gorged with the blood of the prey; and the herd complains not among the rich pastures. The ox knows his owner, and the ass his master's crib, and they are satisfied with their provisions. But human aspirations reach beyond these things. They go out after the unseen and the intangible, the things unknown to sense and but faintly apprehended by reason, because man's nature is *spiritual*, and transcends the material and the merely rational; and as our physical and social wants all find their complements in the provisions made for them and adapted to them, so it may be inferred that there are provisions made for the satisfying of our spiritual cravings and necessities; and the discovery of such adapted provisions anywhere would be accepted as sufficient evidence that the one was designed for the other. The agreement together of related things, especially if the points of adaptation are many and complicated, indicate that such things were intended for each other.

From these somewhat general and comprehensive

views, we come to consider more definitely the proposition assigned for our present discussion: "The adaptation of the Holy Scriptures to man's moral and spiritual nature." And if we succeed in showing that the instinctive appetences of the soul indicate its want of such things as the Scriptures bring to it; or if the things set forth in the Scriptures are found to answer to the felt wants of the soul,—then we shall have accomplished our purpose, and not only proved the adaptation of the Bible to human wants, but also rendered evident the truth and the Divine origin of the sacred records. Then shall we have demonstrated the oneness of the origin of the *Word* of God and of man as a spiritual being.

It is not our business at this time to present proofs of either the multitude or greatness of man's wants. If it shall be objected that many have lived and died without being aware of some of them, we may partly concede the fact, but not its force as an objection. Only sound and healthy subjects properly answer to the normal conditions of their kinds; and only a slight examination of man's spiritual condition detects indications of derangement and disorder. The instincts of the soul are in many things sadly perverted, and its healthful and life-diffusing appetences are dwarfed, or held in abeyance. But even such cases prove the reality of these wants. The soul so perverted in its spiritual instincts, and depraved in its tastes and instinctive desires, is itself balked in its growth and deformed in its development. Growth is an essential condition of life, in all immature natures; and if, in man, the higher and more spiritual elements of his nature remain inactive and undeveloped, the lower and more brutish will be relatively enlarged, and made predominant in his life. In such cases the reality of the wants is evinced, not indeed by the conscious longings of the soul for spiritual good, but clearly and very painfully by the ruin induced through the absence of the things requisite for the soul's well-being. We legitimately argue the requirements of any given case, not only by the good that results from the possession of the things presumed to be needful, but equally certainly by the evil results of the lack of such things; and no class of men more forcibly, though sadly, demonstrate the reality and the greatness of their spiritual wants, than those who are the least spiritually minded. The sensualist and the worldling, the man of pleasure and the devotee of wealth or of the honors that come from men,—these of all men manifest continually the restlessness caused by the unappeased hungerings and thirstings of the soul.

Nor is it true that such persons have no recognized and defined spiritual cravings. The world is full of pains and travail and sorrow; and an almost universal *unrest* is characteristic of the race. The most worldly passions and impulses give intimations of others back of them, of quite another kind. The ambition that aims at only worldly greatness, is but the prostitution and misdirection of a Divine impulse designed to bring the soul to "glory and honor and immortality." The covetousness that clutches convulsively at worldly wealth, is but the unappeased thirst of the spirit for its unattained, perhaps unrecognized, spiritual sustenance. The discontents, the perpetual strivings for something better, the dissatisfaction and disgust with what is really possessed,—what are these but the expressions of the wants of the soul, which can not be satisfied with the things of time and sense? He was indeed justly styled a *fool*, who, with only material wealth, congratulated his soul on the abundance of his possessions. Infallible wisdom and truth has said, that "man shall not live by bread alone;" "that a man's life consisteth not in the abundance of the things which he possesseth;" and a groaning world utters its *Amen* to this Scripture. The reality of man's spiritual wants is matter of universal consciousness; though often both the source whence they come, and the objects for which they are calling, may be but faintly, if at all, recognized.

But no man is at all times precisely equal to his own average. To even the most sensual and worldly, there come seasons when the spiritual being will assert itself—times between the gusts of passion, or intervals in the active domination of worldly or sensual desires, when a still small voice is heard in the soul, calling to higher purposes and more spiritual occupations. And to such calls the enthralled spirit responds with the passionate, but often hopeless, earnestness of the caged bird answering to its free companions, when the voice of Spring invites to the joys of love. Deep down in the hearts of even the least spiritual of men, are yearnings and complainings and askings for something better. Because man in his essential nature is a spiritual being, with spiritual wants that can neither be crushed out nor yet satisfied with earthly goods, he longs for and requires spiritual supplies and consolations; and the adaptations of the lessons and revealings of Holy Scripture to answer to these wants, and, in doing that, to bestow the highest good, indicate an anterior design in placing the one over against the other.

Among the earliest felt requirements of the unfolding intelligence, is an appropriate object upon which to rest the vagrant thoughts that go out into the limitless ranges of existence. The problems of being force themselves upon the mind of childhood, and weigh like a nightmare upon the maturest intellect, till some suitable objective is gained, some potent and sufficient Source and Foundation of all life and being is recognized. Human intuitions spurn all limitations to the range of thought, and, while confessing its inability to measure the infinite, the mind clearly apprehends its reality as a necessary fact. But without a personal and almighty *First Cause*, such as is known only through the revelations of Scripture, Eternity and Immensity are but horrible chaotic wastes; and even the finite and conditioned then seem unreal and chimerical. For every phenomenon we intuitively require a cause, and all secondary causes imply others beyond them; and so the recognition of a *First Cause* is a philosophical necessity. And this great First Cause, in order to its purpose as the prime factor in all the problems of being, must be apprehended as infinite. In considering the ages of the past eternity, the mind rejects as absurd the idea of a time when God was not; and in contemplating the unfolding cycles of the coming eternity, it requires always the presence of the infinitely potent Original. Reason, alike in its simplest and its loftiest processes, requires an infinite original of all secondary beings, uncaused, eternal, almighty. But nature presents only the finite; all its phenomenal beings are limited and conditioned upon all sides. The postulating of a personal God, himself embodying and dwelling in the infinite, is exclusively the work of the Holy Scriptures. God, as revealed only in his works, is unreal, shadowy, and hypothetical; but when once seen and recognized in his Word, all nature becomes vocal and eloquent in confessing him; and especially does the human intellect find, in that primary truth, that wonderful revelation surpassing its clearest intuitions, an answer to its most painful and perplexing questionings. God, self-revealed, is the only sure basis of a sound philosophy.

Man's spiritual requirements are chiefly of the moral and religious kind. So largely does that kind predominate, that in that relation the epithets *moral* and *spiritual* are often used convertibly. There can be no doubt that the religious wants and capabilities preponderate, and that man's religious instincts demand their appropriate objects with a peculiar importunity. The normal development of the powers of the soul present them in controlling activity, and with proper culture they increase and expand till they come at length to characterise the whole spiritual being. In proportion as the religious elements of man's nature are developed into a full and healthy maturity, is the character ennobled, and the man becomes Godlike. But these religious aspirations especially require an object beyond the soul itself, towards which they may tend, and upon which they may rest, and which shall embody, in all fullness, those properties of character that answer to their cravings—just those, indeed, which the Holy Scriptures reveal as dwelling in infinite perfection in the God of the Bible.

A primary requirement of the soul is that the object of its religious devotion shall possess all the attributes of a perfect personality. An impersonal and intangible principle, a blind, unreasoning force, a diffused and insubstantial spirit, without will, or self-consciousness, or purposed action, can not command the worship of an intelligent soul. Love always, and necessarily, demands responsive love. Prayer itself is an unmeaning exercise, till faith confesses the object addressed as the Hearer of prayer; and penitence is perfected, only where the Divine placability is recognized. Back of the attributes which we admire, and which seem to command our worship, we intuitively postulate a personality, of whom those admired characteristics are predicates. Nature reveals to us a mighty force and an all-pervading order, and it intimates design and wisdom, but does not fully prove them. But it is the peculiar province of the Divine Word to respond with all clearness to the felt wants of humanity, by presenting the person of *Jehovah*, the infinite I AM.

Again, it is required that the object of the soul's worship shall be enthroned in the majesty of rectorial power. Love, admiration, and a qualified reverence may be given to the powerless and the unauthoritative; but worship is given only to the Almighty and the All-provident. It is eminently in the revelation of the Divine greatness, the majesty and power of the Ruler and Dispenser of man's destiny, that the Scriptures effectively command our worship to God. If apprehended as less than the Almighty, or as neither the Keeper nor the Judge of all men, God no longer commands the highest devotion of the soul.

The ethical element enters very largely into all our intuitions and conceptions of religious worship. The idea of moral rectitude—the *essential good*—is intuitive and spontaneous; and to no other susceptibility of its own nature does the spirit render such profound deference. The logical faculty may control the judgment, and the æsthetical may minister to the emotional nature; but the ethical, developed and exercised in the form of conscience, dictates the conduct, and extends its authority even to the feelings, tempers, and sentiments of the heart. And it is especially in his ethical character that the Holy Scriptures seem to delight to portray to us our God. Righteousness, justice, truth, are among his moral attributes, the perfections of his nature, in which he is perpetually presented to our adoring contemplation. We gaze upon such excellences, and are drawn to adore and worship the Being in whom they subsist, and we confess their authority over our own lives and hearts. But chiefly when we contemplate these things, not as abstract qualities, or segregated individual properties, but as concentrated into a glowing focus of intense moral worth, under the name of *holiness*, do we fully or adequately appreciate the ethical side of the Divine character, or rise to that lofty height of pure worship which is alike due to God and profitable to man. Only when we contemplate the Divine Being as a devouring fire of holy wrath towards sin, and of intensest, purest love towards all that bear the image of his holiness, do we find in Him the inspiration and the sacred joy that are, as for ourselves, the great end of worship. And need we more than intimate how fully, as well as exclusively, the Holy Scriptures teach these things, and present to us the Divine character, in the fullness of holiness, perpetually and effectively active throughout the moral world?

The æsthetical element of man's nature, though less prominently, yet in no inconsiderable degree, enters into his religious life and its exercises. Worship itself is the highest form of the æsthetical. Angelic and seraphic praises of the Most High are the devout outpourings of sacred admiration of that uncreated glory upon which they gaze, or veil their faces before its insufferable splendor. Even to human apprehension there is a "beauty of holiness," which commands the ravished hearts of all capable of its appreciation, and which, when perceived, casts a pall of dimness over all earthly glories. All kinds of earth's lesser beauties are but the forms and shadows of the heavenly, that essential beauty that dwells in absolute fullness only in the Divine holiness, whether contemplated in the effulgence of the sacred person, or viewed in finite spiritual natures, made in the image of God. The development and culture of this really spiritual element of human nature requires models of essential holiness, both absolute and proximate, such as are given in the revelations of the sacred persons of the Godhead, and illustrated in the lives and characters of holy men in the Scriptures. There, and there only, may be found the models that can both form and satisfy the highest and noblest tastes; and there, too, are given the processes for gaining and reproducing the highest forms of virtue.

The human conscience, untaught by aught besides its own deep intuitions, confesses the need of some remedial agency to deliver the soul from its thralldom. It is not for us to discuss learned questions in theology; but we may safely venture the statement that, somehow, there is found widely prevalent among the most thoughtful classes of mankind a deep interior consciousness of *sin*, with heartfelt yearnings for a *better life*. At those seasons, which come perhaps to all, when men are better than their own average, there is a painful consciousness of deep-seated moral evils in the soul. Sin is then seen in its real character; and, though perhaps but faintly resisted, it is abhorred as a loathsome evil. The lowly breathings of the soul in such an hour, impotent and perhaps purposeless, are for a better heart and a new life. But, though these aspirations may be feeble and quite insufficient to restrain the passions and control the will, they are manifestly real, and sufficiently powerful to disturb the guilty quiet of the soul, and to check, at least momentarily, the headlong currents of vicious pleasures. Learned and thoughtful heathen, especially, have confessed these whisperings of the soul, and some of them have both forcibly and feelingly declared their utterances. But to them these things were, necessarily, only as some delightsome dream, the imagination of an ideal quite too lovely to be realized, as if a light from heaven had fallen upon the camera of the soul, and formed an image of surpassing loveliness, which remained but for a moment, and then melted away into darkness.

And even among these there have been efforts towards the realization of that bright but evanescent ideal. A few of them have told us of their efforts to retain in their minds the lovely image of virtue, and to realize in their own characters and lives its sublime lessons; but in all such cases utter failure is the only result. Each, in his own manner, confesses that, while he perceives and admires and longs to pursue the good, and abhors and struggles against the evil, still the evil, and not the good, is pursued.

That phenomenon of experimental Christianity, known as *conviction of sin*, or *religious awakening*, differs in degree, rather than in kind, from these heart-yearnings of the best class of heathen minds. The more adequate teachings, enjoyed wherever Bible truth is diffused abroad, illustrating the vileness of sin and the contrasted excellence of holiness, the one devolving guilt upon its subject, and the other demanding purity of heart and earnest devotion of life, give largely increased force to these spiritual impulses. But even then the resistance against the steady undercurrent of the inbred sin of the soul is usually feeble and transient. A schism in the soul is, however, not only detected, but made active. Two antagonistic impulses now war against each other. The individual self becomes dual, and the conflict is waged within the soul itself. "That which *I* do, *I* allow not; what *I* would, *I* do not; but what *I* hate, that *I* do." But notice that, always in these conflicts, if conducted under the guidance of reason and by human agencies alone, the victory is uniformly on the side of evil. "The *good* that I would, I do not; but the *evil* that I would not, that I do." Just at this point the most earnest resistant against sin is brought to despair; and just where self-despair ensues, the hopes of the Gospel, as revealed in Holy Scripture, become both strong and very precious. By these we are taught not only the transcendent excellence of essential virtue, but also tne way to its attainment.

The sacred Volume is replete with images of transcendent goodness, not shown as merely beautiful ideals, to be gazed upon and admired, as quite unattainable, but each is presented as a spiritual study, to be considered and reproduced in the susceptible soul, and copied into active life. Over against the depressing sense of guilt stands the promise of free pardon; against the dominion of sin is the assurance of emancipation by the power of renovating grace; for its defilement a fountain is opened that cleanses from all spiritual uncleanness; and for all them that "hunger and thirst after righteousness" is the beatific assurance of eternal fullness.

But chief among man's felt wants is that of a competent protector, guide, and defense. Viewing himself among his surroundings, no thoughtful man can fail to be painfully conscious of his utter helplessness. He knows that his life was not given, nor is it sustained, by his own power. He has not ordered his own surroundings, nor appointed the time and place of his habitation. Instinctively he looks outward and recognizes a potent energy, an awful and resistless Power about him and pressing upon him, and yet utterly unknown. Men call it *destiny*, or *fate;* they make it a negation and a contradiction, under the name of *chance;* or they belittle it by calling it *luck*. It is their ruling *star*, or good *angel*, or *demon*. The recognition of such a Power, so intimately near, and ever active in our affairs, so resistless and unapproachable, can not fail to be fearfully oppressive to the spirit and dwarfing to the whole soul. Against its resistless and oppressive tyranny, reason and philosophy are powerless. The stoic sullenly confronts it, and in desperation defies it; the Epicurean, because of his conscious helplessness for both the *present* and the *future*, makes haste to "eat and drink, for to-morrow we die." The faint glimmerings of a surer faith, giving rise to a better hope, in a very few of the best minds of both Greece and Rome, were little more than fitful shadows, too faint and evanescent to deliver the soul from its painful uncertainties. There were, indeed, among them religions enough, and divinities more than enough; but the former brought no consolations, and the latter were careless of human welfare, or mpotent to help. Under this burden, and in this absence of any assured hope or rational dependence, "the whole creation travaileth and groaneth together." The religions of heathendom are every-where a horrid and hopeless slavery, in which the soul is, by turns, tortured with superstition, or blasted by an arid and desolating atheism; between which two the spirit sighs in the desolation of orphanage, or drifts helplessly and hopelessly onward to the unsearchable abyss of the future.

Nor are the lessons of simple *Theism*, however comprehensive its recognition of the Great Author of being, adequate to the requirements of the soul. God's greatness may, to the apprehension of reason, seem to place him at too great a remove from us either to take knowledge of us or to care for our affairs. The sons of our forests and prairies confessed the "Great Spirit;" and they thought they heard his voice, or felt his power, in the thunder and the tempest; but he was quite above their trivial, every-day affairs, and in the absence of *his* watch-care, their whole lives were a prey to their miserable demons. Even the inspired Psalmist seems to have fallen, for the moment, under this oppressive sense of God's stupendous greatness, removing him far above all human concerns: "When I consider the heavens, the work of thy fingers, the moon and the stars, which thou hast ordained; what is *man*, that thou art mindful of him? and the son of man, that thou visitest him?"* It were not enough, then, if reason and nature were equal to the task of revealing God; we need to be assured that God

* Psalm viii, 3, 4.

cares for us, keeps us, and will be our support and defense always.

The wonderful adaptation of the lessons of Holy Scripture to the requirements of our case, at this point, can not fail of attention. Its great Author and subject is there revealed, as not only the Almighty, the Eternal, and the All-wise God; he is more than all of these, and in them all he comes near to us and teaches us to call him *Our Father.* While upholding all worlds, and directing the course of universal nature, he is still "not far from every one of us." Though his omnipotence and ubiquity may imply that, in some sense, "in him we live and move and have our being," and though his moral perfections may indicate his regard for the *right,* and render it certain that his judgments will be in equity, we still require, as the basis of our confidence, the direct lessons of his *Word* to assure us of his peculiar nearness to us and his fatherly care for us. Nearer and and better than all that reason can teach us of the Divine character, and stronger in affections than any thing suggested by the mutual relations of creatures and Creator, is the fact that the God of the Bible, though infinite in Majesty and power, chooses to be recognized and addressed by us as "*Our Father,*" and specifically entitles us to claim from him all the benefits of that relation.

Assured of God's *fatherhood,* we cease to be dismayed by the awful powers of nature, which, indeed, under his control are changed to ministers of mercy. Our confessed helplessness is more than compensated for by the assurance that the Almighty Ruler of all things in heaven and earth is our loving *Father*. With what triumph and confidence does the Psalmist exclaim: "God is our refuge and strength, a very present help in trouble. Therefore will not we fear, though the earth be removed, and though the mountains be carried into the midst of the sea."*

Man's inmost nature asks for security, for some sure ground of confidence upon which he may rely without doubtings and misgivings. This is essential to his peace, and it is found only in an abiding conviction of the Divine providence, exercised always with fatherly kindness. All this, indeed, is compatible with a life of labors and perplexities, needful discipline in our present imperfect state; but with it life can not be sad or fearful. In this confidence, the soul is staid upon God; and from its depths it utters anew that inspired song in whose sacred exultations unnumbered multitudes have confessed the sufficiency of the Divine providence: "The Lord is my shepherd; I shall not want. He maketh me to lie down in green pastures: he leadeth me beside the still waters. He restoreth my soul: he leadeth me in the paths of righteousness for his name's sake. Yea, though I walk through the valley of the shadow of death, I will fear no evil: for thou art with me; thy rod and thy staff they comfort me. Thou preparest a table before me in the presence of mine enemies: thou anointest my head with oil; my cup runneth over. *Surely goodness and mercy shall follow me all the days of my life: and I will dwell in the house of the Lord forever.*"†

* Psalm xlvi, 1, 2. † Psalm xxiii.

The revelation of God's fatherhood, assuring us of his wonderful providence over us, thus meets our wants; and, if accepted in the spirit of faith, it is sufficient to stay the soul in devout confidence. But a still more wonderful display of his care for us is shown in the teachings and the work of Christ. Here are exhibitions of mercy yearning to save the ruined and guilty. Here is love, rising above all obstacles, stopping at no sacrifices, and hastening, through tears and blood, to redeem the fallen and to rescue the perishing. If to be loved is among the cravings of the human heart, how abundant the provisions made to answer to it in that transcendent display of tenderest, strongest affection in the Divine heart for helpless and guilty men. Here is the miracle of Divine compassion, the love that "passes all understanding," but that which only and alone reaches to the yearning necessities of the soul. Our spiritual nature demands a present Christ; the Bible is itself the revelation of the Christ to the soul.

At the risk of transcending our allotted space, we must present yet another instance of a chief want of man's spiritual nature, to which only the Word of God, the revelations of the Gospel, respond. We speak of the soul's earnest cravings for immortality and future blessedness.

Love of existence is a perpetually active sentiment of the heart. No help of reasoning is needed, either to awaken it to activity or to preserve its unflagging intensity. It grows with the growth of our years, and gathers force as the toils and pains of life multiply; and as burdened age stoops downward to the tomb, the instinctive longings of the soul call for a new life, for which there shall be neither old age nor decrepitude nor death. But over against these longings nature presents the mementos of mortality. Among the earliest learned of earth's lessons is the astounding fact that people die. Larger experience of human affairs detects the shadow of death everywhere. Thus, with perpetual and passionate longing for immortality, men pass as a vapor through time, with the dark wings of the Destroyer spread over them. In nature there is thus found the ill-assorted companionship of intense desire and despair.

The pencil of inspiration has painted most truthfully the dark background of the picture of human destiny, by simply setting forth the confessed truths of our mortality: "Man that is born of a woman is of few days, and full of trouble. He cometh forth like a flower, and is cut down: he fleeth also as a shadow, and continueth not. . . . Man dieth, and wasteth away: yea, man giveth up the ghost, and where is he? . . . So man lieth down, and riseth not: till the heavens be no more, they shall not awake, nor be raised out of their sleep."* And at the close of this sad tale, and as if to crush the feeblest strugglings of hope, comes the despair-enforcing question, "If a man die, shall he live again?" uttered with the assurance that earth's oracles could answer only with a universal negative.

The question of immortality and the future life has been an ever-present and deeply interesting one among all the races of mankind. Their religious

* Job xiv, 1, 2, 10, 12.

instincts suggest it, require it, and recognize it, as the necessary complement to our present existence; but the sense-encumbered intellect and the cold logic of merely mundane facts give the lie to all these fond suggestions. Thus, though the idea of immortality is every-where cherished, it is rather as a beautiful, but unreal, fancy than as an assurance ever to be realized. Socrates, at the approach of death, spoke with apparent confidence of his passage at once into the society of the "immortal gods," declaring his persuasion that men live after death; but every careful student of the life and teachings of the great Athenian sage knows but too well that his hopes were much more largely made up of desires than of confident assurance. Plato, too, reasoned of immortality, and seemed to show that it was *reasonably possible;* and he could do no more; and Cato, in his extremity, cast himself upon death, preferring that dim possibility to the wretchedness of his earthly being; but even the faint hope that impelled him to such rashness was the child of his despair. Men of every form of religious faith have hoped for immortality, but their hopes have been as destitute of assurance as their creeds have been deficient in rational evidence; so that in the presence of death, in nearly all cases, life and hope perish together.

This, then, is the humiliating result reached by human reason, under the guidance of nature, as announced by the greatest of merely human expositors of the heart of man:

"—— *Death is a fearful thing.*"

And, O! how true to nature is his picture of the

soul, contemplating, as near at hand, the terrible catastrophe of being!

> "Ay, but to die, and go we know not where;
> To lie in cold obstruction and to rot;
> This sensible, warm nature to become
> A kneaded clod. . . .
> . . . Or to be worse than worst
> Of those, that lawless and uncertain thoughts
> Imagine howling! 't is too horrible!
> The weariest and most loathed worldly life,
> That age, ache, penury, imprisonment,
> Can lay on nature, is a paradise
> To what we fear of death."*

And if such is nature's picture of death, to escape such terrors is man's greatest and ultimate want. But death is inevitable. On every hand is the concurrent declaration or confession, "It is appointed to men once to die." To escape death, therefore, is not an object of rational hope, but to find out some sure and sufficient way to rob death of its terrors through the hope of immortality after death. This is attempted by almost all forms of religion; and all alike of the religions of men's devising have failed in the endeavor. To every heathen mind not maddened by fanaticism, or to the mere philosopher, *Death* is truly and fearfully the *King of Terrors*. Only the faith of the Gospel has ever sufficed to overcome the fear of death.

Holy Scripture teaches the doctrine of immortality, not chiefly by positive and direct declarations, but rather by showing man's proper spirituality, by virtue of which he is incapable of dissolution. The sacred narrative of the creation tells of man as the

* "Measure for Measure," act iii, sc. 1.

one spiritual creature upon the earth, inspired with "the breath of lives," and constituted for perpetual existence. And these primary statements in man's history are steadily recognized in the after-records of the Divine Word. God's providences towards men imply their transcendent worth among the creatures of God's hand, a worth that is found chiefly in their spirituality and consequent immortality. The one crowning truth of Holy Scripture, the manifestation of the Son of God in the flesh, would appear purposeless and unwarranted, except that man's immortality justifies the Divine regard for him. Without that recognition, the wonderful history of JESUS would be something worse than an enigma, a strange misuse of the richest resources of Heaven. Granting man's immortality, that history is the grandest ever enacted. He came to bring "life and immortality to light." He reveals himself as "*the light.*" He shows that, by his personal union with our nature, humanity itself is quickened and redeemed. And to those who receive him as their life, he declares that where he is—in the glory of immortality—there shall his servants be also. Thus every assurance of the future life that the truth can declare, or love make precious, is infolded in the very substance of the Gospel. The largest desires of the aspiring spirit are fulfilled by what is there taught respecting the life after death; and the fear of death gives place to devout joy and the triumphant song of faith. Thus, through the Gospel—and by no other means—there is found out a way of escape from the dread of death. While suffering that fear, the soul is dwarfed and bowed down to the earth; but in the clear vision of that Heaven-given light, it rises into the ennobling and purifying atmosphere of revealed "life and immortality."

Here we must cease; not that we have gone over the whole field of either the evidences or the illustrations of our subject, but our utmost limits are reached. Our examinations prove to us that, if there is any harmony in the spiritual universe, if the Creator has not written contradictions in the human character, and, contrary to his economy in nature, given appetences and needs for which he has provided nothing to answer, or has set forth only mocking and delusive answers, then has he made provisions to respond to the instinctive desires and spontaneous cravings of man's spiritual nature. And since the Holy Scriptures with such wonderful adaptations answer to those wants of the spirit, the evidence seems beyond rational cavil, that the Framer of man's interior nature is the Author of the Sacred Scriptures, and that he has, of purpose, set the one over against the other, to be the life, the light, and the culturing agency for the soul.

Lecture X.

THE PERSON OF JESUS CHRIST.

BY THE

REV. WILLIAM D. GODMAN, D. D.,

President of Baldwin University,

Berea, Ohio.

Cui enim veritas comperta sine Deo? Cui Deus cognitus sine Christo? Cui Christus exploratus sine Spiritu Sancto? Cui Spiritus Sanctus accommodatus sine fidei sacramento?

TERTULLIANI DE ANIMA, I.

LECTURE X.

THE PERSON OF JESUS CHRIST.

"He saith unto them, But whom say ye that I am? And Simon Peter answered and said, Thou art the Christ, the Son of the living God. And Jesus answered and said unto him, Blessed art thou, Simon Bar-Jona; for flesh and blood hath not revealed it unto thee, but my Father which is in heaven." MATTHEW XVI, 15–17.

ABOUT eighteen hundred and thirty-seven years ago this day,* if the received chronology and calendar be correct, occurred the great event which secured the triumph of Christianity. The rolling away of the stone from the holy sepulcher, the reappearing of Jesus, was more to the new faith than the patronage of the Cæsars or the protection of a thousand legions of trained soldiers. It is a pleasing arrangement of Providence that permits us to-day to come into this learned presence, before this Christian assembly, with so Divine a theme. May He of whom we are called to speak be present, and verify in our hearts His ascended glory! We beseech the guidance of "the Spirit of Truth." May he that "searcheth the deep things of God" impart to us such of his treasures of knowledge as our exceeding weakness may be able to receive! If we

* Easter Sunday, 1870.

may, without presumption, borrow the words of a prince in the world of letters, we may pray:

> "And chiefly Thou, O Spirit, that dost prefer
> Before all temples, the upright heart and pure,
> Instruct me, for thou know'st: . . . . .
> . . . . what in me is dark
> Illumine! what is low, raise and support."

The most stirring question of the civilized world is this: "*What think ye of Christ?*" Not only the monk in the cloister meditates upon it; not only the surpliced cleric and the zealous evangelist strive to give it a fond or a professional answer; but grave philosophers, who make least account of popular enthusiasm, leave their speculations about development and spontaneous generation to utter their thoughts about Jesus. The jurist, forgetting the eminent claims of legal antiquities and the current exigencies of the administration of justice, lays aside the ermine and takes the pen to record an opinion concerning that Nazarene of whom the least that can be said is, that the world can not forget him. Men of letters, the familiars of every muse, turn themselves from the ravishments of polite learning and of high art, to enrich the imagination with the ideal beauties of "the Man of Sorrows," and to expend the resources of the most cultivated taste in the reproduction of what transcends all else in nature's growth—all else in history's life. Men of action, trained to politics, or married to gold, ask themselves, *What of this man Jesus? Why should we have an opinion concerning him? What is it makes him essential to us?*

This question, agitated for eighteen centuries, addresses now more minds than ever before, and receives more various answers. Responses, in other days, were given in the cannon's roar and in the dying groans of martyrs. Now they are given with the voice and the pen. Once given in reply to threatening power, now they are made in conflict with defiant reason. Unbelief is better equipped and more self-reliant to-day than in any former age. Metaphysics, history, art, never furnished her such effective weapons as she draws now from the armories of natural science. The Christian religion in its infancy was trodden beneath the iron heel of power, despised, hated, crushed, as is every good thing when it is weak. But every drop of the Church's blood was prolific, and she throve amidst her agonies. Now that the millions train in her steps; now that she has a record of glory in history; now that the veneration of centuries is enthroned upon her brow; now, in the days of her hallowed maturity, and in the exuberance of her maternal goodness,—there are found those who glory in their enmity, not to Christians, but to Christianity, who attack the fortress of her strength, and, seizing her own guns, turn them inward upon her vital defenses. *Rationalism*—which is an affectation of rationalness, just as theism is of godliness, and as Romanism is of Catholicism—rationalism is the name of the prevailing tendency of unbelief, the cover to all the attacks against Gospel truth. Men are zealous to be disciples of Reason, as if the ages before us had been only irrational. This is the general name for the skeptical reactions of two centuries against the Reformation of the sixteenth century. This tendency began with a so-called *rational interpretation* of Scripture, so explaining supernatural events as to bring them within the domain of the natural. There followed the attempt to reduce the *narratives* of miraculous occurrences to *myths*. This, failing to account satisfactorily for the rise of Christianity and the Christian Church, was succeeded by the endeavor to invalidate the apostolic origin of the *four Gospels*, and to father upon St. Paul the *invention* of the supernatural in the Christian records and faith. This having been defeated by historical criticism, the enemies of the faith have turned, as with one accord, directly to the *person of Jesus Christ*, as if to take the citadel of our religion and thereby secure capitulation of the outposts. Many proclaim the victory already won, and are but waiting, as they think, the rapidly approaching hour when the Christian world shall strike the colors of Immanuel. A highly cultivated French gentleman pronounces Jesus to have been a young man of great talent, a much refined and very subtle sinner; a German professor discovers that he was a sinless man and an uncompromising low-churchman; an American conventioner calls him Mr. Jesus; and a St. Louis Councilman, learned in "lager beer," decides that his religion is an "*exploded humbug*."

Abating our contempt for the pretensions of ignorance, and our disappointment with the ill-disguised sophistries of learned men, there is one view of the activity of skepticism which commands respect, and bids us heed its honest utterances. So far as the

Christian Church has sought to impose her beliefs by authority; and so far as skepticism is a protest against this procedure, a demand for light and a denial of prerogative,—so far it merits a respectful consideration, and an effort to attain the middle ground whereon faith and reason, prescription and inquiry may find themselves at one. All do not discriminate between Christianity and the Church. Imposture, rampant around ecclesiastical altars, may cast the shadow of its rottenness over the sacred origins of religion and Church. Strauss's declaration, that "he who would banish priests from the Church must first banish miracles from religion," is but the outgrowth of hatred towards ignorance, bigotry, and imposture in the living representatives of the Founder of the Christian Church.

Furthermore, the discoveries of modern science and the achievements of criticism have annihilated so many hypotheses of ancient thinkers; have swept away so many traditions, venerable with age and consecrated in the prejudices of nations; have re-written the histories of so many men and so many peoples; have unlocked so many secrets, and explained so many mysteries; have reduced so many fog-mountains to molehills; and have found but a calf in the sanctum of so many temples; in short, have brought us so much daylight, and left the ancients so benighted,—that a presumption has been created against every ancient belief; and that which can not verify itself anew in inward experience or by outward experiment and observation, must fall to the ground. We are in the midst of such a crisis. We rejoice that it is so. Truth has nothing to fear. The more numerous the tests, and the hotter the fires, the brighter will be the luster of her after-glory.

PRESUPPOSITIONS.

Since some things must be taken for granted in any writing; and whereas many things, closely connected with our theme, have been amply discussed and satisfactorily determined elsewhere, by other writers, we must, therefore, request the hearer, at the outset, to concede to us the following presuppositions:

(*a*) AN HISTORICAL PRESUPPOSITION; namely, *The several books of the New Testament were written by the persons whose names they bear; that is, they are genuine.*

(*b*) AN ONTOLOGICAL PRESUPPOSITION; namely, *The supernatural in history is not repugnant to reason.*

(*c*) A PSYCHOLOGICAL PRESUPPOSITION; namely, *There is something in man which may be called faith, or intuition;* be it a faculty of intellect, or a power of feeling, or a mere receptivity—something which mediates to us the knowledge of God.

When the apostle John says, "And we beheld his glory, the glory as of the only-begotten of the Father,"* he appears to assume, not a miraculous power of perception in the disciples, but a power resident in us all, more developed in some than in others; a power whereby, had we, who are here,

* John i, 14.

been there, with Jesus and his disciples, we should have perceived the same thing, the *Divinity* incorporate in Jesus.

Jesus taught that this perceptive power, this organon of spiritual knowledge, might be dimmed, and even blinded. "If the light that is in thee be darkness, how great is that darkness!"* If this eye be "single"—that is, incorrupt—we may with it discover the treasures of the unseen world, and our hearts will be ravished with their beauty. If it be "evil," we may think there is no unseen world, because we perceive it not; that is, have gone past perceiving it. Are there not those who "having eyes see not, and having ears hear not?" Are there not things which "eye hath not seen, nor ear heard, neither have entered into the heart of man, but God hath *revealed* them unto us by his Spirit?" This may be, and doubtless is, in most of us, a feeble faculty, a power but little developed. But let us not doubt its reality for that reason. Perhaps if we should try, we might rub these eyes open, and see worlds of beauty hitherto concealed. This *spiritual vision* made Peter eminent among the chosen, who were all, probably, selected because of their superior endowment therewith; and upon it was pronounced the blessing: "Blessed art thou, Simon Bar-Jona, for flesh and blood hath not revealed it unto thee, but my Father which is in heaven." Tertullian would, doubtless, grant us what we claim, for he says:† "Who ascertains truth without God? To whom is God known without Christ? By whom is Christ explored with-

* Matt. vi, 22, 23.

† *Vide* our motto.

out the Holy Spirit? And to whom is the Holy Spirit granted without the sacrament of *faith?*" The mystic discoveries and triumphs of Christian experience rest upon such a spiritual power. We all, in the heart, admit it. We preach it, pray it, sing it.

> "My prayer hath power with God; the grace
> Unspeakable I now receive;
> *Through faith I see Thee face to face;*
> I see thee face to face, and live!
> In vain I have not wept and strove:
> Thy nature and thy name is Love."

Here, then, we stand. The Gospel narratives have adequate historic verity. The mysterious person of Christ is not to be rejected at the outset because it is supernatural; and there is in us a power of such a nature as, if cultivated, will aid us in discerning the wonderful verities of our Lord's person.

And now we approach more directly our theme, beseeching our Lord to pardon the shortcomings of thought, and by his own illumination to fill up, and complete in your minds, the necessarily imperfect picture we shall draw.

We humbly propose to show that Jesus Christ is *very God*, and *very man.*

I. DIVINITY: *That he is very God.*

Let us bear in mind that we speak of an historical character; of one who has actually lived among men, sharing all the lowly conditions of our mortality, having human infirmities, speaking in a human language, enjoying the friendships and incurring the hatred of men and women, and closing a laborious, self-denying life with a most tragic and humiliating death. Of such a person we speak, who, notwithstanding all, claimed to be much more than a man; and his claim was accepted and honored by all who knew him well, and has wrought itself into the foundation and the essence of the religion bearing his name. It has been well said, by Dr. Schenkel, that "no religion has its fortunes and its results so closely connected with the person of its founder, as the Christian religion."* It is equally true that no religion is so well prepared to risk its existence upon the person of its founder, because it has the requisite historic basis. Much as infidels ridicule a historic religion, there is nothing but history, that is, *authenticated facts*, that can substantiate a revelation and verify a deity. An invented religion may serve the purposes of a philosopher; but dying men and women call for a revelation and a "living God." We are not, therefore, appalled by the greatness of the problem before us, seeing Divine Wisdom has graciously provided abundant material for its solution.

But we are met, at the outset, with the assertion that *the incarnation of Deity is impossible and absurd.* The Infinite, it is claimed, can not impose limitations on itself. The writer last quoted says:

"Statements like these, namely, that he imposed limitations on himself in regard to his Divine fullness; that, during his earthly life, he made no use, or only a partial use, of his Divine powers,—are not only empty and unmeaning subterfuges, they are derogatory to the perfections and majesty of God. A

* "Character of Jesus Portrayed," Am. ed., Vol. I, chap. i.

god who limits himself, is a god who ceases to be God; for to the being of God it belongs, above all things, to be unlimited. By propositions of this sort, Christian theology sinks to the level of heathen representations of God. It makes him a being changeable and divisible; that is, a mere personification of forces and powers."*

If this be sound philosophy, there is an end of controversy. We should not care to defend an unphilosophic and self-contradictory theology. But we must confess our surprise at the raising of this objection by one who must be so familiar with the history of thought. Let the objector reconcile creation and providence and revelation with the infinitude of God if he can. Let him solve the problem of the individuation of the absolute—a favorite with the schoolmen. When he has done this, he may consistently apply his dialectics to the doctrine of the Incarnation. We shall not need to tarry here, because of the prominence given, of late years, to the philosophy of the Infinite, and because of the large circulation, in our country, of the works of Cousin, Hamilton, and Mansel.

Now, remembering the authenticity of the Gospels, assuming metaphysical or ontological difficulties to be satisfactorily adjusted, looking upon this historical personage, and, for the time, thinking of him only as a man, too good to deceive, and too wise to be himself deluded, let us inquire what is his testimony concerning himself. A man who exacts no pay, while perpetually rendering most inestimable services;

* "Character of Jesus Portrayed," Am. ed., Vol. I, p. 4.

who courts not popularity, but shrinks from applause; who aims at no advantage for himself, and cherishes not a shadow of ambition for fame or power; who finds his delight in relieving the poor, in healing the sick, in restoring outcasts to the society of their kind; who is happy when he can make a blind man see, and when he can restore a widow's son from the embrace of death to his mother's arms,—such a man, if he lived in our midst, without property, without office, without party, without social distinction, without clique, or clan, or cure, or cunning; such a man, we repeat, would command our confidence. Nay, more; we would accept his testimony on any subject with which he ought to be familiar, in preference to that of any other man in the community. Nay, yet further; we should not feel ourselves justified in differing from such a man. If he testified at all of himself; if he spake of himself with such reserve and candor as his great deeds would require,—we should receive his testimony, as much more likely to be true than the opinions of others; especially if those others were unfriendly, and rendered so by the claims of selfishness.

Though we have not space for a complete and exhaustive view of this testimony, we notice, briefly:

1. *Some indirect testimonies to the nature of His own person.*

a. "Wist ye not that I must be about *my Father's* business?"* This seems to be something more than a presentiment of a future prophetic vocation. Samuel received a Divine call when a child, a call from

* Luke ii, 49.

without, which took him by surprise, and, to fulfill which, he was educated. Jesus, a lad of twelve years, speaks of God as from an *abiding consciousness*, and calls him his "Father." This betrays an inner light, which could not have proceeded from maternal instruction, and which was not derived from the study of the prophets. Whence can it have come? Does it not suggest a possible grandeur and mystery of person, not inclusible within the ordinary limitations of humanity?

b. The wonderful child, whose strange birth, history, and sayings were treasured up in a mother's pondering heart; the lone and inspired man whom the unsoiled and beautiful souls* sought, and, when they found, exclaimed, "We have found him of whom Moses, in the law and the prophets, did write;"† this man, just emerged from obscurity, but brimful of "grace and truth"—the truth that overtopped all written laws, all recorded prophecies, and the grace that warmed and won, like the morning's glory on dew-laden flowers,—this man said, "Follow me." The love-smitten souls of fishermen and tax-gatherers left pelf and toil, profit and pleasure, to rot away in their boats and coffers, while they companied with him, who chained them to himself by a spell, which was the sign of the mysterious and unmeasured power within the man. What was it that gave authority to the summons, "*Follow me?*" Something in the man; but what was it? And what

* "What dost thou call a beautiful soul? Thou callest a beautiful soul one that is quick to perceive the good, that gives it due prominence, and holds it immovably fast."—*Jacobi.*

† John i, 45.

did he assume when he said *"follow?"* We interpret as if he said: "I have that to give which is better than your trades and gains, better than your homes and friends; that which ye have longed for; that which men every-where would have, if they could buy it or work for it. It is in me. It is my birthright. No other man has it." They saw the reflection of the inner light, did they not? They felt the attraction of the hidden power, did they not?

c. The first sermon of Jesus proclaimed a *kingdom.* "Repent, for the kingdom of heaven is at hand."* He proclaimed the restoration of the theocracy, as says the author of "Ecce Homo."† But he pointed to no successor whose credentials he would publish. He spake not of a king yet to come, beneath whose scepter the "quickening fire" of a golden age of peace should make beauty and blessing start from every desert soil of life. But, calmly taking to himself the royal prerogatives, he lays down, upon his own authority, the laws of a sovereignty as broad as the human race and more enduring than time. As Jehovah, under the ancient theocracy, pronounced the blessing and the curse, so now, Jesus declares "blessing" on the man of love, "hell-fire" on the man of hate. When he would heal the palsied man, he declares his sins forgiven; when his disciples gather and eat their food on the Sabbath, he stops the mouth of caviling by announcing himself the Lord of the Sabbath; when his dear friend has been four days dead, and the sisters doubt and weep, he cries, "Lazarus, come

* Matthew iv, 17. † Chapter iii.

forth." Among the living and the dead, in nature's unconscious laboratories, and in the quick spiritualities of human hearts, he moves alike with sovereign composure and undisputed command. Nature never revolted. Where human perverseness resisted and seemed to triumph, it was evident he chose not to use his power. Human beings, fanatics, have fancied themselves kings; but when have they, without purse and without armies, persuaded others of their royalty? When and where have they consistently, composedly, beneficently, maintained their claim, amid the hearty responses of grateful friends and indebted thousands?

d. But among the indirect testimonies of Jesus to his superhuman excellence, the chief importance must be attached to *the interior, spiritual functions which he takes to himself in relation to the souls of men.*

e. He is legislator for the spiritual kingdom in his own right. "Jehovah spake unto Moses, saying," etc.; but Jesus says, "*I say unto you.*" Whosoever kept not the law given by Jehovah to Moses, was to be "cut off from his people." But Jesus says, "Whosoever heareth these sayings of *mine*, and doeth them, I will liken him unto a wise man which built his house upon a rock," etc.*

He speaks not in another's name. He retires to no oracle for instructions in critical moments. He shelters his opinions and advices under cover of no ancient and revered names. He commands our virtues, denounces our vices, and wields with serenity

* Matthew vii, 24, etc.

the awful decrees of irrevocable fate. He set out upon his ministry with the assertion of this prerogative, armed as yet with the sole might of his person, and before he had wrought the wonderful works that drew all eyes to him. Out of his own consciousness of inherent majesty and right comes his legislating; not from the consent of the popular voice.

f. He is the supreme object of our heart-devotion. With a keen glance, and without any knowingness, he fathomed the human heart. He saw it, a tender dove, in its weather-beaten ark, floating over the comfortless waters of submerged joys and extinguished hopes. He saw its panting, its worrying, its longing; its fretted wings, its disappointed efforts, its untried powers. He spake to it: "O, suffering humanity! leave all thy crushed treasures and come to *me.* Forget the wild roar of the troubled waters beneath thee in the peaceful haven of my bosom. Cease thy strivings, and the beating of thy frail wings. Take the 'olive-branch' of my promise, and be at rest. I will assuage the waters." "Come unto me, all ye that labor and are heavy-laden, and I will give you rest."* How great was his heart, that could take us all in! How vast the resources of a nature that can drink up all the depths of our sorrow! Did ever man speak so before? Was he but a man? If he were, did he not wofully deceive himself when he thought he could comfort us?

But, again, he saw that man could be redeemed only through his affectional nature; that he could not be permanently withdrawn from his sins except by

* Matt. xi, 28.

attaching him to some better being, as a ship is moored to the dock. He knew, too, the supremacy of conscience in man, the indisputable and indefeasible sovereignty of rectitude, even in the fallen nature; so that there could be no mooring of the soul to an imperfect, fallible being. The attempt to tie our hearts in supreme devotion to a less than infallible being, would inevitably create internal dissension and warfare. But Jesus proposed peace and righteousness. Hence, to demand our sovereign affections for himself, were treason, not only to God, but to us, if he were only a man like ourselves, however pure and refined. Yet, although he says, "Thou shalt love the Lord thy God with all thy heart," etc.,* he also says: "If ye love *me*, keep my commandments;"† "He that loveth father or mother more than *me* is not worthy of me;"‡ "He that loseth his life for *my sake* shall find it."§ Many a time friendship has laid human lives on the altar of sacrifice. Many a time have loyal heroes, fired with passion for glory, followed chivalric leaders to bloody graves. But who ever, before or since Jesus, challenged our dying love for himself? Many a one has said, "Fight and die for your country;" but who else than this one has said, "Fight and die for me?" Who, besides him, has ever said, "When the issue is made between father and mother and *me*, choose me?" Who but him has said, "When thy wife and children stand between thee and *me*, put them aside?" How like the mandates of conscience! This inward monitor

*Matt. xxii, 37; Mark xii, 30; Luke x, 27. †John xiv, 15.
‡Matt. x, 37. §Matt. x, 39.

says, "Die, rather than lie, or cheat, or murder." Jesus says, "Die, rather than betray me." May it be that our fealty to rectitude and to Jesus is all one and the same? Does he not assume it?

g. But, again, *he presents himself as the world's Savior*. "No man cometh unto the Father, but *by me*."* "No descent from Abraham, no covenant privilege, no keeping of laws, can give one acceptance with the Father. This comes only of my mediation." "I am the way, the truth, and the life."† "I mediate access to the Father. None other can. I illuminate the human mind. I give the knowledge of the Father. I bestow the power of a new life. I raise souls, that are dead in sin, to the life of righteousness." Could Paul use such language? Could he give life? Or did he count "all things loss for the excellency of the knowledge of Christ Jesus?"‡ Did Paul imagine a new creation, originating with himself? Or did he say, "If any man be in Christ, he is a new creature?"§ Was it, then, as a man among men that Jesus said, "I am the way, the truth, and the life?"‖ Let prophet or holy man say,

* John xiv, 6. † Idem. ‡ Phil. iii, 8. § 2 Cor. v, 17.

‖ We quote here with pleasure the words of Dr. Gess: "The position which Jesus takes toward us corresponds to that which he wishes us to take towards him. A Moses may well desire the Israelites to believe in him and to trust him (cf. Exodus xiv, 31: "And the people feared the Lord, and believed the Lord, and his servant Moses"); but only by reason of the commission and the prophetic endowment which God has given the prophet, not because of the inner essence of his person. The purpose of that Divine endowment being attained, the relation of subordination between the prophet and the people ceases, and another prophet may step into the place of the first. Every prophet, the truer a prophet he is, the more certainly, must desire his own decrease, his own retreat (cf. John iii, 30), and

"Ye believe in God, believe also in me;"* shall it not sound as blasphemy in our ears? But the words drop from the lips of Jesus, and create no shock. He is about to leave his disciples—*to die.* But he assures them he dies not as others die. "I go to prepare a place for you. And if I go and prepare a place for you, I will come again, and receive you unto myself; that where I am, there ye may be also."† Is it blasphemy? The disciples do not think it. Is he beside himself? The words are very sober, for a lunatic. If this were lunacy, then the disciples also were lunatics, and so continued, until they became martyrs for their lunacy. This is a lunacy, too, that has had a strange power of self-propagation, a marvelous pertinacity of endurance, a fertile productiveness of every thing good, and the power to organize society and erect social institutions, surpassing the highest achievements of reason. Is there not in him, that so addresses us, a consciousness of excellence more than human; a feeling that he can do for us what all the good and great might strive in vain to do? But who can utter the bitterness of the mockery, and the stupendous sottishness of the imposture, if these be the words of one who is but wrought up by enthusiasm to the counting on imag-

the ascending of all to his prophetic elevation. On the contrary, Jesus, at the approach of his departure, says to his disciples, "Ye believe in God, believe also in *me.*" (John xiv, 1.) And, while a prophet exacts more faith in his person of the less experienced, but is obligated to direct those of riper religious experience to their own immediate experience of communion with God, *Jesus*, on the other hand, induced much rather the most experienced—namely, his disciples—to build their entire inner life upon communion with his person." (Die Lehre von der Person Christi, u. s. w., 1856, p. 5.)

* John xiv, 1.

† Id., 2, 3.

inary powers; or, still worse, if they proceed from one who, being delegated by the Supreme Benefactor of the world to do us a great service, practices upon our credulity, by drawing our attention to himself instead of the Universal Father.

But turn to another scene, and behold this same person in the crowded temple, confronting his persistent enemies and rejecters. He is weary of denouncing sin, and longs for some sign of relenting. See the risings of his heart towards his recreant household. Behold the forgetting of conventions, and the oblivion of the machinations of enemies and of the selfish artifices of a cold world. It is one of the most beautiful pictures in the records of this wonderful life. Looking into the faces of sordid money-changers, of loose debauchees, of flaunting courtesans, of wily demagogues, of hypocritical Pharisees, of artless countrymen and countrywomen, and thoughtless of all but their souls' worth, he exclaims: "O Jerusalem, Jerusalem, thou that killest the prophets, and stonest them which are sent unto thee, how often would I have gathered thy children together, even as a hen gathereth her chickens under her wings, and ye would not!"* Are we mistaken? or is there in the words "how often" a backward glance of a more than human memory over ages gone by, when this gracious presence, not yet become incarnate, watched over his chosen people and endured their rebellions?

2. But, secondly, we introduce the more direct testimonies of Jesus to the nature of his own person;

* Matt. xxiii, 37.

testimonies which unequivocally avow his divinity, or at least assume for him the attributes of Deity.

a. He claims *a pre-mundane and eternal existence.* He "came down from heaven;"* he was in heaven before his earthly existence: "What and if ye shall see the Son of man ascend up where he was before?"† He was in glory with the Father, before the world was: "And now, O Father, glorify thou me with thine own self with the glory which I had with thee before the world was."‡ He was, nay he IS, before Abraham: "Before Abraham was, I am."§

When we endeavor to understand the words "before the world was," shall we conceive a limitless stretch of time antecedent to the creation of the world? Shall we banish from conception all rolling worlds, all shining light, all marked periods, all revolutions, and all sounds; and conceive the solitary, soundless rush of the thoughts of God, like a spiritual Tequendama in an unfrequented Andes? Shall we behold one separate thought spring out from the dread abyss, and by Divine volition become a conscious being, an armed Minerva, an angel of light, a companion of a hitherto solitary God? Does he spring into a splendid florescence of beauty? a gorgeous affluence of majesty and power? Does he receive much and bestow much? Does he call into existence many ranks of intelligent and social beings? Does he form abodes of paradisiac beauty and elegance for their entertainment and delectation? Does he lead a life of untarnished glory and triumph

* John iii, 13; vi, 38.
† John vi, 62.
‡ John xvii, 5.
§ John viii, 58.

through the skies, in perpetual ovation? Does the wealth of his love pour floods of blessing through the worlds, and meet responsive songs of grateful hallelujahs from thronging millions of happy creatures? Is this the being who now, a traveling Prince, turns his eye, from a distant and disordered world, back to his Father's throne, and prays, "Glorify thou me with thine own self with the glory which I had with thee before the world was?"* Such was the doctrine of Arius, an accomplished man of the early part of the fourth century, a doctrine which gave rise to the Ecumenical Council of Nice, wherein it was condemned. It must be rejected by us, not because it was thus condemned by the Council, but because, whatever Gordian knots of metaphysical obscurity it severs, it does not meet the demands of Biblical interpretation. Take due note of the words, "*The glory which I had with thee.*" Is this the language of a created being? What creature, however exalted, may share the Divine glory? How vast, how incomprehensible, the gulf between the Infinite God and the highest of his creatures! Indeed, the most exalted creature, no more than the meanest, could partake of the ineffable glory of God. It is the creatureship, not any relative degree of littleness, that forbids the participation. Then the added words, "*Before the world was,*" were it not puerile to explain thus: "Before the earth was formed and its inhabitants created, but still after creation had begun?" This is as if we should interpret "before Abraham was, I am," thus: "Before

* John xvii, 5.

Abraham, to be sure, but not earlier than Adam; or, if earlier than Adam, at least contemporaneous with Gabriel; or, at farthest, just a little before Gabriel; a few years, at most." This is a *reductio ad absurdum* of our Savior's words. He spake too seriously and too grandly to be thus understood. In his thought, "before the world was," and "before Abraham was," signify before the creation, and antecedent to the course of time.* The glory he had enjoyed, and had laid aside, was a pre-mundane glory, without conditions and limits, outside of all the befores and afters of our human life. Otherwise, why did he employ the peculiar phraseology, "Before Abraham was, *I am*," when, if a creature, "I was," was the language he should have employed, both for truth's and grammar's sake? Did he not know that "I AM" was the peculiar and most dreadful name of the God of the Jews? Did he not know that they so reverenced it as to substitute for it another word, on ordinary occasions, so that they might not profane the holy name? And were they not exasperated by his self-

* "'I came down from heaven;' 'I came out from the Father;' 'Glorify thou me with the glory which I had with thee before the world was;' 'That they may behold the glory which thou hast given me: for thou lovedst me before the foundation of the world;' 'Before Abraham was, I AM;'—in these expressions Jesus, in a plain and incontrovertible manner, ascribes to himself a glory before the temporal world was, and, therefore, *before time itself*. He was with the Father, in the same glory which he has in his post-temporal life, wherein all power in heaven and upon earth is given over to him; and he has power to bestow the Holy Ghost. He also ascribes to himself a changeless life; not one of becoming and of passing away, but one of *being*. Is not this just what we should expect of him who says: I am the life; baptize in my name; my voice shall wake the dead?" (Gess, "Die Lehre v. d. Person Christi," p. 28.)

appropriation of this supreme name? Did they not take up stones to put him to death, as a capital offender? Again, if he were the good and true man we have believed him to be, what are we now forced to concede? *Either that he was God, as he claimed to be, or that he was wofully deceived concerning himself.* Was he likely to be deceived? Could the author of the Sermon on the Mount be easily mistaken on any subject pertaining to morals and religion? Keep this point steadily in view. Is there any intellectual production in the world, in all the literatures of all the ages, equal to that mountain discourse? Did Confucius ever rise to its placid elevation? Did Plato ever attain its sublime vision? Did any other discourse ever so vindicate its truthfulness in the consciences of men? Here are teachings at the very top of all the wisdom of time. Was their author an enthusiast? Was he a sciolist? Was he fanciful? Was he sentimental? Was he weak-minded?

Again, his enemies were Pharisees and scribes, men who taught that it was a great offense to eat without washing, or to send for a physician on the Sabbath; but it was venial to profane the common name by which Jehovah was known, or to defraud parents in the name of sanctity. These men said Jesus was an impostor, and denied his Messiahship. Who was more likely to be mistaken—the casuistic Pharisee, or Jesus? We must renounce our common sense, or accept the testimony of Jesus.

b. He claims *self-existence* in the words, "Before Abraham was, I *am*."

c. He assumes *essential equality with the Father.* "He that hath seen me hath seen the Father."* "I and my Father are one."† "No man knoweth the Son, but the Father; neither knoweth any man the Father, save the Son."‡

d. He makes himself the *source of spiritual life,* and the *quickener of the physically dead.* "I am the way, the truth, and the life."§ "For as the Father raiseth up the dead, and quickeneth them; even so the Son quickeneth whom he will."‖ "For as the Father hath life in himself; so hath he given to the Son to have life in himself."¶ Can he have life in himself whose existence is derived and has a beginning? Is there not a contradiction in the conception of a *created life-giver?*

e. In concluding our meager notice of the direct testimonies of Jesus to his divinity, we may not omit what is perhaps the plainest and most emphatic of all, and which is often called the baptismal formula: "Go ye therefore, and teach all nations, baptizing them *in the name of the Father, and of the Son, and of the Holy Ghost.*"** This is not only a substantial, but also a formal, assumption of the prerogatives of Deity. Baptism formally devoted the man to the exclusive worship and service of God. Creatures have no place as the objects of baptismal worship and service. But here is a careful and deliberate array of the Son and the Holy Ghost along with the Father, as the united object of baptism. Criticism has sometimes attempted to expunge the words from

* John xiv, 9. † John x, 30. ‡ Matt. xi, 27. § John xiv, 6. ‖ John v, 21. ¶ John v, 26. ** Matt. xxviii, 19.

the text, but authority fails. Anti-trinitarians usually evade the passage in their arguments. Here, however, is the attempt of one who is bold enough to hazard his cause against this stronghold of the truth:

"This teaches no trinity of persons, much less of equal persons in the Godhead. On the contrary, the use of the word Son implies inferiority. The words mean that we should be baptized into faith in God as our Father, in the Son of God as our Savior, and in the Holy Spirit as the guiding influence which proceeds from God. This comprises the whole Christian faith. It is sometimes said that to be baptized in the Son is a proof of his deity; but it is not so, for Paul speaks of the Jews as having been baptized into Moses.* Nor does it follow, because the three are spoken of together, that they are equal to each other, for we read: 'The people came to Moses and said, We have sinned; we have spoken against Jehovah and against thee.'† And, again, 'All the congregation blessed Jehovah, God of their fathers, and bowed down their heads, and worshiped Jehovah and the king.'‡ And, 'David said to Abigail, Blessed be Jehovah, God of Israel, who sent thee this day to meet me: and blessed be thy advice, and blessed be thou, who hast kept me this day from coming to shed blood.'§ You will observe the strength of this language. It is an ascription of praise, first to Jehovah, God of Israel, then to her advice, and then to herself. But the ascription is to be understood differently in each case. So, when we read that they

* 1 Cor. x, 2.
† Numb. xxi, 7.
‡ 1 Chron. xxix, 20.
§ 1 Sam. xxv, 32.

worshiped Jehovah and the king, we understand the first as supreme worship, and the second as the homage of respect. In all such cases, which are frequent in the Bible, common sense saves us from error. Although two or three subjects are spoken of in the same connection, it does not follow that they are spoken of in the same sense, much less that they are the same thing, or equal to each other. Nor does it follow that the Holy Spirit is a person because we are baptized into its name; for, according to a common mode of expression among the Jews, the name of a thing often meant the thing itself. So the Rabbins speak of being baptized into the name of liberty, and the Samaritans circumcised their converts into the name of Mt. Gerizim."*

Let it be observed, in reply, that we are forbidden to infer the Divine nature of the Son of God from his position as an object of baptismal honor, because in one place it is declared that the Israelites were baptized unto Moses. Now, we remember that baptism is made an antitype of the deliverance from the flood.† It will doubtless be conceded, on all hands, that, in the passage cited from Corinthians, St. Paul makes it the antitype of the deliverance of Israel from the Red Sea. Therefore the baptism unto Moses is not *real,* but figurative; and the putting Moses in such a relation to that figurative baptism, is only an acknowledgment of his historic position as leader and deliverer of Israel. Moses, as a prophet, was, in some sense, an object of faith to

* "Doctrines of Christianity," by Wm. G. Elliot, pp. 22, 23.
† 1 Peter, iii, 21.

Israel; but, in the passage in question, there is no allusion to Moses other than historical. The connection requires, simply, a forgetting of Moses, and an absorbing of the mind in the deliverance. There is, therefore, in this use, by the apostle, of the words "baptized unto Moses," as compared with the other places of the New Testament, wherein universally God or Christ is made the object of baptism, a good opportunity for the application of the above writer's words, "Common sense saves us from error."

As regards the import of mentioning the names of Father, Son, and Holy Ghost together, it is vain to cite instances of the kind mentioned. It is universally held by scholars that a purely doctrinal passage is to be interpreted more rigidly than an incidental bit of narrative. Where there is a conscious regard to the doctrinal import of one's words, and an intention of teaching something, we may find a ground of valid inference, which may not be justified in an incidental remark of the historian. When Jesus, the sublimest of all teachers, enjoins baptism in the name of the Father, and of the Son, and of the Holy Ghost, he is unquestionably teaching his disciples to co-ordinate those blessed hypostases of the Divine Nature. For this utterance does not stand alone. It must be taken in connection with the other sayings of our Lord: "I and my Father are one;"* "He that hath seen me hath seen the Father."† And, again, "But when the Comforter is come, whom I will send unto you from the Father, even the Spirit of truth, which proceedeth from the Father, . . .

*John x, 30. †John xiv, 9.

he will guide you into all truth; . . . he will shew you things to come; . . . he shall glorify me."* It is evident, too, although the writer to whom we reply, ignores it, that the Father, the Son, and the Holy Ghost are, in baptism, a personal object of faith, not a mere subject of propositions. The recipient of baptism signified, in his recipiency, something more than a mere confession of the existence of God, and of Jesus Christ, his Son, our Savior, and of an influence from God delusively called the Holy Spirit. John Baptist proclaimed, "He shall baptize you with the Holy Ghost, and with fire."† Jesus said, "Except a man be born of water and of the Spirit, he can not enter into the kingdom of God."‡ Do these words import that the Holy Ghost is but a name? Do they signify that the baptized merely acknowledges a creed? Or do they assume that the subject of baptism receives a Divine power, and enters into a new spiritual relation? To whom does he hold this relation, if not to the being in whose name he is baptized? To the Unitarian these grand distinctions and titles, pertaining to the Divinity, may be only subjects of belief; but to us they are *objects of faith.* We do not insist on the word "*person,*" as applied to them. It has never been regarded, from Augustine to our own time, as adequate to the truth. It misleads, of necessity, until we put ourselves on guard against it. But it is our infirmity, that we have not found a word fitted to take its place.

When we remember that Jesus has continually demanded our unlimited faith in his person, our

*John xv, 26; xvi, 13, 14. †Matt. iii, 11. ‡John iii, 5.

resting of all spiritual hopes thereon, we can not doubt that when he places himself alongside the Father, in the formula of baptism, he still aims at our immortal, saving trust in himself, as in God.

We have noticed but few of the utterances of Jesus which more or less plainly avow his Divine nature. Time and space forbid an attempt at exhausting this review. The sayings of Jesus, suffice it to say, are all permeated with the idea of his superhuman and Divine nature. When this is not expressly avowed and brought into the foreground of the picture, it lies in the background, and throws its coloring over the whole. When he speaks as "one having authority;" when he names himself "the Bridegroom," as did Jehovah in the Old Covenant; when he bids the world come to him and live; when he raises the widow's son upon his bier; when he rises, himself, from the grave,—in all these things are conspicuous to the unbiased reader now, as to the pious disciple of old, *the manner and the power of God!*

3. We have reserved for this place a brief discussion of the import of the phrase, "*Son of God,*" although the understanding of it is indispensable to the right appreciation of the baptismal formula, of which we have already treated.

We assume that we are all sufficiently familiar with the fact that the phrase, "Son of God," is sometimes applied, in the Old Testament, to *holy men,* and *men of exalted position* in the Theocracy. We need, also, only to advert, in passing, to the fact that the same title is employed, as in the second

Psalm, to designate the promised Messiah. The question now is, whether the title, as applied to Jesus, was any thing more than the official Messianic title; *whether it signified his Divine essence.* It may be granted that, in the announcement of his Sonship at the baptism of Jesus, and afterwards at the transfiguration, the primary object was to point him out as the Messiah, rather than to declare any thing concerning his nature. The same may be true of John Baptist's confession, "And I saw and bare record that this is the Son of God;"* and of that of Nathaniel, "Thou art the Son of God; thou art the King of Israel."† But, it is evident, a different and higher relation is indicated in the words of Jesus, "All things are delivered unto me of my Father: and no man knoweth the Son, but the Father; neither knoweth any man the Father, save the Son."‡ This is no official dignity, but a vital and pre-mundane relation between the Everlasting Father and the Son, a mystic union which only Divine Wisdom comprehends. He assumes the same relation, not of identity, but of *Sonship,* when he says, "He that hath seen me hath seen the Father."§ It is only a theoretical prepossession and bias that can resist the force of such declarations. Compare, moreover, the words, "For God so loved the world, that he gave his *only begotten Son,* that whosoever believeth in him should not perish, but have everlasting life."‖ That the term "only begotten" does not refer to the temporal phenomenon of the birth from Mary,

*John i, 34. †John i, 49. ‡Matt. xi, 27.
§John xiv, 9. ‖John iii, 16.

is evident from such passages as I have already quoted;* and from this, "And now, O Father, glorify thou me with thine own self with the glory which I had with thee before the world was;"† and from many other utterances of the Savior himself, not to speak, now, of those of his apostles. The opinion that the appellation, "Son of God," was given in a distinctive sense to Jesus, only because of his supernatural incarnation, has been maintained by some scholars; but no profound scholar or capable critic of the present day would risk his reputation on such a hypothesis. The Jews themselves, unless John has deceived us, understood the title in its highest sense when Jesus said, "My Father worketh hitherto, and I work;"‡ for "they sought the more to kill him, because he not only had broken the Sabbath, but said also that God was his Father, *making himself equal with God*."§

If we turn, now, to inquire how the apostles understood this peculiar name, and how they employed it, we find John, who knew him best as a human being, most decidedly impressed with his Divinity, and clearly conveying it in the use of the name *Son*, and its equivalent, "*only begotten*." "And the Word was made flesh, and dwelt among us, full of grace and truth; and we beheld his glory, the glory as of the *only begotten* of the Father."‖ And, again, "No man hath seen God at any time; the *only begotten Son*, which is in the bosom of the Father, he hath declared him."¶ "In this was manifested the love

* Matt. xi, 27. † John xvii, 5. ‡ John v, 17.
§ John v, 18. ‖ John i, 14. ¶ Id., 18.

of God toward us, because that God sent his *only begotten Son* into the world, that we might live through him."* "Who is a liar but he that denieth that Jesus is the Christ? He is antichrist, that denieth the Father and the Son. Whosever denieth the Son, the same hath not the Father."† To St. Peter, God is "the Father of our Lord Jesus Christ." St. Paul sets him before us as "made of the seed of David according to the flesh;" but "declared to be the Son of God with power, according to the Spirit of holiness, by the resurrection from the dead."‡ He says, "The life which I now live in the flesh I live by the faith of the Son of God, who loved me, and gave himself for me."§ We may well believe St. Paul did not live by faith in one whom he esteemed a creature. In the Epistle to the Philippians he speaks of this Son of God as having been in the form of God, but at his incarnation taking on him *the form of a servant;*|| which is an implicit contradiction of the opinion that his Sonship pertained to his incarnate existence. The author of the Epistle to the Hebrews, whoever he was, is most explicit in his use of the name Son, in the divinest sense: "God . . . hath in these last days spoken unto us by his Son."¶ "And again, when he bringeth in the first-begotten into the world, he saith, And let all the angels of God worship him."** "And of the angels he saith, Who maketh his angels spirits, and his ministers a flame of fire. But unto the Son he saith, Thy throne, O God, is for ever and ever."††

* 1 John iv, 9. † 1 John ii, 22, 23. ‡ Rom. i, 3, 4. § Gal. ii, 20. || Phil. ii, 6, ff. ¶ Heb. i, 1. 2. ** Id., 6. †† Id., 7, 8.

Now, taking the pervading thought of the New Testament, that *divinity* is couched in the appellation, "Son of God," or, in other words, an equality of essence with the Father, wherein is this idea of Sonship superior to that of creatureship? Do not we that worship the Son, after all, worship a creature, and so violate the first command of the Decalogue? The Son was *begotten*. Was he not begotten at a particular point of time? Is not *begetting* a process as necessarily finite as *creating?* Let the distinction be whatever it may between these two acts; let the one be a transient exertion of power, the other a passing over of the Divine essence into a new embodiment; let it be further assumed that this passing over of the essence is *perpetual and eternal*, after it begins,—still, since the begotten existence *began*, did it not begin as the result of a volition of the Father? Does not the Son, therefore, hold his existence by substantially the same tenure as creatures hold theirs—namely, by the Divine will? However exalted, therefore, his being, yet, in its dependence, it stands on the same plane with the rest of creation. Can he, therefore, be worshiped? Must we not attain to some different conception of the Son, or else get rid of such Scriptures as, "Let all the angels of God worship him?" The Church has felt this from the beginning, and has found a solution, which, however, is not exactly a solution, but an answer. Now, let it be premised that the terms employed in Scripture are not presumed to be adequate to the mystic and transcendent truths they represent; nor is it assumed that human language has any terms adequate to their expression. Our words are adequate only to those things which we comprehend. When we do not comprehend, words are only symbols, with a very loose and indefinite adaptation to their objects. Sometimes they are like the algebraic x, y, z; sometimes they are like the hieroglyphics on ancient monuments. Their contents are obscure, and have to be sought out and rendered definite. It may be long before, at the end of the process, we can precisely state the value of the unknown quantity. Of this vague and inadequate nature are the correlatives, *Father* and *Son*, in the names of the Godhead; the words *begetting* and *proceeding*. They are the best words which we have to represent the truth intended, but it is very little of that truth which they distinctly convey. They can, therefore, be better understood negatively than positively. We can much more easily say what the "Only Begotten" is not, than what he is.

The Church met the difficulty by teaching, in the "Nicene Creed," "*The only begotten Son of God; begotten before all worlds; God of God; Light of Light; very God of very God; being of one substance with the Father.*" The "Athanasian Creed" puts it thus: "Such as the Father is, such is the Son, and such is the Holy Ghost; the Father uncreate, the Son uncreate, and the Holy Ghost uncreate; the Father incomprehensible, the Son incomprehensible, and the Holy Ghost incomprehensible; the Father eternal, *the Son eternal*, and the Holy Ghost eternal." Theologians, taking up the question, have forged the apparently self-contradictory phrase, "*eternal genera-*

tion," to express the mysterious and incomprehensible relation of Father and Son. Now, let us only remember that these terms are employed, not as adequate, but as constituting for us a sign of these two thoughts; namely, that the essence of the Father is participated in by him who is called the Son; and that this participation takes place outside of time and space, where spatial and temporal limitations of thought do not have place. This phrase thus becomes to us simply a terminus beyond which we can not think; and, instead of answering all the questions we can raise, only preserves, like a casket, the germs of truth we have secured.

We are aware of the finiteness of the thought embodied in the word "*participation*," which we have employed above; and if any one prefer, he may substitute the word *fellowship*, if it seem less liable to objection. We are here again reminded of the hopeless disability under which our thought labors; a disability which can only be mitigated, not remedied. There may be some force in the following:

"For our conceiving, or for the sensuous investiture of our thought which is necessary to our spiritu-corporeal nature, in its present earthly stage of development, the notion of *bringing forth* presents itself as *a calling into being of that which hitherto has not been;* from which arises the presumption that the *cause*, under all circumstances, *must be older than the effect*, and *the effect younger than the cause*. So long as our thinking is mediated by the activity of the brain, or of any material organism, so long can not our thought free itself from conceptions; and we are, therefore, with our idea of causality, compelled to think of the *being-effected* as an emerging out of non-existence into existence, and therefore the effect as a something beginning before the eye of our imagination. How, then, is it related to the thought and the self-consciousness of God? Are not effects wrought by God? None will contradict it. Is there, then, any time wherein God was without his thoughts, and without self-consciousness? Certainly not. Herein we perceive that God's working must be timeless, and his operations without beginning. Therefore, the beginningless begetting of the Son can involve no difficulty."*

No; it contains no other difficulty than belongs to all the doing and thinking of the Infinite God. It is therefore consistent with all that we believe concerning God. Our inability to comprehend it is of a piece with our inability to comprehend God himself. We may therefore accept this subtle doctrinal statement as a very near approach, for our minds, to the verity of revelation. And let us bear in mind, too, that a begetting which is without beginning is also *without ending*—an *eternal process*, of which the very creation itself, with all its history, may be but the type and the outflowing. This may serve to impress upon us, yet more forcibly, how far this truth is raised above our power to conceive; how inadequate our terms are to shadow it forth; and how futile must be our controversies about our forms of stating doctrines which are so far above all forms.

*Dr. Gess, "Die Lehre v. d. Person Christi," pp. 192, 193.

II. HUMANITY.—*That he is very Man.*

But omitting the apostolic testimonies to the Divinity of Christ, which are themselves worthy of a separate treatise, it is time we should give attention to the *humanity* of our Divine Lord and Redeemer.

a. He is a real Man.

The received doctrine of the Church concerning our Lord's humanity is found concisely expressed in the Athanasian Creed (so-called), as follows: "Perfect God, and perfect man; of a reasonable soul, and human flesh subsisting; equal to the Father as touching his Godhead, and inferior to the Father as touching his manhood; who, although he be God and man, yet is he not two, but one Christ; one not by conversion of the Godhead into flesh, but by taking of the manhood into God. One altogether, not by confusion of substance, but by unity of person. For, as the reasonable soul and flesh is one man, so God and man is one Christ."

This is beautiful, precious doctrine; sublime in mystery, but touching to the heart.

What a Savior is a perfect God and a whole man! How warmly did the earliest Church grasp her risen Savior, glorying in him as her "Lord and her God;" at the same time apprehending him as "the Man, Christ Jesus!" But when the fervor of religion became mixed at length with the vagaries of speculation, other and various views arose. Some thought the humanity of the Savior was unreal, and a mere appearance or vision. To them he was God, descended "in fashion as a man," without either the body or the soul of a man. Others, among them Arius, as chief, maintained that the Logos, who was not God, but the first and most exalted of creatures, became incarnate in a human body, without a human soul.

In later, and in present times, we are not aware that any can be found who deny the reality of the Lord's body. But there are many who stand with Arius, and deny both his deity and his human soul. Of these views, Dr. Channing is the ablest and worthiest expounder. He insists that Jesus is not God. He does not say that he is not man. But he uses such language as the following: "There is one God, even the Father; and Jesus Christ is not this one God, but *his Son and Messenger*, who derived all his powers and glories from the Universal Parent, and who *came into the world* not to claim supreme homage for himself, but to carry up the soul to his Father, as the only Divine Person, the only ultimate object of religious worship."* Again, he says, "We believe that Jesus is one mind, one soul, one being, as truly one as we are, and equally distinct from the one God." † Such views are variously repeated in his religious discourses. They show that while he did not in words, so far as these published discourses show, deny the actual humanity of Jesus, yet he held Jesus to be a lofty creature, "the express and unsullied image of the Divinity," ‡ who was united to a human body, making one simple person.

To this view there are several objections, which should have been decisive against the hypothesis, in so acute a mind as Dr. Channing's.

* Works, III, p. 165, published by the American Unitarian Association. † Works, III, p. 75. ‡ Works, III, p. 232.

1. It is necessary, in order to maintain it, to expunge a considerable part of the New Testament.

2. It does not relieve us of speculative difficulties. Did Dr. Channing ever undertake to show that it was more reasonable a creature-spirit should become incarnate, than God? Did he even presume to suggest that it was easier to domicile a spirit in an empty body than in one already en-souled? Who would be so presumptuous? What then is gained for rationality of doctrine? Indeed, could it not be made to appear somewhat probable that a superior spirit would find an inferior soul, already inhabiting a body, a convenient point of contact for his own incarnation? Just as man's bodily nature more easily digests material that has already undergone one transformation in vegetable life, and still more easily that which has undergone a second transformation in animal life; so, analogously, it might be, that a pure and lofty spirit, that never had contact with matter, might find in a soul that had been born and brought up in contact with matter a congenial medium for its incarnation, such as would be lacking in a soulless body.

But, be this as it may, we are still environed with mystery. If, therefore, one is seeking *simplicity* in the person of Christ, why not at once call him a *man?* For although man is not a very simple being, still we know something of him; and we know nothing of such a being as Dr. Channing believed in. And, if we put ourselves upon the task of burdening a creature with the awful attributes and wonderful achievements assigned in the Scripture to the Son of God, why not take man? For aught we know, he can as well intercede for the world as an angel; for aught we know, his death might signify as much as an angel's. Hence it is, that a large proportion of the Unitarians of our country have gone forward to carry out the tendency generated by Dr. Channing, and have held to the simple humanity of Jesus. In this they are fully as consistent as he, and, we think, have the better doctrine of the two.

The inner relation, subsisting in the person of Jesus Christ, between the Divine Logos and the human Ego, is a profound mystery which is not, probably, penetrable by our minds. Two natures, so wide apart, compounded into a grand, complex, unique personality, construct a problem of gigantic proportions, and, for the metaphysician, tougher than the geometrician's problem of squaring the circle. But as the one, so the other may be indefinitely approached. Man may, for the gratification of a speculative tendency, invent plausible and rational hypotheses of this hypostatic union. Thank God, these speculations have no practical value to the believer. They are not necessary to faith; nay, they may be a hinderance to it. That is, the tendency of mind they generate may be unfavorable to the sweet repose of faith. But whether they be a hinderance or not, our faith works on in triumph, whatever form of hypothesis our understanding may adopt for simplifying or systematizing this mystery.

The Athanasian Creed has the well-chosen words: "*One*, not by conversion of the Godhead into flesh, but by *taking of the manhood into God*." What this "taking into God" is, we may not be able to conceive.

It is not important that we should think or say much about it. It is safer, for clear understanding as well as for faith, to speak negatively rather than positively. Remembering that we hold our Christ to be *both God and man*, we must then deny such commingling of the two natures in Christ, as to confound the attributes of both, and present us a being who is *neither God nor man*. We must also deny such separation of the two natures as will be inconsistent with their unity in the theanthropic person of the Redeemer. Further than this it will avail us little to go. But theologians have gone further, and Churches have their distinctive forms of apprehending the mystery. We have seen how the early Church, the Catholic Church, expressed her thought about it.

Among modern Churches, the Lutheran holds that in Christ the Divine and human natures *blended*, each imparting to the other its qualities and conditions. According to her theologians, the human lent to the Divine its sensations, its limited consciousness, its feelings of privation, its pains and griefs. The Divine gave to the human a participation in the splendors of almightiness, omniscience, omnipresence, and holiness. While the Divinity actively employed the acquired human faculties and susceptibilities, the humanity was for the most part quiet in the possession of its acquired Divine powers, and seldom brought them into requisition. The Reformed Church holds the distinctness of the two natures and their co-ordinate, parallel, and co-operative development.

These are the two leading forms of conception

imposed by Christians of the present day on this Divine mystery. The Church of England stands upon the Athanasian creed. Dr. Gess argues with great ability and subtlety for a strictly human development of the Divine Logos during his earthly existence.* That is, in his estimation, the Son of God *surrendered his eternal self-consciousness in his incarnation, and actually became man,* recovering his Divine self-consciousness at his glorification.

In all these attempts to understand so subtle a mystery, we get little light, while we discover great revelations of darkness. And this, the discovery of our intellectual impotency, is often most wholesome. It will be to us a great blessing if it humble the aspiring mind in lowly and adoring reception of truth too sublime for our philosophy, too vast for our logic.

But so long as it stands in the Word of God that Jesus Christ "*was made sin for us,*" so long as our consciousness of sin recognizes the need of a Mediator, so long will the *real humanity*, the actual manhood of fleshly body and reasonable soul, in our Savior, be to us a truth above all price.

b. He is a perfect man.

His manhood was without defect, corporeal or spiritual. It was not common, but extraordinary. It was not commonplace, but marvelously unique. He was "the seed of the woman" standing alone in all history. He was "the Star of Jacob," brighter than all the patriarchs and prophets. He was "the Scepter of Israel," loftier, greater than all her historic

* "Die Lehre v. d. Pers. Christi," p. 288, ff.

kings. He was "the Son of Man," not the offspring of this or that particular man, but a divinely constituted "branch" of the common stock of humanity. He was "the second Adam." From the first Adam have come all colors and kinds of the races of men; from the second, come, and shall come, in all the future of eternity, all the varieties of the spiritual life, as it shall bloom and ripen in immortal men and women. He is thus the head Man of the race. He is the ripe fruit of humanity's tree. He is the most complete and beautiful flower of the life that began in Eden. He realizes all the good possibilities that were wrapped up in the first man. All that intellect can be; all that can grow in the pure heart; all beautiful thoughts; all best affections; whatsoever we can conceive of perfect good in the possible experiences of a man; whatsoever is grand in moral power; whatsoever is beautiful in sentiment,—all gather harmoniously into the oneness of this glorious Person. Privation, pain, and sorrow dim not the brightness of his perfection, but seem to be the media for its happiest manifestation. He has not where to lay his head; but yet he is at home every-where. He has no lot to seek; there is none whereof he complains. He hates nothing but sin. He loves all forms of being. Human feelings are all known to him, and every one of them is to him a jewel. He loves men. He is at home with them every-where—in hut and harbor and palace. His presence is a charm. He brings with it attraction. He uses that attraction to bring men nearer to his ideal self, up towards the measure of his spiritual stature. He has the most perfect equipoise ever known in man. He strives not. He cries not. He is never in a hurry. He is never agitated. He is not storm-tossed with passion. The cloud-shadows of our life seem not to fleck the sublime serenity of his interior life. He is not up and down like the ocean's billows, as most of us are. He is as composed amid the crowd of crafty, vulgar, stormy adversaries as is the sleeping infant in its mother's arms. He sleeps when nature is enraged, and rises in calmness to chide the winds. This sunny sweetness, this grand composure, made him a grateful refuge to the weary-hearted. Like a mountain, he could furnish a quiet retreat for weary flocks. Like a great rock, he casts his shadow over the fainting traveler. He had nothing in him exclusively Jewish. He cherished no fondness for the traditions of his ancestor David. He had no family pride, no pride of intellect, no vanity of achievements, no conceit. There was in him no littleness, no narrowness, no blind prejudice, no obstinacy. He loved that which was human; rising above all his surroundings, transcending all antecedents. His thoughts are human and humane. They are as fresh to-day as when they were uttered. They bear no marks of Jewish master. They bear no partial reference to times and countries. They are of universal import and of immortal excellence.

Such a human being is a *perfect* man, filling out our ideal of the highest human excellence and leaving nothing yet to be attained. The race culminates in him. All history before sought after him, and looked forward to him. All history since looks back to him, and moves forward in his light.

Perfect as was this humanity in its inception and growth, the history makes it plain that its acme of refined completeness was realized by the instrumentality of suffering. This is it that brings it nearest to our sympathies. 'T is this that opens the innermost depths of our hearts for its fellowship. That such a being suffered as we do, and yet was perfect, sheds a radiance on our sorrows, and relieves them of their harsher aspects. His suffering makes his love for us deeper and stronger, in proportion as his perfection stands in contrast with our unworthiness. His trials add to his inherent excellence the grandeur of heroism, and his humanity shines the more perfectly human, inasmuch as it stands secure, while all others of human kind have fallen in the hour of trial. And herein we see how "it became Him, for whom are all things and by whom are all things, in bringing many sons unto glory, to make the Captain of their salvation *perfect* through sufferings."* We "love Him because he first loved us." The sin-smitten heart in agony of self-despair, will gladly cling to Jesus. Clinging to him, it will sing, in the words of an old hymn:

"Tecum volo vulnerari,
Te libenter amplexari
In cruce desidero."

With the apostle, "counting all things but loss for the excellency of the knowledge of Christ Jesus,"

* Hebrews ii, 10.

and even suffering the loss of all things, we may say with St. Bernard, of Clairvaux:

> "Let me true communion know
> With Thee in thy sacred woe;
> Counting all besides but dross,
> Dying with thee on thy Cross;
> 'Neath it will I die!
>
> Thanks to thee, with every breath,
> Jesus, for thy bitter death;
> Grant thy guilty one this prayer,
> When my dying hour is near,
> Gracious God, be nigh!"

c. Thirdly, *he was a sinless man.*

Although we have almost anticipated this thought, yet it is sufficiently distinct from that of his complete and fully developed human-ness, to form the subject of a few concluding thoughts, and is worthy of more attention than we can give it.

That he could not have remained a *perfect man* if he had sinned, is clear. He would in that case have fallen down into the ranks of those who train in the gloomy footsteps of Adam. What a loss this had been to the world, we can appreciate, who look back to him now as the *man who never sinned.* Who can utter the value of this one thought in history, *that Jesus committed no sin?* Does it not illuminate every dark page of our human record? Does it not surround the very savage of Africa's dark wastes with the halo of possibilities otherwise not to be imagined? Does it not kindle hope in the criminal's bosom, the victim of society's justice, the doomed wretch, who has no hope for this life? Ah! who can tell how deep a pall would have rested on the spirit of the modern world if it had inherited the mistakes and miseries of the ancient world without the glory of Jesus? Who can tell us how much of the hopefulness, the cheer, and the triumph, of our modern civilization is owing to the sinlessness of this one man? For it is this that makes him dear—makes him a Savior.

He could not have been our exemplar if it had not been said by an apostle, "He knew no sin;" if he had not himself said, "Which of you convinceth me of sin?" Neither could he be our Mediator and Intercessor with God if he had, in the slightest shadowing, come short of moral perfection. "If any man sin, we have an advocate with the Father, Jesus Christ, the righteous." This sinlessness is sunshine over all lands, and in all hearts. It gives emphasis to the commands of conscience in the bosoms of the great and of the humble. It overhangs the oracles of justice, and makes the utterances of human law more sacred. It enters the noisy marts of trade, and reveals to the worshiper of Mammon a more entrancing luster than that of gold. It glows in the sacred desk, and sanctions every claim of the Divine law, while it glorifies the benignity of the Gospel.

This sinlessness of the Savior is the very essence of his glory, the very core of his saving excellence. We can not suffer it to be tarnished. And while men now, as in other times, will contradict the testimony of Scripture concerning him, it delights us to know, that now, as in the days of his flesh, he can triumphantly say to his enemies, "Which of you convinceth me of sin?" Men can not prove that he sinned, they can not make out even a plausible case against him; they can only avow that, *since he was human*, in their judgment he *must have sinned*. His sinlessness would be too much of a miracle for Rénan, and though it is assumed by Schenkel, it is nevertheless frittered away. But in the simple, honest story of the evangelists, without parade of learning, and without a touch of vanity, there shines forth the glory of such spotless purity as can not be gainsaid. That exalted goodness, too great for our common humanity, too great to have been invented, speaks to the world's heart. The human need of Jesus is too great ever to suffer his place to be vacated.

Now, if any one choose to say that this sinless Savior *could have sinned*, we may not care to controvert it, if he means that in him was only the *physical possibility* or capability of sinning. But if he mean that there was a *moral possibility* of his sinning, then we must demur. Had the moral possibility existed, he could not be the Savior of whom we have spoken, nay, of whom the word of God speaks. Could he who was "tempted in all points like as we are, yet without sin," have possessed even the most germinal desire to sin, and have been free from taint? Could he, in that case, be our High-priest, "holy, harmless, and undefiled?" There is only one view of this to be taken by those who trust in Christ for salvation. If he had the moral possibilities of sin in him, we must seek some other object of our faith. Absolute holiness is required by the Christian faith, in the object of trust. Jesus himself taught, and insisted upon, this spirit of faith in his followers, and he directed their faith continually toward himself—toward his own person. He had proved himself a deceiver, therefore, if, after soliciting the absolute trust of the human spirit for its eternal purity and felicity, he had shown himself to have the merest initials of sinful desire.

Now, the faith of his disciples recognized in him a perfectly stainless purity. And for love of this they bade farewell to earthly friendships; they sacrificed all worldly prospects; they brooked poverty, and dared persecution; they took up their lives as a little thing, and flung them into the very jaws of death, feeling assured that in him whom they loved they were rich, though "suffering the loss of all things," and in him they were superior to death, that masters all besides. Their faith and love have been transmitted, not as fanaticism propagates itself, but as life and love travel, through the convictions and the affections of men. Ages have come and gone, and the testimony of Jesus still lives. Great men have lived, triumphed, perished, and been forgotten; but the name of Jesus is mighty in all lands, and more honored as time rolls on. This is the might of holiness, this the success of charity. Well might the exiled Napoleon say: "What a wide abyss between my deep misery and the eternal kingdom of Christ, which is proclaimed, loved, adored, and which is extending over all the earth! Is this death? Is it not life, rather? The death of Christ is the death of a God!"